JRF; BEYOND THE HATRED

TOSH MCINTOSH
GILLY BLACK

**Britain's Next
BESTSELLER**

First published in 2017 by:
Britain's Next Bestseller (English translation)
An imprint of Live It Ventures LTD
126 Kirkleatham Lane,
Redcar.
Cleveland.
TS10 5DD
01642 285722

All enquiries should be addressed to - info@bnbsbooks.co.uk
Cover design by Yordan Damyanov (Slavena Publishers)
www.bnbsbooks.co.uk
@BNBSbooks
ISBN 978 191 0565 346

Pat Dolan & Donch McPench

CONTENTS

A FEW WORDS...

KELLY and I know nothing about football.

There it is.

So, when we were contacted by Tosh and Gilly regarding publication of an English imprint of JRF: Beyond the Hatred, we were slightly reluctant.

How can you publish a book when you don't follow the sport? Despite reservations, we kindly accepted the opportunity to read the manuscript... and it was a mini revelation!

Upon first glance, some may think this is just a book about hooliganism and football violence. But they would be so very wrong.

I learnt about the history of a country, the culture of a people and more importantly, the true meaning of loyalty and friendship.

Anything talking about violence was secondary to what was actually a refection on the world today and how people can bond over a commonality; a passion for something that, unless you are a fan, you can never hope to truly understand.

It was our pleasure and privilege to be able to work with Tosh and Gilly on this book.

We feel like we made some true friends and discovered a little more about the world as we went along.

In the end, that is why we all do what we do.

Enjoy your time with the Jolly Roger Firm!

David and Kelly
Live It Ventures LTD/Britain's Next Bestseller

FOREWORD

First, we would like to make it clear for you what this book is about and what is hidden behind its gripping title *Beyond the Hatred*.

It is the original history of the hooligan *Jolly Roger Firm* and it depicts our involvement during the last two decades. It would be a pleasure for us to mention every single fight and event in chronological order, but this would be simply impossible and, besides, we do not intend to introduce sheer statistics to our readers. The book will try to follow our history from when we were just kids who loved watching not only football but also what was happening on the terraces to the times we grew up as adults seriously involved in football-related violence. We will also make an effort to devote some time to sociological theories and psychological profiles that stand behind the phenomenon of football hooliganism.

A number of books have been written on this topic in academic circles, so we will put forward our particular reasons for becoming part of this culture. This is the authentic point of view on how the idea was born, what happened in the past (mainly), what the present is and what hopefully the future holds for us. We won't be able to answer all questions, such as "*why young men from wealthy backgrounds and men who hold responsible positions in society would gather on a Saturday afternoon with men from poorer backgrounds and with those who have nothing to lose just to meet a rival firm?"* Maybe it is a phenomenon, maybe its the kind of rush you cannot feel anywhere else.

When fighting against larger firms and smaller ones, it is usually the numbers that prevail and decide on the winner, but sometimes it is down to the lads you have around and behind you. Sometimes bigger clubs would bring hundreds of fans and, quite logically, we expected to lose the battle off the pitch, but it wasn't always like that because, although outnumbered, we would stand our ground and would never let our home (Lokomotiv stadium) to be taken over. As years went by, our reputation as a tough firm spread in those circles and soon we were amongst the major "players". Having started from scratch, we would always try to get involved and be wherever there were riots.

The roar of those around you, the sounds of kicks and punches, the adrenaline rushing to your brain, the thought you were protecting your beloved club's honour, the feeling of infinite freedom – believe us, those were the most exciting things in the world. It is hard to explain to those who have never been involved, but we will try. Our personal opinion is that it was a basic instinct for us and that, weird or not, it was all related to the football game. It was a feeling that money can't buy! We felt pride in our hearts. For us Lokomotiv (GO) was certainly not the best team, but it was our home team, the one and only!

This is a travel back in time when there was no football firm in Gorna Oryahovitsa (GO) and the founders of *Jolly Roger Firm* (JRF) were innovators and pioneers in football clashes. Our intention is not to encourage any form of violence. We do not expect anyone to approve of the path we followed and we will not make any excuses whatsoever. We have heard people say that blokes like us who cause trouble during football games are not real fans. However, we find such comments as downright stupid and revealing of the incompetence and misunderstanding surrounding football hooliganism. Back in those days we were young and we had no responsibilities, but we never used to be "mindless thugs". We always used to avoid any confrontation with those who only came to watch the game. In addition, there was also some quite old-fashioned values such as fidelity, friendship and loyalty, which unfortunately are now nowhere to be found. It is exactly that loyalty and the respect we had for each other that shaped our personalities. In our case, almost all of the close friendships we made both in Bulgaria and England were as a result of our love for football.

This is a book about the JRF era, about the days that could only be relived in our memories and in the lines to follow. It was a unique stretch of time, our golden age and undoubtedly some of the best years in our lives. Unfortunately, things would never be the same again.

Now we are married and have children. Our hooligan outrage years are gone, but we are still proud to be Lokomotiv (GO) supporters and it's been like that since the first time we started supporting the team in the mid-1980s. Football has changed a lot recently, but nevertheless, we still get that buzz, we remain black-and-white fanatics and we will always be like that. And we are sure this is something that will never change.

And since this, hopefully fascinating, story is now published in English, we would like to provide our readers with a brief history of our club, firm and town... the beginning and development of football in it. We will provide names and facts that contributed to the reputation of this football town. The nine-year participation of Lokomotiv (GO) in the top flight, where they played 268 games, and more than 1000 games in the second division, are remarkable sports achievements.

The book does not claim comprehensiveness and accuracy as far as any statistical and historical data is concerned. We just tried to recreate the story of our lives alongside the pleasure and pain we have had with our beloved team. We hope we have succeeded, but it is you who will estimate our efforts while reading the pages to follow.

The people we would like to thank from the bottom of our hearts are: our families – parents, wives, sons and daughters, brothers and sisters, close friends and relatives – for their tolerance and endurance through all those years and for their unconditional devotion, support and patience while we were working to finish this project of ours.

Tosh would like to thank: Desi, Nadya (Senior), Nadya (Junior), Georgi (the Bambina –RIP)

Gilly would like to thank: Mimka (my guardian angel who has always loved and supported me), my beloved son Tony and my daughter Eliya (my lovely princess).

Our special thanks go to: Nikolai (Vacheto), Stoyan (Stobby), Proletin (Prolyo), Berkov (Ritchie), Mladen (the Smurf), Ventsi (the Pedagogue), Victor (the Docent), Chavdar (the Sprat), Kuncho (GMU), Venelin (NUP), Ivan (the Plevener), Anto Platt (Notts County) for their valuable contribution and for sharing their memories with us.

Thanks to our special guests (terrace legends) from Britain: Martin King (Chelsea Headhunters), Gary "Boatsy" Clarke (Forest Executive Crew), Mark Fisher (Barnsley Five-O), Annis Abraham (Soul Crew), Andy Frain (Chelsea Headhunters), Angus Nutt (City Service Firm), Sandy Chugg (Inter City Firm), Lee Spence (Fine Young Casuals), Rob Sanders ex S.C.F. (Feyenoord's firm) for their nice words and in advance for their possible future support for publishing this book in English.

Unfortunately, some lads and mates we would also like to thank to are no longer with us: Donch (Doncho - RIP), Pat Dolan (Fat Pat − RIP), Kalin (Kalkata - RIP), Gosho (the Cur - RIP). They will never be forgotten and our BIG THANKS go somewhere out there, wherever they may be now.

Last but not least, we would like to thank: Slavena Publishers (Vitaly Zarkov & Yordan Damyanov), Britain's Next Bestseller (David & Kelly McCaffrey), Milen Panayotov (English translation) for the opportunity given to us to publish this book in Bulgaria and England.

It was entirely our pleasure to let us work with you.

PREFACE

I was born and raised in a fairly good working-class family. My mother was a nurse and my father a construction worker. I can't say we were poor, but despite all my parents' efforts, there was always some kind of deficiency. It was just that the economic situation in our country and the political regime did not allow anything better. My parents were rather old since, for one reason or another, they had not been able to have children for quite a long time. After 15 years of waiting I was born to this world, but due to their age and deteriorating health I had no brothers or sisters. That fact made my parents feel obligated to ensure I had everything I needed for a good life, though sometimes it was far beyond their powers. As a result of the long years of hard manual labour, my father got ill and the last 5 or 6 years of his life were a real torment for all of us at home.

Those were the years when I was 12-18 years old, the time when a boy grows up to be a man and shapes up his character. Having to live through that at such a tender age was rather depressing for me and as I was to understand later, left a lasting mark on me. In 1995, when he was 58, my father left this world (rest in peace, Dad!).

During his last years, alive he managed to get through to me his messages. As a perfect representative of the working class, he was a tough and demanding man and like most of his colleagues – a devoted football fan and Lokomotiv supporter. He was well qualified and very good at his job. Steel and concrete were his life and his 'bread and butter'. By the way, he contributed greatly to the repair works needed for the modernisation of the football ground in our town (the modern-day grandstand). He had quite a lot of subordinates, a team of 30-40 people, all of them tough blokes, hard as rocks, their hands as huge as of a longshoreman's. Their team was known as "The Steel Hearts". Every day those fellas managed to conquer steel and shape it the way they wanted. When I was a young boy I remember I loved looking at a photo of his, on which he and his workmates were proudly standing in front of an enormous statue of an elephant they had made from steel in a children's theme park in Germany. They were really proud of what they were doing and felt recognised and renowned in their town, but would also not miss any opportunity to prove who they were in any towns where Lokomotiv (GO) would play an away game.

Quite a few fans of other teams did suffer from their huge fists made even harder by the hard manual labour. The years of strenuous work had led to the accumulation of a lot of malice and they would let off steam when Saturdays came. They were the absolute Bulgarian equivalents of English dockers. This was the harsh environment I grew up in. I quite often attended their binges at home because my mother worked night shifts and there was no one to be left at the cares of but my Dad.

Imagine a little boy amidst all those giant, drunk, rowdy and hyped up men. Of course, they loved me as if I was their own son and they respected me since my father was their leader. He would often praise me but not for being a good student or for what profession I would acquire, but for being skilful at boxing and fighting. I remember him taking out a hard pillow out of somewhere and made me hit it till I would drop. I almost always had a large audience in the person of his mates who used to surround me as if in a real boxing ring and cheer me with their shouts: "*Come on, boy, bring it on! That's right, boy, well-done!*" Finally, my father would say: "*You see what my boy can do, don't you?*" It was not long after that when I saw those men use their fists in a real football related fight. Mum was just the opposite. If Dad stood on the North Pole, she was far away on the South one.

Having taken the Hippocratic Oath while quite young, she was brought up with the sole purpose of looking after people. Kind-hearted, humble and quiet, she did her best trying to teach me some basic virtues. She wanted me to learn my lessons, help her with the household chores and believe in good. As a devoted believer in the virtues of Christianity, she wanted me to be a modest, good-hearted and kind man.

Even nowadays, when she is well advanced in years, she still helps my family. She persistently teaches my daughter the same virtues and without any hesitation I would call her "Mother Teresa". She often had conflicts with Dad since he wanted me to be the exact opposite, to be tough like him, geared up for the difficulties and injustice of life. Looking back now I see that they were both right in their own different ways and I do believe I have managed to benefit from them both. Yeah, I had to be tough in order to face the challenges of fate, but also, I had to acquire all human virtues.

It was exactly that dilemma that deeply confused me back then and when my Dad was gone I felt a void inside me. I didn't know what path to take and what to do with my life. It was as if like being on another planet. I felt spite, rage, hunger for revenge, and all of those were directed to people who were not guilty of anything. I blamed everyone, even my father, for leaving me at such times, though I was not that young anymore. I knew death was inevitable and had its logical explanation, but it was just that I was not prepared for the day it would come. If I had to personify my perceptions and my image in those years I would do it with the character of Anakin Skywalker before becoming Darth Vader.

So, it was exactly then that I chose the dark side and I decided to take my love for my football club to a place where I would be able to direct all the malice built-up inside me. I am telling this story in order to try and answer one of all those *whys*. You cannot so easily stigmatise someone without knowing what they have been through and what lies deep down in their souls. Everything has its roots, its own origin and can be attributed to and explained. As I said in the beginning, everyone has their own destiny but no one can choose it. Just like no one can choose their parents. Even if I could, I would choose mine once again because I am extremely proud of them both!

Best wishes,

TOSH

Below is the fate of my longtime close friend and co-author Gilly, with who I've been together since our first steps at football grounds.

I was born in the small industrial town of Gorna Oryahovitsa and I grew up on the outskirts of a working-class neighbourhood located along the town hills close to the railway station. The town was a typical working class site, a concrete jungle of high-rise residential buildings and factories, all of them constructed in the dawn of the communist regime. The neighbourhood I grew up and spent most of my life in was notorious for being one of the harshest and most hostile for both people from other parts of the town and those visiting fans who dared to walk along its streets. The only way from the train station to the Lokomotiv stadium passed through this neighbourhood. They used to call me Phil (short for Philip), but my nickname is Gilly.

My parents were from a middle-class family of its own rules and principles. I was not an only child as I have a younger brother who at some point became one of the regular football players in Lokomotiv (GO). He played for the club for many years, going through all of its levels. My mother was a piano teacher and my father – a construction technician. In his past, he used to play football for FC Dunav Ruse and afterwards he was a coach at Lokomotiv youth academy. Both my parents were highly respected in our town. It was my father who I inherited the love for football from. As a kid, I used to play as a goalkeeper in the local football academy, but since I was overweight and had to put up with my coach's mockery I had nothing left to do but quit training. Obviously, I was destined to follow my favourite team as a supporter. Even my primary school was located near the stadium, which was named Dimitar Dyulgerov at the time. The arena that was home and fortress not only for the railway men (as you know, it was the club's nickname), but also for all black-and-white supporters. A sacred place that remains forever in my heart.

Unlike my mate, Tosh, my childhood was not so difficult. I'd rather say it was contradictory, as deep inside I would fight against stern parenting. My parents' methods were strict and there were even occasions when I would get a slap or two. They wanted me to have good education, to prepare me for the harsh reality of life and pass on our family values to me. As I was rather naughty and expansive I got into a lot of trouble both at school and at home. I would get into fights after school and come home nose bleeding, bruised and with my clothes torn. I was frequently guilty of what not, my parents were often called at school and they, poor folks, would blush with shame and put even more efforts to bring me into line. Fighting peers and bullying gypsies were the standard acts of violence. I felt hatred, fury and hunger for that in spite of my parents' advice. That accumulated aggression had to find its way out and the only place for that to happen was on and off the pitch.

As I said before, I inherited my love for football from my father. Though he was a demanding parent and had good command over himself suppressing his anger, there used to be occasions (that I witnessed) when even he would let off. Of course, that would sometimes happen on Saturdays and Sundays at football grounds, mostly when we played away from home.

I first went to a football game with my Dad during the 1986/87 season. It was our team's last game in the second division. I was a 10-year-old kid then. It was 7th June 1987, a hot and sunny day, and Lokomotiv (GO) played its last decisive game for promotion in Division One against a team called Svetkavitsa (Targovishte), which had already been relegated. However, such teams would always try to make things go wrong and on that day we just hoped they wouldn't. The atmosphere was unbelievable; chants were being heard everywhere, even beyond the ground. A real town festival. Fans wouldn't stop singing and cheering their team. In front of a crowd of 6000 having the presentiment that their 24-year-old dream would finally come true, Lokomotiv deservedly won 3-0 and so we were promoted. In addition to my brilliant impressions from the team's performance and the astounding win, my eyes were riveted to the opposite stand where our fanatics stood. A huge mob of black-and-white fans famous for being one of the most passionate and dangerous supporters in the country. Time and again, the police would have problems dealing with them. I enjoyed their unruly temper and hooligan behaviour and I dreamt about the day I would be one of them.

Best Regards,

GILLY

INTRODUCTION

The first evidence of living in settlements dates back to the second half of the 5th millennium BC (Middle Neolithic period) and is connected with the remains found in the area called "Blatoto" (the "marsh"). It is now an inner town area. The rectangular houses above ground level were made of hedge and clay. Traces of the earliest Thracian settlement can be seen in the area called "Pchelno Myasto" ("bee place"), about 2–3 km east of the town, between the "Kamuka" (the "stone") height and the "Arbanasi" Ridge. Its inhabitants belonged to the Krobyzoi tribe. The settlement was quite large (its area was more than 100.000 m²). It was guarded by a fortress called "Kamuka" (the "stone"). It existed from 5th to the 1st century BC when the Romans came and on its remains they built a fortified settlement of their own. It gradually gained economic power producing mainly grapes and wine. In II-III century the Roman province of Lower "Moesia" was the only one that took advantage of the central government's protection of its grapes cultivation and manufacture of high quality wines.

Life in that settlement continued until the arrival of the Slavs (VI–VII c). No verified evidence of life in the settlement exists from the VII–XII century period. After the restoration of the Bulgarian state in the late 12thcentury, there was a need of guarding the new

Bulgarian capital Tarnovgrad. Several sentry fortresses were built, including "Rahovets" (4 km north-west of the modern-day town). This happened between 1187 and 1190 and the purpose of the newly built fortress was to guard the road from Cherven (in Ruse District) to Tarnovgrad. The name of the town "Rahovets" was derived from the Persian word "rah" meaning a "road". Hence, the modern name of the town evolved.

During the Ottoman invasion, the fortress was captured by the Turks after they cut its water supply (without destroying it). "Rahovets" fortress existed until 1444 when it was demolished by Wladyslaw III of Varna. During the first centuries of Ottoman rule there were three separate small villages called Little, Middle and Big Rahovitsa. Gradually Gorna Oryahovitsa (due to some rights it was granted by the Sultan in 1538) turned into an economically strong town, especially during the Bulgarian Renaissance. Crafts thrived and trade was one of the most active in Northern Bulgaria. On Fridays, there were lively markets for cattle, agricultural products, timber and charcoal. Back in 1822, a monastery school was founded and in 1827 Father Gerasim Stoykov opened his private school (later it became a municipal school in 1835). In 1850 the first girls' school opened and in 1859 the first-class school appeared organized by Ivan Momchilov. The community center opened in 1869. In 1870 Gorna Oryahovitsawas declared a town. At that time, it had 4700 citizens, 1200 houses and 5 churches.

The town population took part in almost all national liberation activities in the region. Vasil Levski (a national hero) set up a revolutionary committee here in the early 1869 and after that visited the town twice more. During the preparation for the April uprising, Gorna Oryahovitsa was nominated for the center of the First Revolutionary Districtand Stefan Stambolov was appointed as its main activist. However, the most active campaigners in the town were Ivan Semerdzhiev, Georgi Izmirliev and the Grancharov brothers. Following a series of betrayals, the plan for a massive uprising came unstuck. There was only one battle between a fistful of rebels and Turkish forces and its outcome was tragic. On 28th May 1876, in the town of Tarnovo, the Turks hanged Ivan

Semerdzhiev (together with other rebels like Bacho Kiro, etc.). On that very day, in the center of Gorna Oryahovitsa, they also hanged Georgi Izmirliev whose last words at the gallows were: "How sweet it is to die for the freedom of your Fatherland!" Sider Grancharov (a.k.a. Sider Voivode) died leading his band at Mount Murgash. Gorna Oryahovitsawas in grave danger, but the brave chair of the women's society Elena Grancharova gathered women, old people and children and led them to Tarnovo to ask for Reuf Pasha's protection. The Pasha sent the regular army and so protected the town from the paramilitary forces and bandits. Three men from Gorna Oryahovitsa fought in Botev's band and 132 joined the Bulgarian Volunteer Corps during the Russo-Turkish War of 1877-1878. Gorna Oryahovitsawas liberated by Russian troops on 26th June 1877. Among its liberators was major Emilian Sienkiewicz (brother of Polish writerHenryk Sienkiewicz), who married a girl from Gorna Oryahovitsa.

After the Bulgarian liberation, the town developed as a major transportation (mostly railway) centre and it still is a railway hub. The town, situated in Northern Bulgaria on the boundary between the Balkan range and the Danubian plain, is the second largest town in the district, the first one being Veliko Tarnovo. It is located along the Yantra River and the northern foot of the Tarnovo heights shaped as a giant horseshoe. Those heights are cut through by the river gorge. To the west one can see "Belyakovsko" plateau and to the east −"Kamuka" height and "Arbanasi" plateau. The "Bozhur" ("peony") area located southwest of the town has become one of the symbols of Gorna Oryahovitsadue to the unusual fields of dark red peonies. The town is also an administrative centre.

According to the latest census the citizens of Gorna Oryahovitsa are approximately 35.000. The working class prevails in the small country town. It boasts of its own airport, rich medieval history, relatively well developed economy and the largest railway station inNorthern Bulgaria. Hence the name of the club - Lokomotiv. Its proximity to the former Bulgarian capital Veliko Tarnovo and to "Arbanasi", the beautiful monasteries in the area, the picturesque nature and a number of other landmarks, attract lots of tourists.

Football has been played in Bulgaria since the beginning of XX century. As time went by, the game gained more and more popularity and spread across the country. There is evidence that way back in 1913 the Czech experts constructing a factory in Gorna Oryahovitsa brought two leather balls for the workers to play in their free time.

In 1918–1919, following the Treaty of Neuilly-sur-Seine, French armed forces were deployed in Gorna Oryahovitsa. English troops also stayed in the town in that period. Both parties used to spend their free time playing with a football on a large pitch east of the train station. The game attracted the attention of the locals living in the town and the nearby villages. At almost the same time, sailors training at the marine mechanic school in the town of Varna also used to kick a ball where English and French soldiers played. In the middle of 1921, a football club was founded in Gorna Oryahovitsa uniting the teams from the town neighbourhoods under the name of *SC Levski 1921* and marking the beginning of football in the town. A team made predominantly of working class people, i.e. railway workers, enjoyed the game at weekends finding consolation and delight in their otherwise drab and gloomy routines.

LOKOMOTIV was the name of our beloved team and the representative football club for Gorna Oryahovitsa. The club was founded in 1932 and is considered as *SC Levski*'s successor. After 1945 it was joined by other teams from Gorna Oryahovitsa. In the pre-war years, the team played its official games at the "*Yunak*" ground and later on at the *Kaltinets* ground, which was one of the first stadiums, built in the country. In 1956 FC Lokomotiv (GO) moved to the newly opened all-seater town stadium named after the club with a capacity of 12.000. The club is not very successful and just like the town it represents it is a rather small Bulgarian team. The most successful years for the club were when it played for the second time in League One. This happened after the 1986/87 season, when the "railwayman" from Gorna Oryahovitsa finished second and won promotion to the first division. There, Lokomotiv (GO) played for eight consecutive years, its best seasons being 1989/90, 1990/91 and 1993/94 when they finished eighth. Our older supporters remember that several Bulgarian major clubs were defeated in Gorna Oryahovitsa in those years. The eight years in question coincided with the fall of the communist regime and the period of transition that followed and Lokomotiv's last season in League One, 1993/94, coincided with the USA World Cup, when the Bulgarian national team made its greatest achievement in history.

One of the leading players in the Bulgarian golden generation at the World Cup was Ivaylo Yordanov, who in 1990/91 was Bulgarian top scorer playing for Lokomotiv. Afterwards he was transferred to Sporting Lisbon where he made a fantastic career both in Portugal and Europe. In 1992 the team won the former Intertoto Cup. After playing *Lokomotiv Sofia, Rapid Bucharest* and *Arges Pitesti*, Lokomotiv (GO) finished first in their group. Being the group winner, in the next round our team played the strong Russian side *Rotor Volgograd*. The game in Gorna Oryahovitsa finished in a 1-1 draw and in Russia Lokomotiv (GO) was eliminated after a 2-0 defeat. In 1995 Rotor Volgograd knocked out Manchester United in the very first round of the UEFA Cup.

What followed were years of decline and extended financial crisis that resulted in Lokomotiv (GO) playing in the Bulgarian third division and even one season in the Amateur League. Traditions were abandoned, managements were replaced, interest was flagged and the club was on the verge of closing down. After all those hard times, when there was a real danger for football in the town to sink into oblivion, in 2013/14 season the team finished second in the Third division and won promotion to League Two again and recently the club has been invited to play in the newly formed Premier League. Another distinguishing feature in the club history is the permanent participation in various "railwayman" tournaments at both national and European level. A memorable experience is their fourth place at the1983 European Railways Cup held in former Czechoslovakia.

One may say that Lokomotiv (GO) has quite a lot in common with the English club Crewe Alexandra, not only in terms of nicknames and kits, but also in terms of geographical locations of the corresponding towns. Another interesting parallel could be drawn to the Spanish Athletic. The Basques from Bilbao are famous for using almost only local players, which is also typical of our team not only during its golden years, but nowadays, too. However, like any proper supporter, we cannot agree to such parallels since our beloved local team is unique for us.

During the "golden years" in question, as I said before, Bulgarian leading teams at that time left our ground defeated not just once or twice. It was then when our club earned the nickname "giant-killers". One cannot forget what the legendary Bulgarian footballer Hristo Stoichkov said when he was still playing in Bulgaria: "A really strong football team is a team that can win against Lokomotiv at its home ground in Gorna Oryahovitsa." Words that are still remembered.

Despite its not so impressive history, the team boasts of a constant number of loyal supporters. Even in the darkest of times and after all those long years spent in Division Three, it has been the team's loyal supporters that distinguish Lokomotiv from the other small clubs in the country. What follows below is the story of this group of fans, the Jolly Roger Firm (JRF). I think it is best to introduce you to this story through the eyes of a young member of the firm. Here goes his exciting recount:

"I have been a member of JRF for years. It is a dream comes true for me. As a young boy, I loved watching the black-and-white army of fans surging to the stadium at weekends. I imagined how proud I would be to become one of them. Gorna Oryahovitsa fans knew how to defend their town well. Over the years, my obsession with the firm grew even stronger, day after day. I won't lie to you if I say I wanted to be a hooligan, not just a rank-and-file fan. I would watch them, cheer along with them and dream of growing up faster so that I could be side by side with them in the clashes with rival groups of fans.

The firm has always supported the team, both in its ups and downs. It has always been a matter of loyalty and commitment that fans felt for their club. Lokomotiv is a small-town team but it has incredible and devoted fans. I knew that one day I would be one of them…I would be a hooligan. In times when the "ultras" subculture was the dominant one in Bulgaria, something different was happening among Gorna Oryahovitsa fans. A selected group of black-and-white supporters had established an organization following the English model. While hooligan firms were common in England back then, in Bulgaria this style and way of life were just being introduced. Everyone belonged either to a fan club (which was also a new trend then) or to the "ultras". There were also fans going to games unorganised. In the very beginning when I found out about the ideology of the firm, the idea appealed to me. I was determined to become part of the so called "casual" style (which nowadays has become a synonym for show-off behavior, but then it stood for honour and dignity).

At first I would just watch what the older guys did, and since theirs was a closed circle, it was impossible for youngsters with no proven reputation to enter their firm. I was impressed by the respect the members had for each other. The core consisted of about 20–30 people but sometimes they reached a much larger number. They wore designer clothes such as Burberry, Lacoste, FredPerry, Adidas and plenty of others, to keep the memory for the origin of it all (the hooligan fashion in England in the 1970s and 1980s). As a matter of fact, these brands were hard to find in Bulgaria and in most cases, they were shipped from England. Their firm was called Jolly Roger (named after the song and album of the same name by the German heavy metal band Running Wild). It was a small firm supporting a small-town club that established its own traditions in those circles (or rather, upgraded what the black-and–white army had already achieved).

Just like FC Lokomotiv (GO) was confident enough to challenge the major clubs in Bulgaria, JRF was pursuing this level against larger firms. There were victories and there were defeats both on and off the pitch, but there was only one thing that mattered: NO SURRENDER – one of the mottos of the organisation.

Bulgarians are tough and headstrong (there is a reason behind the common saying that "Bulgarians can break through walls with their heads"). The bravery and heroism, the hot blood in our veins (best proven in the numerous battles in Bulgarian history) have influenced not only our past, but also our present and will continue to determine behaviours even on and off the pitch. If we did this fictional ranking of fans in terms of being loyal and wild (in any brutal sense of the word), Lokomotiv(GO) will definitely make it in the top 10, which would be quite an achievement given the fact that we are not a big-town nor a "spoilt" top team.

Perhaps, the reason for us becoming so united and loyal to each other was exactly the fact that we came from such a small town. I have always had respect for the so called "old school" lads. I used to watch them standing by and I was trying to get closer and be able to hear what they were talking about. Their stories really inspired me and I eagerly wanted to be an active participant, not a mere listener and observer. As time went by, I started to copycat the lads in the firm in terms of thinking (I gained a lot of experience being around them and for that I pay them my RESPECT) as well as appearance.

I was trying to wear designer clothes so that I could merge with them. However, I had no favourite designer brand, I just tried to look tidy. The tolerance the organisation had for us, the younger ones, helped me a lot then. We were not involved in literally everything but they made us feel we were part of them. We knew that if things got tough they would help us. There are several quite good supporters from my generation who later merged with the firm. I must mention my friend (and co-author) Tosh, who was one of the founders of this organisation and to whom I owe my significant development as a fan thanks to his invaluable advice. Thank you, Tosh!

Let's focus again on the organisation itself. Its logo was the skull and bones and its classic flag was the Union Jack with the famous Running Wild band logo on. Even now, I always perceive this band and our firm as an indestructible alloy.

My first closer encounter with the Jolly Roger Firm was in 1998. While walking around with some friends, I saw a small group of people heading swiftly for the railroad station. I was excited because I sassed them out as the "usual suspects" as we used to call them, members of the firm. They were going to an away game. My blood began to boil and I instinctively headed towards them. By the time, I reached the platform they were on the train already, chanting loudly, and beers in their hands.

I approached them and asked if they were going to a game (I knew they were but I just wanted to start a talk with them). They smiled and asked back: "Why, would you like to join us?" I thought they were 'taking the Mickey out of me' but I had so much adrenalin that I just said: "Yes, why not."

To be with JRF on an away game was a dream come true for me. Since the train doors were already shut they pulled me in through a window. As I got in I realised that this was quite reckless of me as I had very 'short' pocket money and my parents were not at all aware I was leaving the town (I was 13-14 years of age at that time). As time passed by, I started to care less about it. Someone gave me a bottle of beer and that definitely brought the smile back on my face. I was the only youngster to travel with them to that game, but everybody was so friendly and I felt free. And it was a game to remember.

Since then I have loved travelling to away games more than the home games, though I attended both. What made the away games different and special was the unique feeling to be in the enemy's den, on others territory, the need to prove yourself to the other team's supporters, the mixed feeling of fear and anxiety of what was to come, the moment when you can't wait to meet the enemy. This was how bravery was steeled along with loyalty to friends and mostly to your favourite team.

What happened then changed everything like the domino effect. I started regularly going to away matches under the wing of the "old school" boys who were still young back then. Everything I had been dreaming of was then becoming reality. The number of my hooligan acts with the firm grew like a snowball being rolled. Even my classmates started thinking of me as somebody anti-social. I don't say it was a good thing, but my age, environment and my temper pushed me into that. Lokomotiv (GO) was playing in the lower echelons, but it was no obstacle for us and everywhere we went we would be remembered for long.

After our team was relegated from the Third division down to the Amateur League for a year, the season was marred by numerous riots. Small and big towns met us with police forces as they knew what to expect from us. It seemed that our hurt pride resulting from our relegation into the eternal hell called Third Division had found release in the form of hooligan acts. Naturally, we were fewer than the group of supporters on the terraces during the "golden age" in the top flight, but the JRF lads always stood by the team. A new organisation called "G.O.BOYS" was established alongside.

The local derby with our deadly rivals Etar Veliko Tarnovo (VT), described in the coming chapters of this book, was 'knocking on the door'. To our joy, they had also been relegated down to Division Three. It was like a dope for us and we used every away game to train for our clash with them. 'Black-and-white junta, you punish and destroy, but always go for the win' was quite a regular soundtrack for the events that happened. We travelled by trains for free as it was dangerous to charge a firm of supporters then. Tosh and many others were the perfect example to me. As I said, times were hard, we had hit rock bottom and no way out was visible because our favourite Lokomotiv was struggling financially. We, however, were able to wipe the shame off our faces as no matter how hard those times were, we always stood behind our team, there was always this core of 40-50 lads who never gave up and served as a worthy example to the present-day young supporters.

I am glad I was part of that core and I can tell the young fans now: "It is all worth it, lads!" In the Jolly Roger Firm and in the whole lot of black-and-white supporters you can find friendship, loyalty and adrenaline in great amounts. Thanks to them, I became a "fine young casual".

All neutral fans still have that respect from their very presence. Actually, as an organisation, they are still untouchable. For me they were the only bunch of people who would always stand behind me. Sticking to them for all these years has been something special that an ordinary fan cannot experience. Those were surely crazy days, but if you ask them they would even say: "Definitely the best days ever."

PART ONE

PROLOGUE

WHY?

QUITE OFTEN, A LOT OF PEOPLE ASK ME: "WHY DO YOU HATE YOUR rivals so much?!" "Why are you so wicked and bad to the bone?!", "Why do you want to harm people so much?!", "Why, why?!" These are all questions that we have to answer somehow. Well, be it so, but I can also ask similar questions like: "Why do politicians lie and steal so much?!", "Why are the police corrupt?!", "Why don't pedophiles and murderers do time in prison?!"

I would try to answer all those questions, but I strongly doubt that anyone would be so kind to even think about mine. We don't always get the answers to every question, especially when they are to be given by the highly esteemed members of the system, by all those who have poorly governed the country for years. In the opposite case, however, you are obliged to give your answers not only because you don't have power and you are down in the dumps, but also because if you don't do it, they regard you as an anti-social person inducing aggression and sedition. The only way to retaliate is to define yourself, find some like-minded folks and respond to the provocation. I define myself as a football fan.

Almost every boy that fails to become a footballer remains close to his favourite game as a fan. The same happened to me, but my family's social status, the hard times and my not so happy childhood contributed to completing the jigsaw puzzle. Spite and hatred prevailed and I was not able to stop them. It was my fate. No one can choose their destiny, can they? So, this is where the touch of "hoolie" appeared in me.

The word "hooligan" is considered as something bad, especially in those years of communist rule in Bulgaria. A long time ago, my grandfather would call me a hooligan when I did some mischief, but now, come to think of it, the word "hajduk"**1** is also a bad one. Or so it was acknowledged in our rudimentary society. Well, can those who used to hide in the forests during the Ottoman rule, fighting for our freedom from tyranny, be bad people?! If we compare the two words, i.e. hooligans and hajduks, both in their positive and negative connotations, we will see that they have a lot in common. In those times hajduks used to wear fur caps, galoshes and national costumes and carried rifles and knives. Nowadays hooligans wear checkered caps, trainers, designer clothes and they use bats and knuckledusters. Of course, such a comparison is a kind of joke, but what matters is that there really are a number of similarities: vigilant mind, being united by an ideal and devotion to that ideal, fighting to the end, and lack of understanding from others, etc.

In modern times, it's the hooligans that form secret organisations and that are the malcontents who join nationwide protests and marches with the clear idea of changing our rotten society. They even started arranging their meets away from the eyes of others in order not to be arrested, convicted and sent to prison. All of this being watched by the remaining apathetic mass of people sitting comfortably in front of their tellies waiting for some corrupted politician to announce that "*The culprits have been taken into custody and will be sued according to the law; they are a bunch of mindless guys, drunk and stoned; they are the dregs of society.*"

Naturally, this is as trustworthy as it is true that I have fought the great Muhammad Ali (Cassius Clay – RIP) in the ring and have knocked him out. Absolute bollocks! If anyone believes such babble, I would dare quote and slightly paraphrase: "Everything will be all right once those who watch football hooligan news become part of them." I do believe that those people who were behind the culprits' backs at some point wanted to do the same but they were afraid to, while those who just sat in silence changing the TV channels have never had the guts to go out and simply be there. Fear is their way of life. Would you mind if I wrote that the words "hooligans" and "hajduks" are synonymous in their positive meanings.

TOSH

There's no easy answer to the question why violence and hooliganism were so common back in those days and still are. Why we hated our rivals so much and why we were that wicked and bad to the bone as my mate Tosh wrote above. Readers may ask *–why we do it, what the point was and what made young people like us behave like vandals?* One may claim that the roots are to be found in the first working class generations after World War II and the advent of the longest regime in our history. From dawn till dusk, in severe working conditions, poverty and starvation, lack of any funds whatsoever – a picture depicting a clear notion of what life was for people back then.

A class of people literally tyrannised by the evil communist regime and the government of a brutal dictatorship for more than 40 years. Those with power nipped in the bud any opposition by the poor and the workers fighting for a piece of bread and better conditions of life. Moreover, intellectuals such as doctors, bankers, teachers, writers and anyone who was against communism and who dared to express freely an opinion on what a normal life should be, were sent to camps (the concentration camp of *Belene* is a vivid example of the brutality of the communist regime). Numerous people were killed and tortured there. In case you did not seem aggressive or discontent with the government regarding their bad policies, you remained passive, became reconciled with being tormented and stayed hungry. Aggression is usually the result of one's way of life, social status, fears and education. It is a behaviour that leads to encroachment upon the personality of others. Its aim is domination over others and undermining their self-confidence and free will. Those are the effects of the regime.

Even after the fall of communism in 1989, they promised a better standard of living but actually continued the old Stalin-like method of government and for that purpose they created a subclass of underpaid people. There was a problem with the shortage of jobs (a number of plants and factories were closed down or privatised for next to nothing) and loss of self-respect and generally the life of misery and sufferings continued. As expected, such people would turn to aggression and revolt. They would be censured, punished and sent to prisons and camps. You would be caught in a vicious circle and there would hardly be any way out. Naturally, you only fight violence with violence. The only way for us to express our discontent with the way of life we lived in those days was by going to football games where we would give vent to all the pressure and aggression that had been building up and that expression was precisely football hooliganism. Football grounds were the places where we would retaliate against provocations. Can anyone define what lies behind the acts of vandalism performed by a group of people destroying only certain material things? Sociologists, journalists... all of them just love writing about the phenomenon called football related hooliganism. Each and every time one and the same questions are asked and one and the same answers are given.

Do any of those people understand hooligans' messages?

The roots of the issue are very different.

As a member of a firm with similar attitudes I can share my observations of this phenomenon and this doesn't mean that a hooligan means some kind of barmy, wacky thug. Hooligans are the outcome of the world we live in. While punks and skinheads fight at concert venues, others decide to fight in disco clubs where, under the influence of drugs and booze, problems also arise quite frequently. Well, hooligans do it at football grounds.

Imagine it is a Saturday or a Sunday. The weather is warm and sunny and promises the next spectacular football clash between two teams that viciously hate each other, for example teams from neighbouring towns or town rivals. Since the break of dawn, police are patrolling the streets as if a civil war is about to break. We all know the score; we all have seen and heard how things are in England, the motherland of football. Groups of young people start gathering in the morning, drinking beer and discussing with who they are going to have a go at in the afternoon. Usually fights between fans occur ahead of games, tensions rise and the main parts are played by their mentality and temper. The essence of hooliganism is to be found in what fans have to state. If it is a game related clash, the reason is down to some kind of difference. If it is rampage, it is a sign of disagreement. A hooligan's mentality comes down to what he can do and show the world. Who he is and what he wants from it.

Our society is way too hypocritical to be able to impartially discuss such controversial topics like the issue of hooliganism. And yet, the overall stratification into social classes leads to the formation of subcultures that are in themselves a kind of self-defense against what is going on around us. As you know, most attention is naturally paid to the public safety threatened by acts of vandalism. Indeed, hooligans are a pain in society's ass, but not a single problem can ever be solved without first being become aware of, understood and discussed. Maybe when the police, journalists and sociologists understand what's going on, we won't be the same anymore…

Nothing can beat the feelings of friendship and unity. Fighting together with your closest friends is a stimulating and highly addictive thrill. The danger lurking around and the feeling that you are with some like-minded mate you can rely on make you strong and resolute. Football violence still exists, though not the way it used to be. Nowadays all those CCTV cameras, draconian police measures and fast track court procedures have significantly reduced the number of acts of hooliganism. Looking back, when we were young in the late 1980s and in the 1990s, I would rather say it was all just a kind of adventure. There was the thrill, the feeling of belonging and what football hooliganism gave us was newly found freedom and excitement. Football violence is an addiction that was a way of life for us. The strong bonds with each other, the territory and setting of our beloved club are major parts of football culture. So, we had the opportunity to feel the instinct of self-preservation when we had to protect our own territory or we were deep in our enemy's one. All those outsiders who have never been involved in hooliganism would never understand it.

GILLY

the steel hearts

It was the autumn of 1987 when I attended my first memorable away game in the town of Pleven accompanied by my father. Lokomotiv (GO) played the local Spartak in a Division One game. Back in those days, trips were usually made by rail not only because of the cheap railway fares, but also because of the excitement felt when a massive support of fans arrived in a strange town. At the railway station in Gorna Oryahovitsa there were about 2000 black-and-white fans armed with carboys and gallons of home-made wine and *rakia*.2 An army waving black and white scarves and flags. An entire train had been especially arranged for the trip to Pleven. Most supporters had been drinking since early morning, lubricating their throats for singing at the game. Naturally, there was chaos and disorder even at the station and the people who took an active part were adults, not children. Those were mainly working-class blokes from the local factories. They had decided to pay their dues to the team by supporting it in its first away game after a 24-year-long exile in the lower divisions. Of course, "The Steel Hearts" team was also there, my father in their ranks holding my hand. I was a 10-year old boy among a bunch of tough men.

Boarding the train was accompanied by chants and cheers, the windows were covered with flags and all across the carriages there was alcohol. The cops tried to force down some lads due to their ongoing alcohol abuse but they were helpless confronting that huge army. A powerful roar echoed all over the place as the train started to pull out of the station, amplified by the sounds of fists and feet thumping like hammers on the carriage metal. The mighty rumble echoed on after the train left the station. Finally we had hit the road. Instantly some compartment parts (racks, seats, tables) were torn off and thrown out of the windows. The streams of wine went on flowing. The *Gamza* **3** was raging inside the men's stomachs and heads.

Upon our arrival at the railway station in Pleven, the youngsters started blowing up minimum-bronze **4** bombs and igniting smoke bombs, while the older lads, just in order to keep step with them, began to hurl empty bottles. What followed was total anarchy. Bystanders waiting to change trains started screaming in terror and running away. Never before had they witnessed such mayhem. It was as if a herd of wild animals had been let loose. A police escort assisted our march to the ground.

During the game the atmosphere on the terraces was tense and uptight. Insulting chants could be heard directed at the locals and their team. There was a pending danger from more severe disorder. Spartak was ahead 2-1. In the dying minutes, a large group of our fans invaded the pitch. The referee had to suspend the game for several minutes. The huge unruly crowd knocked down a concrete fence. Put under the pressure of hundreds of arms and legs it just collapsed as if made of cardboard. The coppers nearby started using their batons, pulling and dragging away some fans like they were animals, while other supporters were being handcuffed. The rest of the crowd was pushing its way to the pitch. After the final whistle, a street war began. On route to the train station the rowdy and arrogant black-and-white army went on a rampage. Stones, bottles and all kind of debris were hurled at shop windows and parked vehicles. A car driven by a woman was attacked. The fans kicked and pushed the vehicle, denting one of its doors. Some natives intervened and it grew into a mass brawl. It was kicks and punches everywhere. The OB could not handle the tidal waves of fans hungry for violence. Some ran into the narrow streets around the stadium chasing their opponents, overturning dust bins, etc. A lot of locals were badly beaten and most of them were lying on the streets noses and heads bleeding. It was a blood bath and it happened in just a few minutes. Bloody scared, I was holding tight my Dad's hand as he was hurrying to the station. Despite my fright, I felt the blood boiling in my veins and all of a sudden I felt an urge to join the battle. I wanted to fight beside the others, but I was still a kid. Trying to protect me, my father punched several men and I watched his giant arms crush their jaws. I distinctly heard the pounding sounds and saw the blood all around us. The cops also saw what was going on and responded by hitting my father with their batons several times. I believed the entire town police force was mobilized.

In the years to follow, I never happened to see again such a massive police escort to guide us back to stations. That game would be long remembered and even to this very day people talk with fear about what happened then. I am pretty certain that day is registered as one of the worst days of violence in the history of football hooliganism in Bulgaria.

On our way back to Gorna Oryahovitsa I asked Dad why our fans were doing that and he replied: *"They do it out of love for their football club. One day you'll understand!"* Deep inside I had already felt it and had understood. The seed of football hooliganism was sown and I was dreaming of becoming one of the thousands of hooligans I saw then.

It was on that very day that I realized football was my love and obsession.

That day was momentous not only because it marked the end of a successful season in the first division after a long exile in the lower ones, but also because of the lasting memories we, the potential football hooligans, were left with. Those very moments set the beginning for some and marked the end for others. There we stood beside our fathers and we felt old enough to continue their work. For them those were their last 'song and dance' while for us those were our first steps and first encounter with what was called football hooliganism. That day I felt like a bird having its last flying lesson and knowing that soon it would be able to fly on its own. Though my mate Gilly already told you about the day in question, I will do it from another perspective, no matter that our stories could sound identical since they reflect the impressions of two children of almost the same age who experienced the day with their fathers side by side.

As correctly written in the article below, it all started with the wine! You may have already read some odd facts about our Balkan culture, which is naturally quite different from the English one. I am well aware that the majority of things are hard to comprehend, but those are the facts and that was the reality in those days. Believe it or not, from the very morning that day I felt it would be quite a special one, taking into account the amounts of alcohol that had been stacked, mostly wine. Not just several glasses or even bottles, but litres of that mighty beverage. I dare call it this way since as part of our customs, we, Bulgarians, produce what we drink and believe me, this drink is different. Now fancy some 5-litre tanks full of wine! Sure we have a special name for them, but what mattered on the particular occasion was that every second man brought such a tank. The event itself had been long considered and well prepared week ago. For days on end people would talk about that game and the word went even across the neighbouring suburbs and villages. Everyone in town was more than happy with the team's performance throughout the season and had decided to support it in its last away game. A free of charge football special had been ensured for that purpose and that train was to take us to a neighbouring town, an hour and a half trip from ours. A kind of football rivalry had developed between our two towns throughout all those years playing in the lower divisions. Well, it was not as bitter as the one between Gorna Oryahovitsa and Tarnovo, but yet, both teams belonged to one and the same geographic area, which was a precondition for quite a good atmosphere.

I remember that morning very well. The station was packed with thousands of supporters, something unprecedented for our country when speaking about travelling fans. Most of the fans were quite colourful, wearing the usual scarves and T-shirts and flying flags, but there were also those who had taken the tanks in question, this time not filled with water, but with something very different. Some had already drunk too much of it and so the police stopped them from going on that so long awaited trip. Indeed, most of them could barely stand on their feet. What greatly impressed me was the presence of plenty of men aged about 50, which was as unusual as our large numbers that day. However, that could be explained by the fact that in those days the tradition was for most workers from the local plants and factories to visit football games in an organized manner even when the team played on a weekday.

In other words, everybody would stop working and everything would close down to pay their dues to professional football that was back in town. "The Steel Hearts" were also there, of course, Dad amidst them. His little boy that used to hit pillows until recently was also ready for his first really big trial. And what a trial it was! In just a few hours he was to see with his own eyes how the rage of those tough men with big fists would push them into unparalleled battle scenes to be remembered and talked about for years.

After the regular quarrels with the police, the train doors were closed and the train set off carrying about 2000 fanatic black-and-white supporters, of them at least 500 considered as dangerous for the public order. Extremely furious and brutal representatives of the lower strata of society and working-class people were on their way not only to support and cheer their beloved team onto victory, but also to give vent to all negative emotions they have accumulated as a result of the daily hard work, privation and poverty they had been put to for so many years by the regime that was about to irrevocably collapse just a year later. What I saw in the eyes of many of them was no joy. On the contrary, it was a clear wish for revenge, battle and conflict. Something that almost always happens when supporters from a smaller town travel to a bigger one or when a small team plays an away game against the champions, for example. However, neither applied to our particular case, although the town we were heading for was much bigger than ours, in general their team was not much successful, but still it was a regional derby, which alone would promise quite an interesting trip. After the very first miles of the train trip I started wondering whether it would reach the town of Pleven in one piece and whether some carriage would not be lost along the way. No doubt the carriages were going to be ravaged. A deafening roar was heard when the train pulled out of the station. I closed my ears since the roar was accompanied by the rumbling thunder of thousands of hands and feet pounding on doors, windows and seats, some of which were actually no longer there as they were incessantly being thrown out of the train. All that noise was devastating and even doubled by the roof of the station. The escorting police were helpless. They tried to nick a bloke or two but soon they realized that for the next hour they just had to obey the rules laid down by the thousands of mouths shouting, fists thumping and boots kicking.

The hour gone, I was surprised to see that the mischievous beverage has left the huge tanks and so they were almost empty. Everybody's throats must have been well lubricated and ready for the cheering to follow. Fists and boots were also prepared for the fight that would inevitably come. Thirty minutes later the train entered the enemy's territory and naturally the crowd wanted to get off with the train still moving, as if they couldn't wait to show what they were capable of. What followed was a complete and utter mayhem, as all hell broke loose. Our police escort had warned their colleagues to brace up in order to meet the massive black-and-white army. We were met by a huge police cordon that wouldn't leave us alone until we reached the stadium.

There, in front of the gates, we started the regular quarrel with the police and hosts about tickets as none of us had or was inclined to buy any. In those days it was unthinkable for travelling fans to buy tickets for a train or game. Every event of this kind would turn into anarchy and no one seemed to care about anything, not to speak of tickets. I felt tensions around me rising and likely to result in something beyond remedy.

Suddenly, a huge mob stormed the reinforced concrete barriers and in just a few seconds they made the solid structure look like made of cardboard. I had the feeling that dozens of beasts were trying to get out of a cage they had been locked in. In the particular case they were trying to get in destroying everything in their way and, believe me, the damage and ruins they left were not minor at all. Some of the more peaceful fans, especially women, denounced such behaviour, confronting firmly the perpetrators without even realising that most of the latter were their own husbands and the children they had just scared were their own sons. That day it was us, me and Gilly and all the other young boys, that would remember that bad example as a good one and would carry it over the years to come. Truth be told, I was simply scared then, but deep inside me I wanted us to win the battle not only on, but also off the pitch, which was later to become my main priority.

The outcome was about 40 people nicked an hour before kickoff and if you ask me what happened on the pitch, I remember almost nothing as all the time my attention was turned to the prevailing extremely hostile atmosphere caused mainly by the visiting fans, whose hot boiling blood mixed with wine had long rushed to their heads, leaving behind all forms of self-control. They just wanted to smash, crush and beat whatever they could lay their hands on. Several pitch invasions followed, one of them resulting in damages to the radio vehicle parked on the racing track. There used to be such vehicles once and they were used for live radio broadcasts of various events. The vehicle in question was smashed, even dismantled, one of its front doors missing. The same things happened to the ambulance that drove back and forth on the track trying to help the injured, as well as to a number of other cars parked outside the ground. By and large, if I have to summarise, that was a Bulgarian little Heysel.

Of course, the locals hit back. They wanted to protect their town from the raging vandals. A fistfight broke out in a park outside the ground where my most vivid memories come from and where I last saw my father and his mates in a real fight. I could clearly hear the muffled sounds of fists and feet hitting their victims' flesh. I don't know how they felt back then, but to this very day I have never seen a more brutal fight, especially when we talk about Bulgarian football hooliganism. I really wouldn't wish anybody the pleasure of confronting hands that had been bending iron for 30 years and that are clenched in fists hitting straight in the teeth. After this fight "The

Steel Hearts" team might as well have been called "The Iron Fists". At least for me, having witnessed what happened in that park, they would forever remain in my mind with the latter nickname. Now many of them are not among the living, unfortunately, including my father, and I can feel nothing else but great respect to the big black-and-white lads from the past. May God have mercy on their souls!

Anyway, the two teams did not play often in the following years. It could be an interesting thought what would have happened if they had to come and play in our town. Nonetheless, this did not happen as that very season they were relegated and they did not manage to win promotion back to Division One while we played there. Their revenge was to be further postponed until the time we were relegated. You know what people say: *"If you don't come, we will!"* And so it happened. No later than the second round in the lower division, fate crossed our paths and after 7 or 8 years of waiting they finally had an opportunity for revenge. It would have been good for them if they had played away in our town that day so that the overall picture could have been the same as it had been years before, but alas! The draw sent us to their town again. I am not in the least sure that if it had been the other way round they would have come in large numbers, all the more that they were not at all famous for being the greatest away game supporters.

So, already grown-up, we and our older lads had the honour of organising our next invasion in the town of Pleven. As one could expect, that turned out to be a much more difficult task than it was before since back then our team was riding on the crest of a wave and the supporters themselves were blissfully swimming along. When a team is successful it usually gets tremendous support; but then things were on the opposite side and after such a painful relegation that we had had the supporters' spirits needed a lift. We did our best to gather the huge army again, but things were really different. Moreover, our country was in the troubled period after the transition and, believe me, football was the last thing people cared about.

I am not trying to find excuses, I have really read a lot about English fans and I do know that when a team is relegated it even increases its attendance in the lower division the very following season, but unfortunately our reality was and still is very different. Anyway, isn't the purpose of all these books to allow anyone to tell about their own experience and let others come inside one's world, sometimes much more different from theirs?

TOSH

---

1 IN THE BULGARIAN FOLKLORIC TRADITION, THE HAJDUK IS A ROMANTICISED HERO FIGURE WHO HELPS THE POOR BY STEALING FROM RICH, AND LEADS HIS FIGHTERS INTO BATTLE AGAINST, THE OTTOMAN AUTHORITIES.

2 A COLLECTIVE TERM FOR FRUIT OR GRAPE BRANDY POPULAR NOT ONLY IN BULGARIA, BUT ALL OVER THE BALKANS WITH AN ALCOHOL CONTENT OF NORMALLY 40% ABV, THOUGH HOME-MADE RAKIA CAN BE MUCH STRONGER (50% TO AS HIGH AS 80%)

3 A DARK-SKINNED VARIETY OF GRAPE USED FOR MAKING RED WINE

4 CHEMICAL MIXTURE-IS A MATERIAL SYSTEM MADE UP OF TWO DIFFERENT SUBSTANCES WHICH ARE MIXED BUT ARE NOT COMBINED CHEMICALLY

АРОДЕН СПОРТ

Когато «гъмзата» лудува

- СЛЕД МАЧА "СПАРТАК" (ПЛ) — "ЛОКОМОТИВ" (ГО)
- ВЕСЕЛА ЕКСКУРЗИЯ С НЕВЕСЕЛ КРАЙ · А МОЖЕ
  ШЕ ДА ИМА И ПО-ТЕЖКИ ПОСЛЕДИЦИ...

ПЛЕВЕН, 4 ноември (От нашия кореспондент). Има такава поговорка: "Човек се учи, докато е жив". Вярна, абсолютно по вярна и точна. Припомни ми я полковник Борис Маринов, началник на градското управление на МВР в Плевен.

РЕПЛИКА

— не само добър събеседник и познавач на футбола, но и мъдър човек. От него научих, че плевенската "Гъмза" била най-немирна от всички нашенски вина, особено есенно време.

— Влез, в което и да е плевенска изба и ще чуеш веселото и звънливо бълбукане в бурето. Извади ли оттам обаче — става лудо. От лудо до — по-лудо! Най-добре е да се стои заключено. Само тогава е мирно и кротко — заключи моят събеседник.

...Последният кръг от първенството на "А" РФГ противопостави, както е известно, един на друг два съседа — два отбора от една област — "Спартак" (Пл) и "Локомотив" (ГО). Оправдан и заслужен е ентусиазмът, който цари сега сред запалянковците от толкова жив център. Нормално е и всеки жител на града да се чувствува малко горд със своя тим, който след толкова години из "изгнание" в "Б" РФГ се завърна най-сетне в групата на майсторите. И не само се завърна, а напоследък радва и с добри игри. Интересът към срещата в Плевен изглежда да е бил голям. За приятелите на футбола от града е уредена специална екскурзия, пуснат е с намаление и извънреден бърз влак. Чудесно. Но... някои решават, че удоволствието им не е пълно, ако не се натъпчат за из път какво и друга бутилка, че и тубичка с домашна "гъмза". И така час преди мача, след едно весело пътуване със знамена, песни, лакардии, туби, шишета, дамаджани и тръби на плевенския стадион "Спартак" акостират около две хиляди "весели" запалянковци.

"Гости, какво да се прави" — ще сподели после пред председателят на ФК "Спартак" Н. Богданов. Но, "гъмзата" не стои мирна. Започват продължавания, обидни скандирания и пр.

— Разшетахме се бързо-бързо и за десетина минути събрахме хич цял куп инвентар — туби и дамаджани с вино и какво ли още не. Най-активните и пияни 30-40 души отнехме от стадиона — споделя старши лейтенантът от милицията Радослав Цолов.

По време на мача на трибуните вираха първи, напрегната обстановка. Чуваха се обидни скандирания по адрес на плевенчани и на техните футболисти. Зрелище, както се казва, опасно и от по-сериозни изстъпления. Не станаха, за щото органите на обществения ред този ден действуваха чевръсто и разумно. Десетки млади (и не съвсем млади) побойници запалянковци бяха задържани и глобени. В ГУ на МВР има цял списък с имената на провинилите се "герои": Кирил Атанасов, Петко Николов, Тотьо Тошков, Димитър Димитров...

— Особено необуздано, агресивно, хулигански и арогантно стана поведението на запалянковците, когато тръгнаха след мача към гарата. — разказва старшината от МВР Венцеслав Хинтоловски. — Такава вакханалия не бях виждал! Нападаха една кола, управлявана от жена, блъскаха колата с тояги и ръце, ритаха, огъна я една от вратите. Нанесоха се гоявания, стана масов побой. Голяма група се нахвърли върху оградата на стадион "Св. Алексей" и тази здрава, желязна маса рухна, като че ли от картон. Нанесоха бе побой на мирни граждани. И всичко това за броени минути. Укротихме бързо самозабравилите се, но поражения оставаха. "Ето още имена: Цв. Станимиров, Ст. Вълчев, Пл. Бойчев... нови "герои" за прокуратурата.

С болка и свито сърце пиша тези редове, защото познавам и уважавам обективната и чиста горнооряховска публика.

Случаят трябва да послужи и за "обица на ухото", за акълна и дълбок размисъл не само за спортните ръководители от Горна Оряховица, но и за всички, които тръгват към стадионите в нетрезво състояние, защото прав е полковник Маринов, когато казва, че гъмзата е мирна и кротка, единствено когато е в бурето...

СВЕТОСЛАВ ОБРЕТЕНОВ

After the Spartak (Pleven) – Lokomotiv (GO) game
A happy trip with unhappy ending
It could have had even more severe consequences

PLEVEN, 4th November 1987 (from our correspondent)

There is this famous quote: "The education of a man is never completed before he dies". It is true; it is absolutely true and correct.

The man who called my attention to this quote was Colonel Borislav Marinov, head of the police department in the town of Pleven

REJOINDER

Not only a good company and an authority on football, but a wise man, too. I learnt from him that the Pleven region *Gamza* was the most mischievous of all Bulgarian wines, especially in autumn.

"Go into any winery and you will hear its jolly and playful bubbling in the cask, but once out of the cask it gets wild … raging wild! So you'd better keep it under lock and key cause only then it stays calm and tender", my companion winds up.

In the last round of the Division One Championship, two teams from neighbouring towns played against each other – Spartak (Pleven) and Lokomotiv (GO).

The enthusiasm among football fans from the major railway centre is justified and well-deserved. It is understandable for every citizen of this town to feel proud of its team, which, after so many years playing in the second division, has finally returned to the top flight … and not only has it returned, but has been playing really well recently.

There must have been a huge surge of interest in the game in Pleven. A special trip was organized for the fans from Gorna Oryahovitsa on a special discount express train. Great! But… some fans decided that their pleasure would not be complete if they didn't bring with them a bottle or two of home-made *Gamza*. So, an hour ahead of the game, after a jolly trip involving flags, chants, jokes, bottles, carboys, gallons and horns, about 2000 jolly black-and-white supporters arrived at *Spartak* Stadium.

"Well, guests they were, what else can you do but welcome them!", would later share N. Bogdanov, Deputy Chairman of FC Spartak. But the *Gamza* wouldn't stay calm. There were provocations, jeers, chants, etc.

- We got quite busy and in just ten minutes we confiscated a whole lot of stock – gallons and carboys of wine, whatnot. We ejected the most drunk and disorderly 30-40 fans", said Senior Police Lieutenant Radoslav Tsolov.

During the game the atmosphere on the terraces was tense and uptight. Insulting chants could be heard directed at the locals and their team. There was a pending danger from more severe disorder. However, the situation was brought under control thanks to the swift and reasonable actions of the police. Dozens of young (and not so young) intoxicated fans were arrested and fined. The Police Department has a long list with the names of those "heroes": Kiril Atanasov, Petko Nikolov, Totko Totkov, Dimitar Dimitrov...

"The fans' behaviour became particularly unruly, aggressive, hooligan and arrogant after the game when they headed for the railway station", said Police Officer Ventsislav Hristolovski, "never before have I witnessed such acts of vandalism! They attacked a car driven by a woman, kicking and pushing the vehicle until they dented one of its doors. Some passers-by intervened and it grew into a massbrawl. A huge mob stormed the fence of Slavi Aleksiev Stadium and the solid iron structure just collapsed as if made of cardboard. A number of peaceful citizens were badly beaten. And all of this happened in just a few minutes. We managed to subdue those insolent fans, but the damages remain. Here are more names: Pl. Suvandziev, St. Valchev, Pl. Boichev..., all of them to be charged by a prosecutor.

I am writing this article in pain and with a sinking heart because I am familiar with and have respect for the impartial and well-behaved Gorna Oryahovitsa supporters. This occasion must serve as an example to others; it must lead to an analysis and in-depth reflection not only for the sports authorities in Gorna Oryahovitsa, but for all those who go to football grounds in a drunken state, because Colonel Marinor is right to say that the *Gamza* stays calm and tender only when in casks…

Svetoslav Obretenov

ONE

HOOLIGENTS

Every one of us has had his idols. Whatever people say, more or less we copy someone's behaviour. It is innate and everyone does it. Though the Bible says that we, people, should stay away from idolatry, which in itself is an excessive admiration or worship of someone or something. However, in their childhood, everyone has his role models to make a cult of and try to imitate. It is always nice to leave a different trail, of course, in order to preserve your identity and individuality. To be unique. For better or for worse, this is exactly what happened to me and my mates.

We were fascinated by everything happening in England only, be it music, football or fashion and even football hooliganism. At this point one would expect once again to hear questions like: *"Why do you idolise them?", "Why do you like English hooligans?", "How are they different from other nations?"* A whole bunch of questions can be asked again and we will try to answer them now. When the English national team was eliminated after the so called "Hand of God goal" at Mexico World Cup in 1986, I didn't get the best of feelings. It was a sheer swindle made by a great football player who later on became a legend. But for me he was a small person both in terms of height and character. What kind of honour and dignity can you have to enjoy the "Hand of God goal" in front of so many people at the ground and before the eyes of millions of TV viewers all over the globe? That is why Latin American football style will never be for me what English football was and will ever be. Brazil and Argentina may have thousands of players that could dribble and juggle with the ball like magicians, but they will never have the charisma of English footballers. That charisma involves courage, dignity, honour, strong character and most of all being and behaving like a gentleman on the pitch. I find people like the "great" Maradona are people who do not value dignity much. I was also ashamed watching that game because the linesman who let that happen and didn't disallow that phantom goal was Bulgarian like me. What a coincidence or maybe fate!

His fault was huge, a lot has been written and spoken about him, but now, when I watch a video of the whole situation it seems more like an optical illusion to me. It was just that the evil genius (in this case) of the small man and great footballer had the say that day. I cannot say that I felt some feeling of guilt due to the Bulgarian linesman's mistake, but definitely, every time I watched the glaring injustice I wished things would be set right as soon as possible. Unfortunately, through all these years, I witnessed many other occasions like that and the worst thing was that they would always involve one and the same team and that was England. That's what made me generally reconsider the game called football. I stood beside justice and decided to support the English national team as if it was my own. A lot of people would laugh at me saying: *"Why did you choose them?"*, *"Why do you like a team that has won the World Cup only once, way back in 1966?"* The truth is that England gave football to the world, the oldest tournament was played there and the first football club in the world was established there.

The dominance England had in Europe in the 1970s and 1980s and all those English fans following their team all over the globe just left a long-lasting memory in my mind. In that memorable 1986, I was 10 years old, but age did not prevent me from realising some aspects of the game and remembering the waist up nude English fans basking in the hot Mexican sun. The army of British wouldn't stop supporting their players. The sight of their flags encircling most of the terraces was definitely a catching one. There were even flags placed on the racing tracks and the fans' roar would smother each singing attempt made by their opponents. This impressive sight made me dream of being like them and why not one of them. In the years to come I tried to get closer to my dream, but that was extremely difficult, even impossible taking into account social life in Bulgaria then. For all Eastern Bloc countries it was a taboo topic, let alone English hooligans. We were buried in poverty and oblivion and we rarely had access to information through the papers, not to mention television. I remember my father managed to buy our first colour TV set in 1985 making Herculean financial efforts so that we could afford it (imagine behind what kind of curtain we used to live). Moreover, those TV sets were manufactured in the town where our rival team and supporters came from. Every time I switched on that great engineering wonder I would see our rival's name (the TV set brand was named after the former Bulgarian capital Veliko Tarnovo) and I wouldn't like it, but it was better than nothing.

Years of darkness and blackout, we were blind to the surrounding world. Living in isolation from the rest of the world, I guess we were also unfamiliar to the others. To a certain degree, we started writing this book with the purpose to draw up the curtain called communism that fell over our motherland and many other countries. We would like to expose the truth so that people finally understand that we are normal human beings, too. And if only someone steps up and says that the communist regime was originally meant as something good! I will spit on that and I would strangle him with my bare hands anyone who says such crap!

The only way for me to see my heroes was again the great forums like the UEFA Euro 1988. I was looking forward to the time I was to sit in front of the telly and see my beloved England and the sea of English fans frenetically supporting their team. We know that Holland played some great games there and made a wonderful impression with their style of play. Lots of my peers were fascinated by the Dutch players, but I already had a clear idea what I would like to be and who I was to support, no matter the score! What I really wanted more and more was to be one of those thousands of

English fans cheering for the homeland of both football and hooliganism. Those were the dreams of an already 12-year-old boy and besides there seemed to be a 'light in the tunnel' because only in two years the monster called "communism" was to leave our country. Of course not completely, but at least we were going to have the freedom to choose what we would like to be and how to define ourselves.

We defined ourselves not only as fans loving the football our team played, but also as people following the example of the English hooligans. I already had a colour TV at home and in 1987 my local and beloved Lokomotiv returned to the top flight after years of exile in the lower divisions of Bulgarian football.

As we said before, football hooliganism is spread all over the world, but in general England is believed to be the homeland not only of the game, but also of hooliganism. Football is the English national sport and occupies a major part of the English way of life.

17th June 2000, Belguim, Charleroi. Germany played England in the UEFA Euro group stage. It was a high-risk game because those who had come to watch the game were tens of thousands while the ground capacity was just 20.000. What more could a football fan and especially a risk-seeker hooligan want? The two deadliest rivals in Europe in terms of football, two teams going for the trophy. Everybody in Charleroiwas ready to celebrate. But instead ... chairs were hurled in the town hall square and the side streets, beer bottles littered the streets, carefully arranged shop windows were smashed, hundreds were arrested. On the pitch it was 1-0 for England, Alan Shearer being the hero. Not much later both teams were eliminated from the tournament. But who cared? The clash of the titans had happened though not on but off the pitch. Everybody talked about one thing only. They had returned, they were there!

Who are they? Europe's football nightmare – the English hooligans. If you look for the roots of hooliganism across English stadia then you are in the know. Hooliganism has existed since the beginning of football in general. It is hard to specify the exact date that marked the start of venting the anger that still reigns over stadia. The more popular and important football became in social aspect, the more brutal the very hooligans became. The English perceive drinking and bullying as their birthright. That's how they manifest their identity. It is a simple fact that England gave the world the word "football" and it was England again where football-related violence was born and later spread elsewhere.

Way back in the early years of the House of Hanover, foreign visitors were horrified by the behaviour of the crowds, namely the constant cursing, shirtless men and the overall loose morals. The addition of a feeling of superiority to that natural rudeness could have some dangerous consequences. During the Victorian period the American writer Ralf Emerson described the arrogance so typical of the English as follows:

"There are multitudes of rude young English who have the self-sufficiency and bluntness of their nation, and who, with their disdain of the rest of mankind, and with this indigestion and choler, have made the English traveler a proverb for uncomfortable and offensive manners."

Every time English hooligans go on rampage in some city or town, flip street café tables and make the noses of all those unfortunate enough to stand in their way bleed, politicians and mass media start asking what that really means. Pugnacity is inherent to the English. The more blood they spill, the more cruel and ruthless they become.

Before the rules of the game were finally established, football games looked more like local riots. There is evidence that during the Edwardian Era (the early XIX century) the crowds of fans already had threatening behaviour:

"Once, at a famous football ground in Northern England, I saw and

heard a thousand-strong crowd assault the referee because of some decision of his. Malicious shouts a torrent of abuse, fists and sticks flying, all those made the crowd look formidable".

The farther back we look into English history, the more understandable becomes the conclusion that besides their good manners and deep faith in personal rights, the English are distinguished for their natural aptitude for rioting. In the spirit of this clearly outlined trend, the number of hooligan acts quite naturally increased in the 1950s and 1960s, and going through the naughty 1970s and 1980s they reached our modern times.

Hooliganism has turned into a game following its specific rules and a certain informal code of honour. Football hooligans are also football fans. The media may think otherwise but it only comes to show how little they understand the bottom line. Fundamentally, any hooligan is a fan of the game and if a fella stops attending games the problem will arise somewhere else. Football is in their blood. Those who indulge in violence do it because it allows them to experience the extremes of any emotion known to man. Anyone who has not been involved would probably find it an astounding phenomenon, but it is actually the truth. Football hooliganism is a kind of extreme sport. Sports like bungee jumping or snowboarding are certainly extreme and everyone runs a risk while overcoming one's fears in order to feel the thrill and relief. The same goes for football hooligans.

Apart from favouring English hooligans and their cultural movement, we tried to copycat their style of dressing and fashion.

In those years of socialism it was inconceivable to find designer clothes in Bulgaria. Our society had not even heard of any fashion designers. All clothes and shoes were manufactured domestically. No one had seen goods "made in the West". So when we were young boys we were not fussy about what we wore. It was prompted by our parents not having much cash and also by the fact that fashionable clothes were imported and accessible only for the privileged as they cost a fortune. That they didn't know anything about those clothes, let alone the casual subculture, was quite a different story. What could an MP's son or daughter know about such culture or football hooliganism?

After the fall of the Iron Curtain such clothes started to appear on the market, but mainly in bigger cities and special stores called *Corecomm* where they sold goods imported from Western Europe. As time went by, around the mid-1990s, designer labels started to penetrate our environment. That was when we began to fully copycat the hooligans from the Albion. The scarves and T-shirts of our favourite teams were replaced by designer clothes. Trains as the major means of transport in the late 1980s were replaced by coaches or cars (we would often get taxis for away games in towns not so far away from ours). We had separated from the general mass of supporters as an independent group of casuals.

The English word *"casual"* means "ordinary, daily" and is used to designate informal attire. It is England where the youth casual subculture originated in the late 1970s and the early 1980s. This subculture was ridiculed and ignored by the media and sociologists. Those ignorant people did not notice how this cultural movement developed at accelerated rates. Its roots were in the Northern working-class cities like Liverpool, Manchester and Leeds. During the boom of football hooliganism when English teams marched triumphantly across Europe, their supporters like a real plague committed outrages everywhere they went.

As a backlash to that aggression and the incessant fights between different "firms" (that's how the organised hooligan groups of English team supporters are called) the English police started to tighten the reins and put up a firm resistance against football-related violence. In such a complicated situation, when anyone wearing their favourite team's colours raised the suspicions of and was subject to a possible check by the Old Bill, hooligans gradually changed their appearance getting rid of the "proper" team uniform and replacing it with casual clothes since those who wore expensive designer clothes were not suspicious for the coppers (then).

1977, when Liverpool won their first European Champions Cup

and their travelling fans would return home with designer clothes, in most cases as a result from looting stores in different European cities where the police was far from being as prepared to fight hooligans as the English cops were, is considered to have set the beginning of the casual era. Football fans became fond of labels like the French Lacoste, the Italian Sergio Tacchini, and the German Adidas, which at that time were not so popular in conservative and resistant to foreign influence Great Britain. Moreover, those labels were much more expensive than locally manufactured ones.

History remains silent as to who first came up with the term "casual" to give a name to that new youth fashion, but gradually the word became a synonym of "hooligan". As a matter of fact it was not established nationwide at once, but had its regional varieties. For instance, In Liverpool "casuals" were preferably called "scallies" – from the slang word "scallywag" meaning "a scamp, rascal". In Manchester they used to call them "perries" because of the Fred Perry brand named after the renowned English tennis player and having the laurel wreath, which had turned into a veritable uniform. Favourite sportswear brands were mostly tennis-related, such as Lacoste, Fred Perry, Sergio Tacchini (not only limited to manufacturing sportswear, but also offering a designer label segment), FILA and Slazenger. Other cult status labels were Adidas and the Italian Kappa and Diadora.

An absolute favourite among casuals became the expensive and high-quality Italian jackets Stone Island with their huge compass logo on their left sleeves, the label becoming an absolute must for firm members. The other two uniform-like elements were white trainers and checkered patterns in shirts, scarves and hats of local English luxury brands like Aquascutum and especially Burberry. Other popular labels (the list not being exhaustive, though) were Lyle & Scott, Paul & Shark, Berghaus, Paul Smith, Lois, Pringle of Scotland, Ralph Lauren, One True Saxon, Ben Sherman, Henry Lloyd, Hackett, Barbour, Emporio Armani, Lambretta, Prada, and The Duffer of St George. If you didn't wear designer trainers, Timberland and Kickers shows were also acceptable.

The rivalry between warring firms expanded from out singing, outwitting and outnumbering to out dressing. Football casual subculture is not related to any political ideology since left-wing, right-wing and liberal coexisted in one and the same firm. It was not necessarily connected with a certain kind of music, either. "Casuals" have pretty varied music tastes – the reestablished mod style, ska, dub, indie rock, new rave, Madchester, punk, post punk, Britpop, etc. Football casual culture allowed fans of all those music style to get together. Probably it was a fashion? Close, but not exactly. First it was about the way you looked and then we turned into slaves of designer labels. Or was it violence? Yeah, to some extent. "Casual" is a product of competition. You are to show the rival firm that you have something more, that you are better than them – both in fights and in the way you look. *"Violence and fashion were the points of competition under the flag of the team you support"*, a veteran hooligan wrote in a very interesting article on casual culture, *"Even when you're down on the ground spitting blood while being kicked by a rival mob, it's important to look good."* It took time for the police and the general public to understand what the idea of designer clothes was and what conspiracy there was.

Before those clothes turned into uniforms, hooligans benefitted from the trick and managed to avoid the attention of the police much more easily. There is this funny case for hooligans when back in 1995, at a Brugge vs Chelsea UEFA Cup Winners Cup game the cops detained a number of Chelsea fans wearing the Stone Island logo as they decided that the logo was a kind of rank insignia given to the most distinguished hooligans. You can imagine what 'analytical and clear' minds coppers have!

Meanwhile, the casual fashion has long been preferred not only by hooligans but by the majority of English football culture fans. You don't have to be a hooligan to wear such attire. This style of dressing has come in strong not only in our country, but all around the globe and now fashion hooligans are everywhere. The football hooligan scene and casual culture still remain misunderstood by a major part of society, hardly noticeable for them regardless of time and space.

These already established hooligan profile and role model, I think, we were trying to follow, defining ourselves as "football casual-hoolies".

Anyway, let's go back to my country in the late 1980s, where, though having bought my first colour TV set, my friends and I faced a task almost beyond our abilities, i.e. keeping up with British football in general! We would listen to BBC Five Live on small transistor radios that used to have antennas because in most cases at the same time we would have a duty to perform and support our native Lokomotiv in its home or away games. Quite often that would happen at the very ground, in the coach or train on our way back from somewhere and at all kinds of other odd places. We would get together at parties, more than 20 people, and, no matter how amusing it may sound, we would flock around the small radio and hold our breath so that we could listen to the sports news coming from the English stadia. The very transmissions were of poor quality accompanied by a lot of static noise (as if a plane was taking off nearby), but we had no other choice then. We didn't have Diema and Nova Sport **5** endless coverage of the Premiership.

My native town didn't have any satellite dish places yet and we, English football fans in the dawn of the Premiership, would have to spend a fortune to travel and watch some weekend game, which, taking into account the poor-quality radio broadcasts, was a great advance in itself! Believe it or not, I would travel many a miles to another town in order to watch English football live in a satellite dish equipped *Eurofootball* betting shop. It was such a thrill for me that I still can't find the words to describe it and I know some of you will not understand and even tell me: *"No, you are not a proper fan of that team, because it is not your native team and you don't belong there, so this is a kind of unnatural fandom…"* Oooh, on the contrary, I am a fan and I am not just an ordinary fan, but a rather extraordinary one! That struggle of ours to watch and listen to football games involved much laughter and dozens of hilarious situations. I remember several of them and even nowadays when I recall them I can't help laughing out loud.

Once there was this friend of mine getting married on a Saturday and so we had to miss the football and instead honour the young couple by attending their wedding ceremony and party. Everything went on as planned, and the formal part being over, we headed for the restaurant to start the party. However, later in the afternoon, the party in full swing, the bride looked for her husband to kiss him as the tradition has it and poor him, she found him hiding outside behind a bush with ten more blokes (all of us) listening to football games on the antenna-type small transistor radio already mentioned. To top it all, displeased with the coming football results, someone had bitten off the antenna and so it became quite clear for all of us that we would not be able to listen to our favourite English games and we decided to go back to the party.

Our ambition to support our favourite native team and at the same time follow our dreams and keep up with the English games from thousands of miles away turned out to be a rather difficult task and before we realised it, maybe even as a joke, we started applying a kind of double standard that was very hard to keep since we would often meet opponents who generally did not accept our ideas. A number of people would ask me: *"Who are you going to support if your local team plays against your TV dream team!?"*

Well now, this is one of the few questions that I can hardly answer. At least not in an unambiguous way. And if I have to be honest, both then and now, I can't see any chance of my two favourite teams playing against each other and as time goes by such likelihood becomes even smaller and subject of probability theory only. It is just because of the modest success and capacities of my team and the absolute contrast with the UK team. Though nowadays I strongly believe in the *"Support Your Local Team"*, motto, in the past it was a real must for us to have a favourite team from England! Naturally, in support of that widely discussed role model, each of us, one way or another, chose such a team. In the early 1990s, or to be more precise during the 1990/91 season, our day finally came. You know what they say that every dog has its day. In 1991, 2 years after the fall of the much loathed communist regime, my town had the honour of topping the chart of towns watching foreign football games via a satellite dish of its own!

Wow, believe me, nothing compared to that joy. The influx of people keen on watching was so huge that the venue would almost burst at its seams… Moreover, the owner of the place had taken the odd (he must have thought it as wise) decision to hire strippers, probably believing that they would entertain the blokes coming to watch football on TV even more and hoping to attract more customers, respectively make greater profits.

Strange or not, it just didn't happen his way and, believe me, those girls were bloody gorgeous. Blond, heavenly bodies, beautiful blue eyes and pale skin, most of them of Russian descent so I guess there's no point in continuing my description of them. Unique beauties! But who cared? Not us, anyway! The magic streaming from the TV screen had fascinated and enthralled everybody and we did not pay even the slightest attention to all the beauty around us. The only beauty we saw was on the TV-screen football pitch.

I remember another funny occasion. I think we were watching Nottingham Forest vs Liverpool (both of them English football giants) and the game had the usual charge and atmosphere, a lot of speed and tension leaving us literally breathless. That especially went for those friends of mine who had chosen those two teams to be their favourites. All of a sudden, one of those blond Russian girls decided to entertain everybody by shaking and grinding her voluptuous body and obstructing the TV set we were watching. One of my mates immediately jumped up and angrily told her to fuck off and so she left in confusion and even started crying. I cannot describe that in any other way but as an obsession and next door to madness. And we've had loads of such occasions through all these years. Years later, when I began to read such literature and for the first time came across the well-known now cliché *"The thrill of watching football is more exciting than of having sex with a beautiful woman"*, I knew what it meant though I was not born in the motherland of football, I did not experience this thrill directly in those years of mass hoolie-phenomenon in Britain and I would rather disagree with such an idea.

At some point of that period, the time came for me to choose my favourite British team and I did it with not much hesitation. I know that lots of you will say: *"For fuck sake! Not another plastic fan that's ignorant and not called upon by the team he has chosen.* "Yeah, probably the team has to find you and not the other way round, or to be more precise you must be born and raised in its locality. However, there's no way I can agree with that, either. As we know, the heart, and hence love, knows no boundaries (just like hatred) and I dare disagree with the way of thinking of those who try to establish any boundaries, norms and rules on something so boundless and mysterious as a man's love for something. In my opinion everyone is free to choose and as we already said at the beginning of this chapter, it is one's primordial right to define oneself and decide what kind of fan one will be and to what extent one is to imitate others and to what one will be oneself!

I've been supporting Manchester United since 1991 when they impressed me by gloriously winning the UEFA Cup Winners Cup final. I still remember well Mark Hughes' deadly finishes and Lee Sharpe's amazing raids on the wing simply destroying Barcelona's defence. Since that very day I have been entirely captivated by that team and its glorious achievements that followed have made me extremely proud of choosing it and not any other. Being a contemporary of the creation of the Premiership and the total domination of my favourite team, enjoying the style of players like King Eric and the newcomer then Ryan Giggs... Just priceless! The only thing I feel sorry about is not coming to England earlier because I could have eye-witnessed all those really grand moments! The years when United did not win trophies but were magnetic and their era of glory started.

Unfortunately, as I said before, my belated arrival in England and the childhood dream realisation deprived me of the opportunity to also witness some "hoolie-stories" related to The Red Army and its divisions. We know that such occasions are now becoming increasingly rare in the UK. I have tried one way or another to 'infiltrate' the "Man In Black" organisation and to some extent I did, but it's not the same. Its members are somehow extremely cautious after all the Iron Lady and its machine did. Dawn raids, life bans, CCTV cameras at every corner, turning grounds into all-seater theatres, etc.

I was also involved in one of the 'battles' of the so called "War of the Roses", but, of course, it's a separate topic.I was relatively well-prepared for the British football scene because, as I already said, I had been listening to English football games on BBC Five Live since an early age, which at that time was the only way to be closer to my favourite British football team! Reading, in particular the specialised Bulgarian newspaper called *'Albion'*, helped me educate in terms of pure statistics and arrive much better geared up for the English scene and not only... all of that helped me learn the language and settle in such a way that I cannot say that my move affected to any significant extent my views, attitudes, conceptions and in general the "hoolifan" side of me.To a certain degree planned, though for a later stage in life, my arrival in England added to my terrace experience, and as far as attending games was concerned, the matches I went to were fewer than the ones in Bulgaria as I am certainly a record-holder following Lokomotiv (GO) in the top flight! I put quality before quantity and 5–6 away games with United per season are just enough for me to satisfy my 'football needs' and I don't need to go to the theatre.I think anyone In-The-Know here will recognise the advantage of away games as pure entertainment for United fans as travel support over their experience at the "Theatre of Dreams".

And so I'll once again go back to the time when gradually things started to arrange for me as a fan, but the sharp contrast I already mentioned and the differences in time remained to make things harder to combine. What do I mean? Gilly already mentioned the specialised stores called *Corecomm* where we could buy certain casual clothes and in particular a pair of cool trainers, jeans and a Polo T-shirt, but not necessarily from the designer labels listed above. In those first years after the collapse of communism it was still difficult for us to get hold of such particular kind of goods.

I remember the times of the communist regime when I was still a student I had a friend whose father used to be a big truck driver and travel across Europe. On returning to Bulgaria he, of course, would bring presents for his son (i.e. my mate) and what he would most often bring were the said designer jeans, trainers and T-shirts. I remember very well how we used to go to his place with my classmates where he would readily show his new stuff and we used to watch with noble envy, agape with wonder, empty-handed, slightly disappointed and sincerely hoping that someday we would also own such things. And there was that particular, even funny case, considered back then as a serious breach to the school rules, naturally in contrast to the communist norms and manners of that time. The boy in question was foolish enough to put on his designer clothes and wear them to school and so he was immediately sent to the principal, punished and warned that he would be expelled from school in case of another similar breach!

After all that has been said so far, you could imagine how I felt when in 1995 I finally got my let's say "hooligan uniform". It consisted of a pair of Wrangler jeans, a Burberry cap and Lacoste trainers! Once again my joy and admiration of what was about to come and what had been by then only a dream and a plan I had shared with few others were beyond description. Somewhere at that point we had the floodgates opened and we did realise that even our wildest dreams have already or were about to come true for sure. So, as you would expect, we followed them without any hesitation.

I dare say and claim with confidence that 20 years ago, even bigger cities in Bulgaria had no indications of casual culture and designer labels whatsoever. Even nowadays these things are still strange for a number of places. No matter that most groups at that time belonged to the so called *ultra* movements, a concept like "casual/ultra" just didn't exist yet, let alone any "hoolie touches" and the style we were willing to establish and promote. No way! We could even say that there were still traces of skin, punk and metal styles, reversible Bomber jackets (orange reverse), sleeveless denim winter jackets with badges and numerous pins (German style) and various other even more colourful items and accessories.

Another memory brings me back in time when we first met some very good football mates of ours (that we will introduce to you later on in this book) and so to say strong allies of ours throughout the years, namely the supporters of a team from the Bulgarian second biggest city, i.e. our black-and-white brothers and team namesakes –

the Smurfs from Lokomotiv (Plovdiv). During one of our frequent friendly visits there at the dawn of their emerging at that time *Lauta Hools* firm, soon after I had acquired the so cherished "casual uniform", I found myself (quite deliberately) on the terraces among them for the all-time red hot Plovdiv derby and their lads were greatly surprised and astonished that someone from a small town like ours can be seen wearing a Burberry cap, for instance!

A really telling example and evidence that in those times such a phenomenon was rare even for bigger and more developed towns in Bulgaria. So if we have to summarise and try to analyse all of the aforesaid in a proper artistic style, the differences between the East and the West in this respect and at that time were more than significant. Probably those 20 years I mentioned seem in this case as a real time difference! In other words, as far as fan culture is concerned nowadays, Bulgarian scene is like travelling back in time to 1995 England. Of course, these days everything is rather relative as the scene is actually quite dynamic and the Eastern countries really made a wonderful development, while in England things have actually been in a decline. But whatever they say, at some point or another, to some extent or another, everybody has been influenced and inspired by the scene in the homeland of football and hooliganism!

I know that while reading this many would say, *"The next wannabies and plastic fans, glory hunters"*, etc. That's why, stating our theories in this book, we are trying to explain our starting positions (then) and convince readers that things were not like that for us.

Not with standing anything in the foregoing, I personally have never blindly followed what has been posh and fashionable and these days everything in football-related fashion is so blurred that there is hardly any more a clear distinction between the different types of fans. Nowadays I'm not a slave to designer labels, but like to dress in plain and tidy informal clothes without any excessive garishness. However, what I have always stood up for are the words that I began this story with, i.e. being and behaving like a gentleman everywhere, even at the fan scene, and, of course, friendship.

Through all those years of football riots and disorder I have witnessed many a sad events (from pure human perspective). Antisocial behaviour such as thefts and mistreatment of elderly people, women, mums, dads and children, at and around the football-related scene. I have always tried to harshly condemn such behaviour, and, if possible, prevent it, but as we know, in any football crowd there will always be those few that can hardly be stopped or controlled. It's just that as the years go by you get used to it and begin to take some not very pleasant aspects of fandom for granted. However, I have always energetically fought against such outrageous behaviour and have vocally expressed my disapproval thereof. Probably that was the reason for the number of differences that eventually appeared between me and some old friends of mine, which differences went on to become a split-up. I'm not saying that I have never taken part in antisocial activities... On the contrary! I remember when all hell broke loose (after the collapse of the totalitarian regime) and we literally would go on a rampage and loot like starving, parched and savage pirates (as if to justify our firm name JRF).

I remember many occasions on which, while we were returning by rail or coach from an away game, roadside shops, cafes and restaurants and railway stations were plundered and ravaged literally in seconds. Beer and soft drink fridges would be looted; bottles of alcohol and food would be downright stolen. During yet another funny incident, I saw one of our blokes step off the coach and in just a few seconds he was back on board carrying a huge pot of freshly grilled sausages. You can imagine what followed next on board of our 'pirate ship' - figuratively speaking. All I could see around me were some kind of enraged cannibals chewing on raw meat!

Another recollection brings me back to an away game when one of our fans, acting like a complete moron, hit an elderly gentleman just in order to take his hamburger and eat it, while another tosser was swearing and throwing insults at a small kid only because the boy had the rival team's crest painted on his face. Here exactly comes the line that I and my closest mates have always tried not to cross.

We had our Code of Honour: fight with bare hands; no weapons allowed; never assault ordinary fans, be it elderly people, mums and dads, kids, etc... In general we used to do our best and follow all those unwritten rules and we would also make sure the younger fans also obeyed them, though the generation gap, the different views and mentality and respectively the increasingly strong opposition would often stand in our way. We reached the point when they started calling us insane just because we were different! Our pursuit of a refined and already completed type of "casual-hoolie" fan who would fight with bare fists only and would support his favourite team also bare handed by just clapping and singing, was in sharp contrast to the generally accepted in Bulgaria fan mentality, which in those times could not be associated even with the ultra-style and all its derivatives.

Real friendship is what I cherished most of all. For me it was of great significance and I strongly insisted on its presence among the firm members. I think I managed to find like-minded mates and we did make a very well organised firm. Naturally, times have changed and so have people, loads of us have scattered all around the world, but one of the good examples and the solid ground for all of this has been my old, real and like-minded friend and co-author Gilly. We already told you in the previous chapter about the great friendship and solidarity between our fathers (and families in general), who initiated us not only into football, but also into this special kind of fandom, and no matter how shocking it may sound to some, taught us not only to fight, but also to battle hard life and remain real friends and most of all human till the end.

In all those years we proved that hooliganism in our case was inherited and was not just a fashionable trend or a negative term, but quite the opposite, it had the positive connotation we mentioned in the beginning. For us, even nowadays, this is not something from the past that we would like to forget, but quite the opposite, we take pride in what we have learnt and in the experience we have gained on the terraces. We still find the words courage, honour, dignity, respecter, broadly speaking 'gentleman's behaviour', meaningful. There is genuine friendship and huge respect between us to this day and they are even stronger than ever, and we will be extremely proud if by writing this book we manage to properly send our messages and leave something of real value as heritage for the future generations of football fans.

Finally I will dare quote the prominent in this genre ("hoolielit") Martin King, who is also feature in this book and who wrote at the end of his book *Hoolifan* (the first book of this genre that I ever read): *"If, after a time, my daughter asks me, "Dad, what are you, a hooligan or a fan!?", I would proudly answer, "A hoolifan!"* I would dare paraphrase him and proudly answer my daughter like that: *"A hooligent!"*

---

5   Diema and Nova Sport are two popular Bulgarian TV channels specialised in broadcasting English and other football games live

TWO

PRO-BRIT (CULMINATION)

- Do you have any hooligan organisation, ultra-group or firm?

— *Yes, we do. We have a firm, it was established in 1995 and it is called J.R.F. (Jolly Roger Firm), or the "Jolly Roger" company. I had the great honour of being one of the founders of the firm, which was, as one might say, originally Pro-British orientated as it was founded by a dozen of lads who besides supporting Lokomotiv (GO) were also fans of British football both at club and national team levels.*

British football and the hoolifan culture and not the ultras culture so typical of the Balkans! You understand that this automatically renders useless some of your next questions like the use of pyro, but never mind, let's go on. On our best days we used to gather about 60 people in just a few minutes by only making a single phone call. I'm speaking of a core of lads who shared absolutely identical views and, taking into account the size of our town, I think that was quite a decent number. I could agree to some extent that the reason for founding the firm was Lokomotiv (GO) relegation from Division One down to the lower echelons, but basically the organisation is focused on real friendship not only on the terraces, but in life in general, which in itself makes the firm pretty unique and distinctive. What we used to prepare as choreography before games were huge flags with our own ideas and symbols on.

– What do you think about the "10 vs 10" or "20 vs 20" type of pre-arranged fights with clear and precise rules as practiced in countries like Russia and Poland that are gradually becoming popular among separate ultras mobs in our country? Would you take part in such a fight?

– By and large I support such ideas and would readily participate, but I find those "anabolic steroid" type of fans way too much cause they practice other sports, do intense workouts and go on strict diets! In other words, the "no-weapons" agreement is a good thing, but being a martial arts master actually turns you into a potential killer!

I have some old-fashioned conceptions. I prefer to get pissed before a game and start a good old time pub or street fight, but to know the names of our starting 11 on that day. I am all for the intelligent and pure type of hardcore fan. You cannot confront football fans by involving professional wrestlers and MMA fighters and then speak of fair rules, equal numbers, fair play and the like...

– Which country would you give as an example of well-developed ultras movement from so that we can draw on their experience and ideas?

– For me the country that invented football and hooliganism is a role model in everything! I can't understand those people who derogate and insult them!

It is as if insulting my father – **NEVER!**

THE QUOTE IS TAKEN FROM IN INTERVIEW IN THE LOCAL PRESS WITH one of the founders of the firm.

The events described in the next chapter can be summarised in one word only: OBSESSION.

In the mid-1990s we officially founded the Jolly Roger Firm and it started growing at a tremendous speed. For some it was only fashion. Lads would gravitate around the main core and in a while they would just be gone as unnoticed as they had appeared. However, for others it became a real drug and they would become more and more addicted and in need of it. Not at all in unison with the relegation of our native Lokomotiv (GO) from the top flight, I would even say in contrast to what was happening (because later on we went further down the lower divisions even reaching the Amateur League). The drop in attendance as a whole (reasonable after such a collapse) was inversely proportional to the growth of our core, which, as if out of spite, kept on growing and we followed our team wherever they played, supporting it even more fervently while at the same time continuing to follow the "English thread".

Watching games on TV in large numbers had turned into a kind of mass sport for us. We would return from the ground our team had just played (home or away) and would immediately occupy some nearby boozer where we would keep on chanting, cheering and hurling abuse, this time at the TV set. Loads of people would wonder at our mentality and would sometimes ask us if there were times when we didn't watch football. Our answer was: *"Yes, when we gather to play football!"* We were more like amateurs kicking around the ball in some neighbourhood than serious football players, but we used to do it quite often at weekends. We even struck up a student team, proudly called *St. George* of course! At one of our student championship games in Veliko Tarnovo we had gone to such great extremes with our fandom mania, respectively with alcohol, that we could hardly move on the pitch. I remember the referee even had to stop the game for several minutes so that our centre-back could throw up in the nearest dust bin.

Going back to the fan side of things, our meetings became more and more attended and remarkable. They would often be just like home meetings. We took turns and each of us sooner or later had to entertain the others at his home. However, some were reluctant to do it, but there were others, like me, who quite often offered their homes for the parties involving the next English football match.

I remember one party at home for the breathtaking CL Final in May 1999 played between Bayern Munich and Manchester United at Camp Nou in Barcelona, after the end of which my flat needed major renovation. Fancy the entire pack of fans, recruited for several years in a row, sitting in front of a small TV set in a flat situated in a tower block. The damages from that weird outrage were still visible until recently. Naturally, my neighbours were furious and I had to allocate some funds for repainting the shared parts since the staircase walls were decorated with loads of various graffiti and even worse, writings by almost all my guests that used to visit me throughout the years were carved in the walls with a coin or something as memorable signs in the shape of different mottos and signatures.

There were the dates of momentous games like the one in 1999, accompanied by, for example, the names of favourite rock groups and of course, the nickname of the respective author. Well, deadly authentic, lads, isn't it! Someone had even carried too far in his desire to go into details and had carved all goal scorers and the times they scored under the historic dates, games and results! And all of that was nothing compared to what was about to happen in my flat on that day after Ole Solskjaer's lethal finish and the spectacular comeback in the dying seconds of injury time.

I won't go into the match details as everybody remembers how much football drama it provided, but I'll brief you on what happened at my place after the final whistle.

We had gathered quite early in order to have several drinks ahead of the game. However, some of us (like me) had been drinking since early morning. As dusk fell, the flow of people coming through my door got out of control, everybody brought booze and some were returning from the nearby shop with the next reload and were literally queuing in front of the gate.

The tower block looked like a dormitory with all kinds of people constantly coming in and out of it. On days like that all informal groups in town would unite around football. There were metal heads, rappers, skaters, spotters and what not. On such occasions we would even totally ignore our English football (club) differences and all of us would support the English team playing in Europe as if it was the national team of England. Chelsea, Arsenal, Tottenham, Liverpool and even Leeds and Nottingham Forest fans rallied behind the "red devils" on that day. I find it impossible to happen here and it was exactly what made us such a unique and attractive (to others) company. Especially as we all knew very well the general disposition in the UK and the attitude of a large number of United fans towards the national team and vice versa. However, we were not familiar yet with the idea of the Republic of Mancunia, and I, being a supporter of that team, also supported the England national football team even more passionately. My mate Gilly and I had long got our tattoos of our favourite club and national team, but, please, don't be mistaken, they were not tattoos of the Bulgarian national lion, but of the Three Lions! There were exceptions, of course, and those were the tattoos of our native club Lokomotiv, which we all had put on a pedestal!

Going back to that momentous day, at about dusk my flat was bursting at the seams and I, squiffed as I was, found it rather hard to control the situation with the constant inflow of old and new guests. I decided to let things go and focus on the much awaited (historically since 1968) final. I had already had the immense pleasure of witnessing the first Premiership champion titles (statistically, after 26 years of waiting), but the Champions League trophy was something very different so I had primed myself well for the occasion. The walls of my entire flat had posters thumbtacked (leaving considerable holes after use) and especially for the occasion all curtains had been replaced with flags!

What followed was a Bulgarian traditional (Christian) prayer for success before kick-off, which after what happened on the pitch would turn into a legend among us, more well-known as "Public Prayer to God Almighty"! The moment Ole "hammered the two rusty nails" into the German coffin, believe it or not, I (wild with joy and under the influence of alcohol) myself lit up a flare in my own living-room (remember Balotelli fireworks?) and thus set the beginning of the greatest revelry you have ever seen indoors.

The smoke spread out through the whole tower block and started going out through the windows of my flat and those of the staircase, where, at the very window sills, there were people throwing up smothered by the thick smoke! Even greater chaos ensued. Everybody was running and jumping around like madmen and the final whistle of the amazing final was followed by frantic screams and shouts. Amidst the already dispersing smoke, I finally was able to see what was going on around me... I saw some lads spraying each other with beer and others pouring water on each other's heads not in the bathroom, but in the corridor in front of the bathroom. As a result of the amounts of spilled, sprayed and most of all drunk liquids someone complained of getting an electric shock... I could hear bottles and plates being smashed against the walls chipping off huge swishing bits of plaster, but what sunk most deeply in my memory that night and I still see clear pictures of was a friend of mine carrying a huge dish (resembling the Community Shield Trophy) high above his head, having naturally emptied its contents somewhere on the floor, a dish very similar to the Bundesliga champions trophy that Bayern had already won that season, though failing to win the CL cup! That was the way for my mate to express his enjoyment making fun of the Germans.

When we got out, it was a really spectacular show and quite an attraction since our ecstasy escalated further and everything got absolutely out of control! My neighbours had come out on their balconies and some had even come down to congratulate us being somewhat aware what that evening really meant to me as a fan! Others were swearing at us and were protesting about the noise and the dust bins scattered about. But what did we care? The night was ours to celebrate till dawn!

I looked up to the third floor just to make sure my flat was still there and I saw smoke still venting out of the windows! I had no time for further inspections because I heard a car engine roar and suddenly I found myself on the roof of another friend of mine's car together with many others clambered up like a circus company (clowns) and so, without me even remembering how, we reached the town centre where it turned out that most of us had taken towels, ready for taking a bath in the town fountains, something that has become a tradition of ours after the USA 94 World Cup! Of course, the cops thought otherwise and after having the usual quarrels with them we were chased away to celebrate in the countryside like wild animals on the loose, something that was also quite typical of our midnight parties.

Those parties were almost always full of swearing, wrangles and longstanding quarrels, there was even that case of a ball-point pen stuck in a geezer's head, merely because not everybody supported Manchester Utd, Liverpool or Arsenal. There were fans of Southampton, Blackburn, Norwich, etc. and that meant huge differences between otherwise good friends. Quite often things would get out of control and quarrels would evolve into fist fights. Imagine two good friends watching a London derby between Tottenham and Arsenal, 1700 miles away from the venue, start a fight after a fierce football-related quarrel in front of the telly, or even funnier, while listening to the radio! It would all be carried over to the street, the coach we were travelling on for yet another Lokomotiv (GO) away game and literally anywhere.

I remember an occasion when I and a friend of mine, an Arsenal fan, went on an away game to the town of Montana and we had a crazy argument at the back seats of the coach for nearly 6 hours, i.e. the entire duration of our trip. All that craze on English football grew into such mass visits to restaurants and pubs that their owners would lock their doors and put on the "Closed" signs the moment they saw us. In those days we had this *Domino* rock bar in our town. It was located on a corner downtown and it had two areas. One was indoors, having some ten tables and a bar, while the other was a huge open terrace used mainly in summer or on other warm days. In winter we would pack indoors and sometimes it would be more than fifty of us and the mixture of cigarette smoke and the smell of booze would make you feel as if in a Wild West bar. Many folks would call it a "hole", but we liked it that way. It was our place, our small home. The music we would play there was only hard rock and heavy metal, which additionally would predispose us to make ourselves at home. The bar owner was also a keen

Lokomotiv fan and you can imagine what happened there at weekends.

The bloke was helpful enough to satisfy our needs to not only watch football, but also to make unbelievable noise as if on the terraces. We would often even demand from the owner to turn up the sound of the TV set, which was sometimes impossible because of the music supposed to come out of the speakers, but anyway, the place was more than appropriate and loud enough for us to drown the shouts of a group of football fans watching their beloved game on TV.

The days when the English national team was to play would turn into celebrations for our small town. We would march in the streets chanting and singing *Rule Britania* draped in Union Jack flags without ever worrying about anything or anyone. Yeah, somewhere in Bulgaria, there was that small town that seemed to belong somewhere else in those times. We all clearly remember England's victory over Germany in Charleroi and the Munich win, when the scenario would be one and the same. We would gather in the bar, watch the games, chant as if were in the ground and then the town would not be able to get any sleep due to our midnight parties that would sometimes feature naked dips in the town centre fountains and police chases in the nearby parks, where we would usually finish our drinks. Truth be told, when I get back to my native town these days, there's not a single place to go. We miss such a magnetic place like *Domino*. Younger fans have no idea what our buzz was in those days. I get goose bumps when I think of all the wonderful memories I have. Unfortunately, the bar is long gone and at its place now there is some kind of a shop, but every time I pass by I feel nostalgic remembering it and I shed a tear recalling all those great times we had there when we were younger.

Other towns would also discover our passion. We had friends studying not only in Veliko Tarnovo (the usual target of our raids), but also in the pretty small student town of Svishtov on the river Danube in Northern Bulgaria. There were days on which we would just catch the afternoon train and go there to party with the girls, but also to get our next fix of English football, which was turning into our trademark, mania and obsession. During one such jolly (at least in the beginning) trip to the Danube town we were drawn into such trouble that we ended up in custody after losing a several-hour hide-and-seek game with the police. It all started with a friend's invitation to celebrate his birthday and, of course, watch footy. As it was quite ordinary for those times, a single phone called resulted in 20 blokes getting on the train to Svishtov in high spirits, a bottle of beer in everyone's hand. For that particular destination you needed to switch trains at another railway station.

Slightly tipsy, we stepped off to change trains, which turned out to be our first obstacle to our final destination. Already on the platform, we saw another group of our mates who must have taken the earlier train and were also heading for Svishtov. We understood that something was wrong. We found out that they had had a scuffle with the locals (some of them being of Romani origin), which for us meant one thing only – an attack. Without thinking any further we directly crossed the tracks and without getting down the subways we were at the main platform in seconds. Then out of the train station we came across the local gang. They were drinking at several plastic tables in a bar outside on the pavement across the street. Without any hesitation and in complete silence (we said not a single word to each other), we crossed the street and went at them offhand. En masse, as a disciplined hit squad and with no ifs, buts or maybes. It was a pure spur-of-the-moment, absolutely unanimous assault and fight. A rain of chairs, tables and parasols poured at us, we returned fire and eventually rammed into them and a hand-to-hand combat started. Jaws and heads were being hit by the parasol aluminium stands and one could hear the familiar sounds of kicks and punches that we were to comment on later. It was our kind of, let's say little Charleroi, as the riots we ran resembled the ones in that Belgian town, though on a much smaller scale. In a few minutes the police arrived at the scene and, naturally, nicked us. We were led into the railroad police narrow room in the station building and they took our IDs.

Inside it was all jokes and laughter when we discussed what had happened and the cops would just stare at us with their usual mean faces. The climax of the fun we had was when we saw the very same train we stepped off on its return trip from Svishtov and the train operator rolled down the locomotive window and shouted at us: *"Come on lads, get a move on as they are waiting for you up there in Svishtov!"* And we were really awaited like celebrities. Our friends there had been made aware of what had happened to us earlier (probably by the train operator himself) and they were waiting for the heroes. We were also awaited by an antisocial behaviour police unit and they warned us to behave ourselves till the end of the evening. However, we ignored their usual blather because we were anyway late and had a birthday party to go to and football to watch.

After a late afternoon lavish treat we indulged in watching footy and enjoying student parties in the local discos and clubs. Some of us once more had conflicts with local lads because of some bird and there we went again, back-to-back, throwing fists and several hours later we ended up standing face to the wall in the local police station. What followed were fights in the downtown area and midnight hide-and-seek with taxi drivers and coppers. We hid in tower block entrances, ran along dark and dead-end streets and finally got nicked (once again) and escorted out of town in the early morning.

In all those years we would often get off at that intermediate station and we would nearly always have fights with the locals and the Old Bill. As they say, *"We had a bad reputation"*. The people in that town are a weird lot and it's just that things there can't go smooth. I remember once there were only few of us (me and 5 or 6 other lads) waiting patiently to change trains when we saw a gang of locals in the waiting room standing in a circle and pushing a young boy in the middle. They were all laughing out loud so our first thought was that they were playing a kind of game and just having fun, but then the young lad's expression told another story. We kinda hesitated and stood there watching only to see how the four bigger lads ran out of the station. Then I asked the boy what had happened and he told me they had stolen all his money. As expected, we chased them, caught up with them and gave them a really good hiding. Time passed and one day I came across the young boy again and he bought me a beer to express his gratitude for protecting him and making those bastards give him his money back.

There were other towns not spared by the Jolly Roger Firm. Our "seaside capital", as they sometimes call the town of Varna, where my friend and co-author Gilly studied later and lives up to this day, would also often become the arena of our endless parties, be it birthday parties or derby games in England. He used to invite us to his lodging, from where on most occasions we would head for the first English pub opened in Bulgaria called *The Three Lions Pub*. We made ourselves at home at that place and after having a few drinks there we would have midnight beach parties and play morning beach football while still intoxicated. The pub was located near Varna railway station, which was just fine for people like us coming straight from a train to have a drink. Its building was also a typically English style featuring red brick walls, wooden furnishing and a huge terrace on the second floor. There were several big screens with *Sky Sports* on, various pictures or photos of famous former English players, club badges and a huge British flag hanging from one side of the pub to the other. The owner was a friend of ours and a dedicated Liverpool fan and maybe that was the reason why the pub was usually full of Liverpool fans, especially in summer, when there were also fans from England. The standard menu was English cuisine plus all kinds of salads and delicacies, local and imported beer and liquor. We would regularly celebrate our birthdays there or come to watch derby games in England, drink huge amounts of alcohol and end up at dawn on the beach stripped to our waists even in winter. We would sometimes bring Lokomotiv (GO) flags or the British Jolly Roger and we hang them all over the pub. We would sing songs of our beloved teams or England chants as we were given carte blanche by the owner. I remember one winter we had gathered more than 30 lads to celebrate Gilly's birthday in March. We had occupied the entire terrace upstairs and we were on the booze, heavily drinking beer and indulging in huge servings of appetisers.

After we got really pissed and almost unable to stand on our feet we headed straight for the beach. It must have been an impressive sight to see 30 naked blokes at the break of dawn swimming in the sea with the water temperature being only 12–14°C. I just wonder what people passing by on their way to work must have thought of us. And then one of our mates, obviously having had way too much to drink, bent sideways and threw up something that looked like a whole meatball! Believe me, we all just burst out laughing as we had never seen anything like that before and we just couldn't believe that we were still able to surprise ourselves with some new crazy shenanigans! We even played beach football then and, not surprisingly, we sustained some injuries. Can you imagine drunken young men diving and tackling on wet sand? The amounts of beer drunk in the pub were never enough and so we would go and buy some more in order to keep on drinking. We would often meet at Gilly's place where we would end up naked from the waist up and fighting each other with our belts.

Once, after such a birthday party in March, I had to travel back short-sleeved, wearing just a shirt, as the previous day when I set off from Gorna Oryahovitsa the weather was quite warm for the season, but on the day that followed our heavy drinking session in Varna there were 20 inches of snow. I still wonder how we managed to go back to our native town. Loads of memories from those midnight parties are still kept alive but some things were just forgotten due to getting blackout drunk in Varna.

Of course, most frequently we visited the Bulgarian capital - Sofia. We had a lot of friends studying there, but mostly we would go to Sofia for more important reasons, i.e. getting in touch with English supporters when Bulgarian major clubs like Levski and CSKA, or our national team of course, played against teams from Britain. Our members were not hardcore fans fond of fighting on the terraces only. We also had collectors and autograph hunters who took advantage of each occasion of that kind. Dawn would quite often find me and those blokes in front of hotels where English teams used to stay or at airports where they were supposed to land and I would help my mates out by taking photos of them with some players, for example. I don't say that I, being a devoted footy fan, was not happy to see my football idols, but that was not my actual reason for being there. I would always secretly look around for those small groups of people arriving from other cities just in order to avoid attention and go undetected. Of course, I would always suss them out and knew from then on that they were in town. That was my obsession. I was not an autograph hunter and if I have to be honest I took quite a few photos of me and British supporters and some of these pictures are included in this book.

There are loads of experiences; some of them I am going to mention only while others I am going to tell in all the details I remember, but if I have to sum up I would say this: from Bulgarians amid Englishmen in Macedonia and Bulgarians in the away stand in Bulgaria to Bulgarians in the away stand at Wembley.

Football was first introduced in Bulgaria with the Bulgarian word *"ritnitop"*, literally meaning ball-kicking, by the Swiss sports teacher Georges de Regibus who was invited to teach in Bulgaria. The very introduction to the new game happened in a schoolyard in Varna in 1893.

Football went on to gain more popularity in the early 20th century when the first Bulgarian clubs were founded. After the European football club tournaments were started in 1955, season after season, Bulgarian teams and generations of Bulgarian footballers have tried to prove their worth in Europe.

We had our moments of glory and failure, ecstasy and disappointment, triumphs and sorrows that still haunt our thoughts and memories. Two Bulgarian greatest achievements were made exactly against English teams, Nottingham and Liverpool in the European Champions Cup way back in 1980 and 1982.

CSKA was the first Bulgarian team to participate in this competition in 1957. At the1981 tournament 1/16-finals CSKA knocked the defending champion, the European Champions Cup double winners Nottingham Forest, by two 1-0 wins, the away victory in England being received as a shock all over the world. 17th

March 1982 marks probably the greatest victory in the history of Bulgarian club football. On that day CSKA defeated European champions Liverpool at the European Champions Cup quarterfinals. In Sofia the English side, led by their legendary manager Bob Paisley, was eliminated after an extra time 2-0 CSKA win. Both goals conceded by Bruce Grobbelaar were scored by Stoicho Mladenov, who is still known by the nickname of "Liverpool's Executioner".

The second Bulgarian team to play in the European club competitions after CSKA was *Spartak Varna*. The club from Varna had the honour of being the first Bulgarians to play in the Cup Winner Cup in 1961. 22 years later, in the late afternoon of 19th October 1983, at *Yuri Gagarin* Stadium in the town of Varna, *Spartak* played against the legendary Manchester United. It was the first and last time for the Red Devils to play on Bulgarian soil.

In the early 1980s United had the burning ambition to achieve something remarkable in Europe since they had been living in the shadow of Liverpool for too long. Manager Ron Atkinson (or Big Ron as they used to call him) brought to Varna his biggest FA Cup winning stars.

It was a really David vs Goliath game as the modest team from Varna confronted one of the greatest English clubs only a year after its comeback to Division One. *Spartak Varna* lost 2-1, but the game will always remain a momentous occasion for them.

Besides the visits from Liverpool, Nottingham and Manchester United in the early 1980s, when we were still small kids, in the late 1990s and after the beginning of the new millennium, other English clubs such as Leeds, Blackburn, Newcastle, Chelsea, Aston Villa and others came to play in Sofia their European club competition away games. We not only attended most of those fixtures but we also made friends with some English fans and now we are going to tell you all about it.

Levski – Glasgow Rangers 2-1, Champions League, 29.09.1993

My first contact with British supporters was quite impressive because 3 or 4 years after the collapse of the totalitarian regime, Sofia was visited not by just anyone, but by the famous Rangers. Until then I had only been told legends of the Tartan Army and the colourful and at times uncontrolled Scots. The time had come for our much tormented country to welcome someone who could not only turn his back on the outdated and obsolete standards of our sick society, but also show off his behinds and blatantly tell the system and its concepts to fuck off. Who's better at doing that than the jolly Jocks? Oh, and they did it all so well in their emblematic loud and offhand way.

Taking into account the times we lived in and the years-long information blackout in the Eastern Bloc we have already told you about several times, I was quite well erudite and knowledgeable and I knew a lot about the hostility between Catholics and Protestants. Not that it was my war or it referred to me from a purely religious point of view, but to tell you the truth, I have always had a preference for Rangers rather than Celtic! Even in terms of colours, we, Bulgarians have never been fond of teams wearing green and Rangers fans probably came closest to the goal we were pursuing. I am talking about the sea of Union Jack Flags they put up everywhere they went and their colours, which, as we already said, were also symbolic of our firm.

On that particular day they were not as numerous as usual, even probably there were more flags than fans, but I think those about 300 blokes supported their team in such a way that even the capacity crowd at *Vasil Levski* National Stadium could not drown their voices. This time I was not in a neutral stand (close to or right among the visiting supporters as it would usually happen), but had joined a couple of mates, die-hard Levski fans, right behind the goal opposite the Scottish. I really dare say that in spite of the great distance from them I could distinctly hear them clap and sing in absolute agreement and see them doing their typical dances and rituals, including turning around and lifting up their kilts. They really made me have fun, lived up to my expectations and I was definitely excited and impressed though it was not Rangers' day.

After a marvellous performance in the second half, Levski made a real miracle and their astounding comeback was completed with a heart-breaking, brilliant screamer scored by the "Bulgarian Kaiser", Nikolai Todorov, which made the ground erupt and I just dipped into the sea of wildly celebrating blue (Levski) fans. The night belonged to them and I (not being able to hide my affections for that team) celebrated side by side with them. As every boy did, when I was young I had an affinity with one of the big Sofia football clubs. It was downright mandatory to choose between Levski and CSKA.

I remember a primary school competition that involved someone running to the nearby sports shop and buying equal numbers of white-and-blue and white-and-red (knitted) scarves. Then we would put them on a desk and everybody had to choose between red and blue. I remember choosing the colour blue. However, it was not quite to my liking (I just had to chose one of the two colours) and after school I went to the same shop and bought a black-and-white scarf that I still keep up to this day!

CSKA – Newcastle United 0-2, UEFA Cup first round, 16.09.1999

I remember the second British team to come to Sofia was Newcastle and they played against CSKA in September 1999 in the first round of the UEFA Cup.Once again there was a tough Northern crowd and so we had some great expectations. The English won 2-0 thanks to goals by Nolberto Solano and Temuri Ketsbaia, but it wasn't exactly the game we were excited about since it was not our beloved Lokomotiv (GO) playing, but one of the teams from Sofia. I have personally never supported any other Bulgarian club, regardless of their history or successes. They may have represented our country, but in Bulgaria I cared only about the club of my native town! Besides, I didn't like the fact that the majority of the bigger clubs from the capital got the support not only of their locals, but also of other fans coming from the country. We were more interested in meeting the famous black-and-white Geordies from Northeast England.

It was rainy and pretty cold for September, as if the English had brought the rain with them as it is a quite common phenomenon for that part of the Albion. It was a late evening game and so we decided to take the noon train from Gorna Oryahovitsa. The train was to come from Varna and so we expected that it would be packed with huge numbers of CSKA before we get aboard. Imagine the number of travelling fans when the train reached Sofia, having stopped at several big towns to pick up more and more of those willing to attend the game. There were CSKA fans from our town, too, but we travelled as a separate group with the special purpose of having a close encounter with the Geordies.

The previous day we had read in the papers that about 600 Newcastle fans were expected to arrive in Bulgaria. We assumed that the number would include only die-hard hooligans from the Albion. Our group comprised of 20 blokes, including some hardcore lads from Jolly Roger. We were dressed in designer clothes and trainers as we wanted to look like typical casuals. We also had our firm (JRF) flag with us. It used to be an inseparable part of us and wherever we would go we would invariably take it. The train station was flocked with fans wearing CSKA T-shirts. A few were from our town and we knew them well, but the majority had come from all corners of the country, waiting to change trains to Sofia. It would happen quite often for the simple reason that, as we said before, the railway station in Gorna Oryahovitsa was an important railway hub and served as a train-switching point for people coming from other districts.

On that day it was decorated with flying red-and-white flags and scarves. We thought it was just a ridiculous masquerade since we didn't like them very much, not to say at all. Well, we had some mates who had affinities with the "blues" or "reds", but those were rather temporary feelings. To be honest, I didn't expect to see so many *"chorbari"*, as we used to derisively call them, on that day. It was hard to find a place to sit in the train and crowds of people had occupied both the compartments and corridors. In addition, there were coppers everywhere as the Old Bill had taken draconian safety measures, and besides CSKA fans are one of the most numerous in our country. They had a number of "ultra" groups and would regularly get in trouble with the police during both home and away games. That was understandable, taking into account that their team was one of the most successful ones in the history of Bulgarian football. We didn't know what to expect during our journey to Sofia.

We got on the last carriages (as the cops had assigned the first ones for the CSKA fans), where we hoped to find somewhere to sit separately from the crowds, but they were also packed (though with rank-and-file red fans). However, we found a compartment with 2 or 3 vacant seats and decided to take turns sitting during the trip. There was noise and chaos all over the train, chants and songs were being sung and the smell of weed, piss and alcohol spoiled the little fresh air that would occasionally squeeze in. Due to the heavy rain the windows were almost constantly shut and we felt like locked up in a coffin.

The reds' songs and the stuffy atmosphere were increasingly getting on our nerves. We were wondering how we were to put up with that for three and a half hours until reaching the capital! Some of our lads were chatting with the CSKA fans regarding English football and in particular the Newcastle fans that were supposed to arrive for the game. The conversation was gradually turning into an argument and one could feel that things were starting to escalate and get real hot. The quarrel was focused on how the *"chorbari"* **6** were going to take down the Geordies ahead of the game or after it, if they were given the opportunity. It went on like that for approximately an hour and then the alcohol started to take its toll on us, too. Two lads of ours opened a window and started chanting *Ingerland, Ingerland, Ingerland*, and then a red stood up and aimed a strike at one of our lads at the window, but he couldn't punch him and just slightly touched his face. 5 or 6 more CSKA fans moved towards us and other at least 4 or 5 *chorbari* jumped out of the compartment behind them, but set off in the opposite direction, obviously to look for backups. At that point the train was already entering a station and sharply reduced its speed. The other bloke standing at the window and having dared to chant was Tosh. Here is what he remembers from that occasion:

'Well stocked with booze, we had drunk a major part of it for the two hours of our trip. The train was jam-packed, the air-conditioning didn't work and so we decided to go out in the corridor and despite the rain pouring outside to open one of the windows. All around us there were *"servicemen"* as CSKA fans would proudly call themselves. Anyway, we didn't give a fuck because, as always, we had set off with the idea of meeting the black-and-whites from Newcastle, who we couldn't help but have an affinity with not only because of the colour of their kits, but also because of the legendary Geordies with their hot blood, so unrepresentative of the northern peoples. We had had enough of the *chorbari*'s banter and so a mate of mine and I decided to start singing an English song.

The train reduced its speed upon entering some station and our chants were getting louder and louder since other JRF lads had joined us. We didn't care at all that we were surrounded by *chorbari* and when the train came to a halt one of our lads took advantage of the silence and started up our favourite *"Black & White Army"*, upon which the red part of the train showed up at the windows and went straight at us. From my window I saw loads of them even get off the train and run along the platform in order to reach us as quickly as possible since the train was to leave any minute then. However, we knew the score well and all those thinking we didn't were about to understand how wrong they had been to underestimate us! Amidst the chaos and disorder we managed to drive back the first waves of attackers quite quickly, though most of them were from our carriage, which in just a few seconds was totally under our control. We knew we were at least 10 times fewer and we had to barricade (something we had already done before).

Once we had managed to push out the first enemies in the direction of the next carriage and had closed the sliding doors in ours (which was the last one in the train), we immediately shut all windows and doors since we expected that stones and bricks would start flying at us any minute. It all happened in seconds and I really understood how good we had become! Without saying a single word to one another (we didn't have time to, anyway) we managed to organise with a precision that anyone could call military. It was just that everybody knew what he was doing and what he had to do, as if we had drilled and trained it a million times. I ran back to check the last train door facing the platform and I saw that the opposite one (facing the tracks) was wide open and it took me several seconds to realise that it was our lads who were literally loading crushed stones (ballast) from the tracks! They had made a huge pile in front of the lavatory with the intention of striking back in case our carriage was attacked from the outside.

I remember that we even found the time to laugh at what was going on though we were in a rather tight spot. We agreed that they would close the doors as soon as possible and would stay and guard them and then I quickly ran to the carriage front doors where the reds were supposed to strike with all of their might. Through the windows we could see the mayhem outside. The coppers had intervened and were doing their best to quell the maddening crowd outside, bring them together and force them back aboard the train as it had a schedule to observe and leave straight away since it was already delayed. We could already hear the hits and kicks on the carriage coming from the outside but we had to focus on keeping the sliding door between the two last carriages tightly shut.

Next thing I saw in the window before me was the hyped up mob of *chorbari* literally ready to lynch us. They were beating on the door glass panels with their fists and kicking the lower part, which was thankfully metal. The same sounds were coming from the outside but they gradually faded away and the train was off. We were still keeping the doors between the carriages shut and as they seemed to be the only threat for us for the time being, we were kinda relieved (once the train had set off and was moving), but a glass panel started yielding and came out of its gaskets hanging out on one side. It was clear that we had to step back, especially as all kinds of objects, mostly bottles, started flying through the gap.

We made a couple of steps back. It has always been a part of the fight and I have always considered the bombastic *"Not one step back!"* as an absolutely ridiculous cliché. We always step back for one reason or another (though few would confess). In that case we retreated just in order to find our next line of defence and it was the swinging door between the vestibule, where the loos are, and the narrow side corridor of the carriage. I'm not saying we didn't step back out of fear. Fear causes adrenaline rush and it is adrenaline that teaches you how to survive in certain situations and on that day we surely needed some.

The scenes in the carriage were increasingly beginning to resemble the ones in the films about the brave Spartans, who, though few in number when compared to the Xerxes' hordes, managed to hold up and drive back the enemy due to their military discipline and skills, the specific terrain and, of course, their immense bravery. We weren't as brave as the Spartans but our tactics worked well and we were able to stop the enemy who became more and more ferocious due to their unsuccessful attempts to get us.

The action had already moved to the narrow swinging door where it was a one-on-one fight between me and my opponent as we had made it to the front line. He was a pretty tough bloke and I have to admit that he outweighed me. Later on we met, exchanged contact details and we hugely respect each other to this very day. He had the fearsome (well, not for me) nickname Principe (like the AS Roma fan). Bro, if you are reading this book, you know the score!

After that incident I understood who he was and that he practiced some kind of boxing, but right then it didn't matter much since we were both actually jammed by the doors and the mobs pushing in behind us! I have never thought of myself as some kind of fighter and apart from my boxing lessons dad used to give me at home, I have never intently practiced any martial arts and I have always been overweight. Well, I did have natural strength and when using certain substances I would become rather aggressive to say the least and I could stand my ground for quite a while. The only sport I ever got to practice and take seriously was wrestling and I dare say I was a pretty promising wrestler, probably because of that very strength that was rooted in my nature.

With a sudden surge and jerk from standstill I managed to push away the enemy to make sure I had enough space to hit him but then I realised that my right hand (my stronger one) was pressed by the door as it was opened in my direction. However, his hand was free and he used it wisely punching me in the jaw. Our eyes met and it was one of those moments that can also be rather funny as they'd be more suitable for romantic TV series. All of a sudden it seemed there were just the two of us and everything around us looked vague and distant or maybe it was only me feeling this way due to the punch I had received. How could I know? His eyes were full of hope that I would probably collapse (not that there was any space), but it didn't happen his way and in no time I struck back with my free left hand, but then the pressure from both sides (behind me and behind him) became even greater.

What followed were the usual attempts to kick the opponent, but that turned out to be even more difficult due to the pushes from behind and the lack of empty space to move your leg. It all continued for not more than 5 or 6 minutes but anyone who's been in such situation knows that it seems like eternity. The Old Bill had made it through the crowd of *chorbari* in the adjacent carriage and managed to reach us and set us apart.

Now it's Gilly's turn again to tell you how exactly he saw the incident from his position, which would most often be right behind my back:

'We stood on both sides of the narrow corridor. They were on the one side and we were on the other, pressing with all our might like rugby players. I knew things were getting rough. We clung to each other, it was a total mayhem. Fists (overhead) and boots were flying all over. One after the other we competed who would punch first. All you could hear were heads and jaws popping. It went on for 2 or 3 minutes and then the railroad police arrived. There were no severe injuries but for several bleeding noses from both sides. Tosh had a bleeding lip as he was frontmost.

They separated our group and pushed us into the last compartments, which were hastily left by the terrified ordinary passengers and fans. We could still hear the reds' threats and insults echoing in the other side of the train. Nothing serious happened before we arrived in Sofia. Mobs of CSKA fans kept on getting on the train at every station it stopped.I had the feeling the carriages were going to burst at the seams.We were guarded for the remainder of the trip and the time passed in chats and comments on English football games from the past as we were trying to kill the boredom. Suddenly one of the *chorbari* (the one who was frontmost) appeared at the compartment door and asked the cops if he could speak to Tosh! As you would expect they didn't like the idea of the two meeting again, but we opened the compartment doors and convinced them to let him in. they agreed after giving lots of warnings and remained there to watch the rendezvous from close range. The bloke held out his hand to Tosh and Tosh returned the gesture by handing him over a bottle of whiskey that he was using to wash out his bashed mouth. We talked to the bloke (he turned out to be a proper lad), we exchanged our contact details and as far as I know Tosh still keeps in touch with him to this day. I remember only part of his words, of course not the exact words he said, but he went something like that: *"Lads, you are fucking mental and so you deserve our respect! I still cannot believe that you held us back!"*

He left in a kind of friendly mood and he promised us that we wouldn't have any problems with them at Sofia railway station. Obviously he was their ringleader and his word was their command because it all went just the way he said it would. When we stepped off the train we heard not a single shout at us. It was as if nothing had happened. We remained alert and chose to catch some cabs to the city center in order to avoid any conflicts with the hordes getting off the train. We knew that a second confrontation would not end up well for us as we were already in the open and it was then that we fully realised what exactly we had been involved in and that a twenty strong mob did not stand a chance against hundreds of them, as they were at least probably 500–600 fans. But for us it was a job done… We had succeeded in standing our ground and deserve the enemy's respect, though heavily outnumbered.

The ground was close to the city center and we decided to have a few beers and eat something in some boozer before kick-off. It had been pouring with rain since early morning. The freezing wind and heavy rain additionally spoiled our plans to take a walk and fulfil our plan. It was such vile weather that only made you want to have a drink or two of aged malt whiskey. We went to a pub, I can't remember its name, but it was near the stadium. There were some reds inside and some ordinary people having their pre-match drinks. Nothing unusual happened for the two hours we spent there; nobody paid attention to the others in the pub.

Kick-off was at 20:45 pm and we hoped that the goddamn rain would stop for at least 90 minutes. We headed for the ground an hour ahead of kick-off. It was still very cold but at least the rain had stopped. There were crowds of *chorbari* in all nearby streets and parks singing, chanting and throwing insults at other teams. As we were approaching the ground we could hear the English chant *"Toon Army, Toon Army"* quite clear as if they were next to us. We bought tickets next to the away sector since, as I already told you, our goal was different and we didn't give a shit about the game in general, not to speak of CSKA! There were buffer zones on both sides of the Geordies. They were segregated with police cordons. And yes, there were at least about 600 English. All around and in front of them there were loads of Newcastle and England flags, a picture so typical of their away games. We stood only inches away from them and watched them for almost the entire 90 minutes. It was unbelievable seeing all of them chant as one and clap their hands in perfect unison during the entire game. No kids or women, just men, awe-inspiring 30 to 40-years old lads. The most admirable sight was some fifty Newcastle fans naked from the waist up showing their emblematic beer bellies and tattoos. They feared no cold or rain and steam was coming off their bodies as if they had just come out of a sauna. Those around us were watching them wondering what kind of people they were, where and in what conditions they could live if they were stripped to their waists in such cold weather. What about summer, eh?!

After Newcastle scored twice the number of waist-up-naked fans increased, all of them hugging and jumping overwhelmed with the frantic joy of their victory. That was the way we wanted to look as well, a compact and awe-inspiring group. We stood there admiring them! Despite the insults thrown and the middle fingers shown by the Bulgarians, they seemed to have even greater fun. Their response to that aggravation included louder chants and clapping. It was a night to remember, one of our first contacts with British hooligans and no one will ever take away those memories from us.'

Spartak Moscow - Leeds United 2-1, UEFA Cup third round, 02.12.1999

Our next meeting with English fans was when Spartak Moscow played Leeds United in Sofia in December 1999 in the UEFA Cup third round. The game was scheduled at a neutral venue due to freezing temperatures in Moscow, so typical of the Russian capital at that time of the year. As far as I can remember the forecast said snowfall and -18°C in Moscow so UEFA had to relocate the game at a place with acceptable temperatures and that was Sofia. The English lost the first leg 2-1 before an audience not exceeding 6000. But as you know, during the season in question, 1999/2000, Leeds with manager David O'Leary reached the UEFA Cup semifinals. Those fixtures were marred by the murders of two English fans in Istanbul on a night full of extreme violence between English hooligans and Galatasaray cutthroats on the streets of the Turkish megalopolis.

We had heard and read a lot about their firm *Service Crew*, which was notorious for being one of the most dangerous not only in Britain, but also in Europe during the late 1970s and 1980s, causing riots and getting into constant troubles with the police. In all honesty, we inspected a full-scale invasion of Leeds fans, but obviously due to the chilly Sofia weather (though not -18°C as in Moscow) not more than 300–350 lads made the trip.Since no Bulgarian team was playing, not many people were interested in that game. There were again some 20 of us travelling by rail from Gorna Oryahovitsa. It was a peaceful trip and the time was spent talking about English football as usual. We had a good stock of several bottles of whiskey in order not to get bored and cold before we arrived in Sofia. We sang songs like *"Rule, Britannia"*, *"God Save The Queen"*, etc. undisturbed.The Jolly Roger flag was draped on one of the compartment walls. After the first two or three bottles boredom was finally gone and we got louder.The purpose of that trip was the same - look for that special group of hooligans, meet them and have a drink together in some boozer.

The weather in Sofia was colder; a chilling wind made you look for shelter indoors and not go outside at all. We were roaming the streets of Sofia in hope to find the English. We saw some groups of rank-and-file Leeds fans wearing scarves and having draped their flags on the pavements beside some roadside bars. They were singing their songs, some were dancing on the cobbled streets and raising their glasses to the passers-by, who were slightly scared and tried to steer clear of them. We couldn't find the ones we'd been looking for. Probably they had not made the trip.

As I told you, it was a cold December day so I guessed their hardcore fans had stayed at home enjoying the coziness of their local pubs and watching the game on telly. However, we got acquainted with several fans drinking beers in a bar close to the ground. We were pleased with our new acquaintances and one of our lads, being a dedicated Leeds fan, exchanged phone numbers and addresses with an English supporter. Chatting and joking, beer in hand, it was time to enter the ground before we knew it. The atmosphere inside was not that remarkable but for the usual English 90-minute nonstop support, though they lost the game. We were impressed by our new acquaintances and by watching 350 fans having travelled 1200 miles to cheer their team not minding the freezing December evening.

CSKA – Blackburn Rovers 3-3, UEFA Cup first round, 03.10.2002

Blackburn Rovers came to play CSKA in Sofia in October 2002 in the UEFA Cup first round. By the way, that was their first visit to

Bulgaria. We knew that their most successful period had been the first half of XX century when they had won the title and FA Cup several times. After 1966 Rovers had a 26-season exile from the English top division and in 1992 they secured promotion to the newly-established FA Premier League. The famous ex-player and Liverpool legend Kenny Dalglish was their manager in those times and in 1995 they became champions of England for the first time in their history. Several participations in the UEFA Cup competitions followed and that was exactly one of those days they played in Europe. Blackburn were the next to remember, this time with their fans having a laugh at my Manchester United tiny logo cap when I entered an Irish pub in Sofia ahead of their game vs CSKA. How foolish I was to wear such a cap on a day like that. Of course, they advised me to *"scrape that shit off my cap"*, which I accepted with a smile pretending not to have heard and understood their words. Our group was large enough again and before the game we had a photo taken together in front of Sofia police department. After that we found some Rovers fans downtown and we had some beers while chatting to them.

Levski Sofia – Liverpool 2-4, UEFA Cup third round, 03.03.2004

In March 2004, on the national holiday of Bulgaria (3rdMarch), Levski contributed to the football history of our country when they played one of the football giants not only in England, but also in Europe – Liverpool. It was a UEFA Cup third round game and the English were managed by Gerard Houllier. There is no point in going into details regarding the history of that great English club as we are all familiar with their domination, especially during the 1970s and 1980s. Football had got them involved in two great tragedies – the Heysel disaster in 1985 during the European Champions Cup final against Juventus and the Hillsborough tragedy in 1989 when Liverpool played Nottingham Forest in an FA Cup semi-final. It was those tragedies that were the reason for the English clubs 5-year ban from European competitions and the urgent measures in the fight against football-related violence undertaken by "Iron Lady" Margaret Thatcher. Liverpool fans were among the founders of the casual culture in the UK. We told you about this fashion trend in the chapter entitled "Hooligents". Anyway, let us go back to the evening of 3rd March 2004. There was an unprecedented hysteria surrounding the game and it was due to the fact that a Bulgarian club was to play one of the leading European clubs exactly on the date of the Bulgarian national holiday. A lot of people had hopes that they would witness a miracle as the "Blues" (Levski's nickname due to the colour of their kits) from Sofia dreamt of eliminating the mighty English club at this stage of the tournament. Also, generations of Bulgarians supporting the English giant were about to make their dreams come true by watching them play in Bulgaria.

The tickets for the game had been sold out in just a day or two after their release. The match was scheduled for Vasil Levski ground. We also had two lads from our Jolly Roger Firm crazy about Liverpool and I would dare say they had more English than Bulgarian blood running through their veins. They were just one of the reasons for us to make another organised trip to Sofia. Those two lads were students in Sofia so they had sorted our tickets and our intention was to travel on the day of the game. I guess we were about 15 lads once again determined to infiltrate in the English stand. We believed a large number of Liverpool fans were going to arrive from England. The weather had been foggy and cold since the morning and we expected the day would be interesting, full of emotions and huge amounts of beer.

We travelled by train (there was a special) from Varna to Sofia, i.e. stopping at Gorna Oryahovitsa, once again bursting at the seams, packed with Levski supporters from different towns. They were in a state of complete euphoria and the train echoed with chants and drum rumbles. At each train station they would throw smoke bombs and flares through the window and sing out loud to the top of their voices. The Old Bill was everywhere. The buffet car smelt of booze, drugs and vomit. Our group had separated there cause anyway there were no vacant seats in the train. We stuck out in our casual clothes among the sea of blue shirts, scarves and flags. There was hardly a Levski fan not dressed in blue. There were probably about 2000 fans and you can imagine the chaos surrounding the entire trip. Some were throwing up, not able to stand properly on their feet after drinking too much booze, others were pissing out the windows and along the corridors, so three and a half hours we sat there surrounded by herds of *"cattle"* (that is the way Levski fans are derisively nicknamed) watching their monkey business. I can't imagine how they cleaned up after them leaving the train, but I was absolutely disgusted and outraged by their vulgar behaviour. I felt ashamed. I approve of football hooliganism, but their conduct was more like next door to stupidity, not anything else.

Having arrived in Sofia, we immediately separated from the crowds of fans and took some cabs downtown. Everywhere the streets were full of English having put up their flags at bars and on restaurant fences, their songs and chants filling up the air. Word went around that almost 3000 Liverpool fans had arrived in Sofia for the last two days. I guessed it was true, judging by the number of Liverpool and England flags draped everywhere. Loads of Scousers were sitting in the parks and gardens around the stadium quenching their thirst with beer. CSKA fans were also expected to turn up en masse since they are Levski's archetypal enemies. Sofia derby between Levski and CSKA is like the Old Firm derby between Rangers and Celtic in Scotland, or like Liverpool vs Everton clash in England, and it is always supposed to be accompanied by riots and quite a few bloody fights.

Besides being deadly foes, most CSKA fans also support Liverpool and Manchester United (while Levski Sofia blues are also Chelsea fans)... Admittedly, that is mainly due to the red or blue colours. Odd and stupid, isn't it?! I personally have never understood them, but I guess they have their reasons. On days like that they would always take advantage of the opportunity to pay off old scores, but the bad thing was that it happened on the day of our national holiday, a day supposed to unite and not divide. It looked like things could get pretty tense both before and during the game and a massive police operation was put in place. We made a pub crawl to oil our dry throats with beer and while doing so introductions were made with a few Merseyside fans.I heard of skirmishes that went on between English and Levski hooligans somewhere in the narrow streets near the ground.

We had been supplied with tickets for the away stand and we raised a toast for that, pleased with the opportunity to be among the English and feel the real atmosphere of standing in their ranks. I didn't know how much beer we had drunk since our arrival, but kickoff time of the so cherished game was much later in the evening so we did have time for more ale. Absolute havoc reigned near the ground, mounted police patrolling all around, riot police guarding each gate, sirens wailing in the distance, crowds of supporters pouring in, chants and songs roaring all over the place, brawls with police going on as some fans were trying to enter the ground earlier than announced. Draconian safety measures were also undertaken by the police while escorting the English to the away sector. There were two, maybe three lines of coppers on both their sides protecting them with shields and batons.

We lined up to enter the ground with the English as our tickets were allocated for their sector. And then something unexpected happened.CSKA hooligans attacked the Levski fans and it all turned into a huge melee. It was kicking off everywhere, punches and kicks, groans and thumps all around. The coppers charged with batons and shields. They had to split the two sets of fighting fans and secure a buffer zone between them and the English supporters.In all that turmoil and confusion, the cops separated and pushed all of us to the adjacent gate where the CSKA ultras were.In spite of our complaints they didn't let us go back to the mass of English fans waiting to enter the ground. We got rather angry and bitter as a result of the failure to fulfil our plans. The attendance exceeded 40 000 and we sneaked right next to the fence (the buffer zone) separating the Liverpool supporters from the Levski fans. The *chorbari* standing next to us were making insulting gestures and hurling abuse at the Levski supporters and so a third set of fans was ultimately formed.

Prior to kick-off, while the two anthems were being played, almost the entire ground booed the English one. What I had seen earlier on the train could not bear comparison with what was going on in the ground. I felt ashamed of everything that was happening. Never before had I seen such behaviour of Bulgarian football audience during a game against a foreign team. I thought they were going to show some respect, especially as on that particular occasion they were playing against one of the most respected and prominent teams in the world. A few Levski ultras even hurled several smoke bombs at the away sector. The Old Bill stepped in again and a shower of batons followed. The English were staring in disbelief, shaken by all that stupidity of Bulgarian fans. We were standing beside the buffer zone and the Liverpool support while the CSKA fans would not cease singing their numerous songs against the *"cattle"*. At some point we even asked ourselves whether we were attending a Sofia derby or a European tournament match. What one could hear most were the chants of both Sofia clubs and the English ones. Levski lost 2-4, with Liverpool fully dominating the game, teaching their opponents a lesson in European football. Upon leaving the ground after the final whistle more brawls between *"chorbari"* and the *"cattle"* followed, but it was already pitch dark and impossible to see what was really going on. Obviously the mayhem was about to continue all night long, as it would most often happen. We moved away from all that chaos and went on walking along dark and dreary alleys. We could not wait to sneak away and find any means of transport that would take us to the place we were to stay over before returning to Gorna Oryahovitsa on the next day.

The first leg of that game was played on 26.02.2004 Liverpool–Levski 2-0.

Two more games followed: on 10.08.2005 CSKA–Liverpool 1-3 and the return leg on 23.08.2005 Liverpool-CSKA 0-1.

Litex – Aston Villa 1-3, Europa League first round, 18.09.2008

Speaking about the recent past or modern days if you like it, memories also become somewhat clearer. Moreover, this game was played just before I departed for England, where I eventually settled down and I am still living with my family. What was interesting on that occasion was that our deadly rivals, the *"Boyars"* **7**, made a huge turnout in the town of Lovech that day. Probably because they found some similarities in colours (which are not exactly the same, though) or they had some other reason I was not aware of, but they had quite a lot of Aston Villa sympathisers. Villa was to play the provincial, but quite strong side of Litex Lovech, which had put an end to the Sofia giants' hegemony for several years. Lovech is also one of our big (well, according to Bulgarian standards) towns and district centers, where we (Lokomotiv) used to experience some tough away games and encounters with the locals. Contrary to us and in inverse proportion to the achievements they had made, their attendance was shite, both home and away! Although Lovech was a district centre and Tarnovo (our rivals' town) a regional one, the team of Aston Villa landed in our native town as neither of the two bigger towns had an airport and Sofia airport was too far away. Villa was on an evening charter flight that landed on the day before the game and naturally, Gorna Oryahovitsa airport was packed with autograph hunters. I was there too, making our traditional preliminary inspection, though I could not expect to see any English fans that night since our airport was closed for official flights though its runway met the international standards.

My reason to be there was to spot some "violet" (that's how we call our biggest rival club's fans) and get an idea and details of their possible turnout on the following day. It went exactly as planned and I obtained the information I needed through an ex-classmate of mine who was from Tarnovo, but used to study in Gorna Oryahovitsa, I don't know why as it usually happened the other way round, i.e. Gorna boys used to study in Tarnovo. The geezer told me that they would be about 40 strong, which meant almost twice as big a mob than ours and so I had to take care of making our organisation better. Due to the already mentioned proximity between the towns, we decided to make the trip by cars. About 30 (6 car loads) of us turned up, our plan being to arrive there as early as possible in order to have a look around and eliminate any surprises. Of course, we were also after a possible encounter (of the third kind) with Villa Hardcore whose firm we had only heard of.

It was quite warm for the second half of September and that became apparent the second we entered the town. It was the usual sight of an English club playing away from home, but this time the host town's capacities were much more limited than those of the capital city and we witnessed their difficulties in the very first pub we sat foot in. There we found some Villa grumbling about the warm beer they were served, not to speak of the tiny boozers around the ground where there was shortage of alcohol and some of the English were raving mad about it. We parked our cars nearby and went into a boozer whose owner decided to close the very moment he saw 30 of us arriving. We met some quite talkative Villa lads and decided not go anywhere further as the place we were at had a good strategic location (a kind of a small platform) and we were able to see anyone coming while at the same time it remained slightly sideways and unnoticed. We proposed to the Birmingham lads that one of us would drive to the nearby shops and stock us with cold drinks and liquor (upon which their faces just lit up) and we stayed there throughout the afternoon drinking, chatting and scanning for our enemies.

Well, right before kickoff time they did appear. Of course, we recognised them from a distance by their looks and the clothes they had (and still have to this day): long hair, denim vests and military boots! I thought to myself, *"For Christ's sake! When are these fellas going to change?!"* Everybody likes to stick to their principles, values, etc. But for fuck's sake, it was not the early 1990s anymore, not to mention that it was more than 30°C and to top it off they were coming seconds before the game when it was full of cops. I was getting angry thinking out loud. Before we knew it, they had already bought their tickets and entered the ground. Most Bulgarian stadia do not have definite sectors, rows, seats, etc. so you buy a ticket and sit wherever you want except in the away end and the main stand, of course.

On that particular occasion Villa were stood beside it and the *Boyars* sat next to them at the corner of the stand behind the goal, while we stood at the opposite corner of the same stand. The first half was rather boring and at half time I decided to play a joke so I followed one of their lads to the lavatories surprising him from behind (it's not what you're thinking), *"Now you're going to get some, you fucking little Boyar"*, I cried out while making a strangling clutch at his neck from behind, first squeezing him tight in order to scare the shit out of him and then gradually loosening the grip so that not to really strangle him! You should have seen his face when I let him go. He was pale as fuck, scared and pissed and he might as well have soiled himself out of fear.

"Go tell your mates that Lokomotiv (GO) are here and we'll be waiting for them outside after the game so that we can settle our scores", I spoke to him spitefully climbing up the steps to the gate while he was standing there lifeless, not able to believe what had just happened to him.

The second half turned a rather different story. The scorching sun had set, goals started flowing (scored by the away team), Villa began to chant out loud and the *Boyars* were kinda agitated as they kept on looking all around wondering where we might be stood. The ground was not full, especially our stand, and the distance between us and them was, let's say, the width of a football pitch, but the violet morons still couldn't see us! We were having a blast. Once I was back from the lavatories and told everyone what had happened they just couldn't help laughing and joking. They would ask me to tell them the story in details again and again and every time I did so they would laugh their heads off. We were definitely having great fun. There was not a single copper between them and us and the distance was suitable even for a head-on attack. Before any cops would step in we could kick the shit out of them right there, in the very stand, taking advantage of the element of surprise and sneaking behind their backs. However, we decided to go on having fun and raising our hands together we started singing *"Black and White Till I Die"*. That was now one of those games attended by four different sets of fans! The violets finally saw us and, in their turn, started throwing insults at us, while we just spread our arms even wider teasing them. Villa fans and everybody in the main stand were wondering what was going on while the few Lovech supporters in the opposite sector didn't have a clue what was happening at the other end of their ground.

The major part of our plan had been fulfilled as we had managed to make the atmosphere red hot, but the most important part, i.e. getting at them, was still there to accomplish. The game finished and we headed for the exit in the direction of their end. The insults and obscene gestures were getting more and more distinct and the possibility for starting a fight on the very stand was becoming increasingly real. The *Boyars* would not move from where they stood and we were menacingly approaching. The travelling supporters were applauding their victorious players off the pitch and the cops were focused on the segregation and protection of the away fans. This was our chance and there was no way we could miss it. The more we advanced (though rather slowly due to the departing spectators), the more nervous the *Boyars* seemed to become and at one point they started to head for the exits melting into the crowd (so typical of cowards). We went outside and gathered in a tight mob. The next moment we saw them also packed tightly together, facing us, waiting (which was a surprise for us). For a brief moment I thought, *"This is it! We are so close!"*, but naturally they had chosen to stand near two coppers guarding the exits and not move any further. They could have gone on and walked the dark streets and found a place where to wait for us and fight us. We were outnumbered but had already gone too far and we just didn't seem to care about numbers. There was time enough for a punch or two and so we went at them!

Panic ensued, the locals didn't know what was going on, who we were and why we were fighting. At the same time the visiting fans had also started to exit the ground and they saw us, though through the fences. I heard some shouts, *"Go on lads, and do them quickly!"* They must have seen the Old Bill coming. We managed to swap some kicks mainly but the cops were really close and they arrived in full force. They set us apart and started questioning us and demanding our IDs. We kept on swearing and insulting each other though separated by the line of coppers. Those around us had finally understood who we are and were ardently discussing that Etar and Lokomotiv (GO) fans had used the occasion of a European game to fight each other. Some Englishmen, having left the away sector, also surrounded us to find out what was happening and, until a while ago vigilantly watched, gradually melted with the crowd of Bulgarian fans (most of them neutral blokes who had come from nearby towns just to watch football). We got thoroughly searched, given back our IDs and escorted to our cars and out of town accompanied by two police cars. It was us, the Jolly Roger Firm, who were the real stars of the night.

Fulham – CSKA 1-0, Europa League, 03.12.2009

A little more than a year after my family and I had changed our place of domicile, I already had some (though vague) idea of the situation here. After everything written so far, you can probably imagine what it meant to me to step on this soil and fulfil some of my wildest childhood dreams. Though at a much later stage, though the scene here had slightly faded away, that change meant so much to me both from a personal and a fan's point of view. Yeah, I did substitute the long years of listening to BBC Five Life, the never-ending following of English football games on TV and the radio and the cutting out of Bulgarian newspaper articles for the real atmosphere and experience of grounds across the UK. Ooh, yeah, it was priceless for me!

Believe me, now I don't want to hear of any TV and radio coverage and newspapers. I avoid them like the plague. I don't even turn on the radio in my car no matter that the game may have started and I am hurrying home to watch it on telly. Of course, I can't see all games in the flesh and I am glad modern technologies provide us with so many ways to get informed and easily keep in touch with others.I hate the other media and I think that to some extent they actually brainwash people. I colleague of mine brings to our office all kinds of papers every day. The minute he has left the office they are already in the waste paper bin. However, I still keep all the editions of the specialised in English football newspaper called

Albion published in Bulgaria in the early 1990s and another two sacks of newspaper cuttings from that period. They just have sentimental value for me! I don't know... my wife keeps on asking me all the time, *"Why do you keep those, why don't you throw them away!?"*, I simply don't have the heart to do it.

I had already been introduced to "Fat" Pat Dolan (RIP) from Chelsea Headhunters, of whom I am about to tell you at the end of this chapter and in the next one (entirely dedicated to him). We had quite a lot of meets here and at some of them he introduced me to a number of lads "In The Know" and I was fully enjoying life in the English capital, soaking as much as I could into football grounds, no matter the club and no matter the league.I was just hungry for football and watching it in the flesh.

Naturally, as a Manchester United fan, my first goal was the "Theatre of dreams", followed by a few away games and fierce derbies against Leeds, Liverpool and Manchester City, but once I had fulfilled that of dream of mine, I got a move on and brought in some variety, adding some practice to my knowledge.

Having worked as a railwayman in Bulgaria, during my first year in England I had free tickets that I could use on National Railways and on ferries and thanks to them I managed to travel all over the UK and visit some legendary grounds such as the Millennium Stadium in Cardiff and the newly built Aviva Stadium in Dublin; as well as attend derbies such as the fiery northern derby between Newcastle and Sunderland and the not less interesting southern one between Southampton and Portsmouth. I remember me and a mate of mine (who also had free tickets) travelled across Britain far and wide. Those tickets had expiry times so once verified we had to use them within 48 hours as we pleased or found most appropriate. So what we'd do was catch the earliest or the latest night trains so that we could sleep on them and at early dawn we would end up in places like Glasgow and Edinburgh, where, of course, we would watch Rangers and Hibernian.

Surely London was the greatest football arena and here I would often meet mates from Bulgaria, most of whom were just like me a year ago making their first real contact with English football or they would just come to watch an away game of their favourite Bulgarian team. This was exactly the case in early December 2009, when CSKA once again drew an English team, i.e. Fulham, in the Europa League group stage. The first leg in Sofia finished 1-1 earlier in September.

A lot of my "red" friends, acquaintances and other fellas contacted me asking to book them (well in advance) rooms in hostels for themselves or for other mates of theirs. Obviously, there was a great interest in the game and the *chorbari* were planning a London invasion. Some of my best "red" mates even stayed with me for several days, but as a whole, the *chorbari* once again showed why we didn't like them much and why so many people generally dislike Sofia clubs.

Due to my contacts with Pat I knew West London quite well. He would often tell me about football rivalries in the British capital (not only) and I learned from him about the hatred between the various firms, which turned out to be different from the common belief, so what we had heard from the media was not the whole truth. For example, I understood that smaller West London clubs such as Q.P.R and Brentford also had their good firms and sometimes, on a good day, could turn out to be more than the bigger ones could chew. Fulham didn't have a top firm, but I was told that they could come turn up with some tough local lads and so I warned my CSKA friends.

On match day a lot of CSKA fans arrived in London, though some of them were sheer tourists. Loads have even taken their families – wives and little kids. Some were shopping on Oxford Street and were visiting museums and other sights, while others were hysterically looking for tickets for the game. I, of course, like the kind host and guide I was, took my guests around London and did my best to be of service to anyone. By "anyone" I generally mean all Bulgarians. I would show the way to people, take pictures of them, advise them on transportation issues and by and large made them feel more comfortable before kick-off time.

In the early afternoon our group suddenly felt thirsty and we decided to go for some pub near the ground quite early. So we did, though after some difficulties because the pubs around the stadium would not let in any away fans, others were fully booked or occupied (at least that was their excuses to us), but anyway, we did find a place, where after a brief conversation with my colleague doormen (I already had a job as a bouncer), I managed to get my already knackered and really thirsty lads inside. As evening closed in, there was complete chaos outside. More and more reds were coming in, some of them being my mates' friends, but they kept on moving in and out and it was me who had to deal with all those petty troubles at the door, so to cut the long story short it was as if I hadn't taken my day off but playing the bouncer stuff again. Nevertheless, there was still plenty of beer, spirits were high, chants and songs got louder, so what else could a football fan need on a match day!? So far, so good...

We headed for the ground, some of us had tickets for the away end and some had for neutral sectors, while others (like me) were still ticketless and were trying to exchange on their way, so it was a complete chaos...

The game itself did not matter to me much, I was attending it out of sheer curiosity and in order to spend some time with my mates, or "for the buzz" as they say. We separated in front of the ground and everybody went to the end specified on their respective tickets and finally I did manage to get one and then I saw some lads from Lokomotiv (Plovdiv) London contingent (LPFC LondonCrew) and I watched the game together with them. The only thing I remember is that we were sat in front of some elderly gentlemen who kept on urging us to sit down (something that has been widely accepted here for a long time).

The atmosphere was not that bad, but generally it was a rather boring game (at least for me). CSKA was defeated 1-0, but long before the final whistle we left the ground and went to the same pub where I had arranged to meet my "red" mates again. We ordered some beers and stood by the windows in order to look at the crowds passing by. The first fans had started leaving the ground and I answered a call notifying me of an inner conflict in the away end, where one of the CSKA firms captured (stole) a Bulgarian national flag (!) on which the name of our club Lokomotiv (GO) was written instead of CSKA and that extremely enraged some *chorbari*! Later on the flag was returned (through one of our mutual friends), but at that time we were also mad, especially I, having understood that the lads who took the flag were actually the ones I most conscientiously helped a lot on that day and they knew who I was and where I was from. The boys who put up the flag in the away sector were just ordinary fans who had come to the game to cheer a Bulgarian club, obviously not aware of any negative consequences.

OK, let's assume there was a misunderstanding and things were settled eventually, but a few days after the game the "red" morons in question proudly posed for a photo with the captured Bulgarian, I repeat Bulgarian national flag (!) hanging upside down! What an act of heroism, what courage! Obviously, for some people words like honour, valour and dignity are completely void of meaning, not to mention words like friendship and mutual aid. Well, I disliked them before that day. I already mentioned about my affinity with their biggest rival Levski, but after that incident I just started to loathe them and there's no way I can ever change that.

Bulgaria – Wales 3-1, 29.03.1995

The first leg was played before a crowd of 20,000 at "Arms Park" in Cardiff in December 1994 and it finished 0-3. As if it was yesterday we sadly remember our brilliant defender Trifon Ivanov (who passed away recently, may he rest in peace!) and his stunning volley lashing into the upper corner of the net, way out of Neville Southall's reach.

We also took interest in the other Great Britain national teams. As we said before, we followed the English thread and were simply obsessed with the way football was played in the UK. In addition to enjoying our beloved clubs, we passionately supported England national team like it was our native one! However, one of the first games of a national team from Great Britain that we were able to see in the flesh was Bulgaria vs Wales. The modest Welsh team arrived in Sofia featuring a number of stars from the newly established Premiership, e.g. Neville Southall, Chris Coleman, Gary Speed (RIP), Ryan Giggs, Vinnie Jones, John Hartson, Dean Saunders... It was a whole constellation of British football stars, but they just didn't stand a chance against our Bulgarian team, which, only months ago, had returned triumphantly from the USA World Cup'94, (having finished 4th, the greatest success to this day) after knocking Germany and losing to Italy in a rather controversial game at the semi-final! Borislav Mihailov, Trifon Ivanov (RIP), Krassimir Balakov, Yordan Letchkov, Emil Kostadinov, Hristo Stoichkov, Lyuboslav Penev... it was really the best generation Bulgaria has ever had!

I, naturally, attended the game and one of my reasons was one of my football idols – Ryan Giggs. I remember there was still snow in Bulgaria on that day and every time he went to take a corner kick, numerous snowballs would be thrown at him! I wasn't very happy with that, but those were the ways on the Balkans. Vinnie Jones made a few of his emblematic tackles and got loudly booed by Bulgarian fans. Though the only goal for Wales was scored by Dean Saunders in the game's final minutes, it was a youngster called John Hartson who made the greatest impression from the Welsh team.

THREE

THE TRILOGY FOLLOWING ENGLAND NATIONAL TEAM

MEET THE CHELSEA HEADHUNTERS

Bulgaria – England 1-1, 09.06.1999

The time came for one of the most memorable games for all of us who were keen on English football.

Bulgaria was to host England in 1999 in a EURO 2000 qualifier. The national team of Bulgaria had played England several times before, the first one being a long time ago, during the 1962 World Cup in Chile. It was our first encounter not only with our adored players like David Seaman, Alan Shearer, Sol Campbell, Jamie Redknapp, Teddy Sheringham, Robbie Fowler, etc., but also with the notorious English hooligans. It was those times that set the beginning of our quite a few dangerous infiltrations (fusions), naturally caused by our desire to be part of them and support England even on our native soil.

A lot of our opponents have questioned our loyalty as Bulgarians through all these years. Others would merely wonder *how we as Bulgarians could support England, the game being played in Bulgaria at that.*

There were also those who would downright call us traitors, believing they were some great patriots! However, the worst thing was, when years after that, one of our lads said he just had some kind of infatuation that he much regretted later. But let me tell you a few words only – whenever I see this date it brings a smile on my face and I remember all those precious moments we spent together with the English; and I have never regretted anything, and I will never, ever, not for a single second, regret anything whatsoever related to the events of that day or to any other day we met them! If there are regretful people now, they can't have had any sincere intentions then or they are nothing else but lying bastards!

At the very beginning of this book we wrote about each fan's primordial right to choose the ideas he is to follow and the ideas that all of us then chose to follow and support were those of the motherland of football and hooliganism! I feel really sorry for those who were misled then, but we are not among them and we will remain faithful and loyal to those ideas until we die!

The evening before the game our group consisted of some 10 lads. As usual, we stayed in the dormitories in the student quarter in Sofia. First thing we did was to leave our backpacks in the rooms and off we went to stroll along *Vitosha* Boulevard, one of the main Sofia streets. As one would expect, we were in high spirits and had great expectations as we always did. It was still lunchtime and one could well meet some tipsy Englishmen, which made us even happier. The way those people communicated was remarkable. We met blokes dressed as knights and we were proud to hug each other and have our pictures taken with them, not a single trace of the so called "English disease" and similar bollocks. Nothing of the kind! They were all friendly, open and well-mannered and they treated us like equals (something I would also feel once I started living in England), and all the rest is just media bias and distortion, as well as attempts to antagonise people, but this is a rather long and different story.

Going back to the main street, it was getting dark already and we had hardly walked in half of the pubs we wanted to visit. We went into a side street to have our picture taken with a well-known six-foot tall English fan carrying the traditional huge red roses and the inflatable Golden Nike Trophy (World Cup). Those lads really brought colour and lively atmosphere wherever they would go. They were charismatic and you could feel their genuine sense of football fandom and that's why we simply adored them.

At the far end of that side street (which turned out to be the street where the Bulgarian Football Union (BFU) headquarters were situated) we saw loads of British flags draped and lads sitting on the pavements. We got there and found our oasis. We didn't hesitate a second before joining them. As the night closed in one could hear the sounds of bottles being knocked over and breaking glass, while the voices got even louder and the police sirens wail never seemed to end. And there we were, right in the BFU backyard, chanting *"Come on England"* at the top of our voices. I remember we met some Wolves fans and it was them we sang with. A group of about 20 tough lads from Burnley appeared and they looked as if they had just had a fight as they turned up together, breathing heavily and some had blood on their shirts. Things must have kicked off somewhere. We had a word with them and they asked us about the local scene and Sofia firms and we found out that they had had a scuffle with CSKA ultras. Our conversation was gradually drowned as someone started another chant and everybody joined. I noticed I had stood up and stretched my arms. I looked up and saw some people at the windows of the surrounding buildings. A woman complained of the hell of a noise we were making but I shouted at her to fuck off (in pure Bulgarian) and went on singing along madly with the English. I found myself shaking with excitement.

As we have always done in such moments of glory, I stood side by side with my brother-in-arms Gilly. Here's how he saw the events of that momentous day:

On the following day Jolly Roger Firm was in its full strength... The morning was sunny and hot even in those early hours as summer had just begun in Bulgaria. It was 9th June 1999, a Wednesday. The day that was one of the most exciting days in my youth and the day I will remember till I die! It was a late evening game but we had agreed to set off early at dawn and catch the first train from Gorna Oryahovitsa to Sofia. All the JRF hardcore were there (Tosh, me and a lot of other lads). The euphoria surrounding the game was unbelievable. Sofia expected the arrival of huge crowds of fans, not only Bulgarian football team supporters, but also English football fans. Papers said that about 3000 English would make the trip from Britain on charter flights, some of them coming straight from Varna and Bourgas Black Sea beaches.

For the first time Bulgarian fans and visiting supporters were to become one, united by their love for football instead of being separated by national or club belonging. Bulgarians were to plunge into an atmosphere typical of the most passionate football loving nations. We were going to Sofia not only to watch the game but also with the hope to find and meet those small groups of hooligans keeping low profile. The trip itself was not very eventful, the usual noise and chaos, fans' chants and songs, huge amounts of beer and the typical banter between supporters of different clubs. We arrived in Sofia shortly before noon and took the public transport downtown.

Stepping off the bus I got the feeling that our capital had been taken over by the English. Never before had I seen so many people at one and the same place. They were scattered all over, in restaurants and bars, wearing their traditional colours and singing songs like *"Rule Britannia"*, *"God Save The Queen"*, etc. Their flags were hanging from windows and fences and the sounds of their chants and toasts were drowning any other noises around. It was as if our country had been invaded and conquered by the English. Here and there we could see English fans stripped down to their waists lying on the grass and pavements and drinking to excess beer undisturbed by anyone. Some were already sunburned as the midday sun was scorching hot and burning their skin.

We were walking en masse to Bulgarian Army Stadium, the venue chosen for the game between Bulgaria and England. The English players were expected to arrive there several hours before kick-off time and that could be the right time for us to make the much desired photos of them.On our way to the ground we had our pictures taken with fans of Wigan, Nottingham Forest, Burney, Blackpool and other smaller English clubs. We knew that England national team got more support among smaller club fans than among the fans of the big clubs, although a few of the latter could also be seen. My excitement was unprecedented, my heart was beating wild and I would get the goosebumps every time we struck a conversation with them, be it long or short. The dream we had cherished and pursued for so long, watching them on TV or reading about them in the papers, was now coming true. Indeed, Bulgarian fans had mingled with the English talking about football and what not. Some were showing their tattoos of their favourite English clubs in order to impress English fans or prove their unconditional love for their beloved teams.

The sun wouldn't stop beating down on our faces; we were thirsty and needed to oil our throats a bit after the usual autographs and pictures taken in front of the ground's main entrance, where the English players had arrived. One of our lads who used to speak the language of Shakespeare fluently was interviewed by BBC Television reporters. If there had been a fountain nearby, I'm absolutely certain we would have jumped in and cooled down with our clothes on as that was something that had become our trademark throughout all those years.

2–3 hours to go before kick-off. As we had agreed on in advance, if we wanted to infiltrate in the away section, we would have to keep silent and not talk to each other or if a copper asked us something we would either answer in English or not respond at all, as if not understanding. That was the only way to achieve our much desired goal. We had some lads wearing England shirts or English club jerseys, which would even facilitate things. We killed the time left to kick-off by drinking beer in the park by the ground, where we stood sat among the English and we chatted to them, no matter that some of us did not speak their language. It was for real, our dreams had come true. The time had come to join the English supporters, sing the British anthem and feel like a small part of them. We didn't give a fuck what people would call us, xenophiles or anything else. It was the Bulgarian national team playing and we were to support England. English football was like a drug for us and we were hooked, it was our obsession, frenzy, mania, call it what you will, but we have always followed this specific thread and we'll keep on doing it.

Shortly before approaching the gate leading to the away end we scattered about, though still sticking to the English and going with their steady flow. Some of us (like Tosh) had hurried to the front while the others lagged behind. We already had that feeling that our plan was working well and so little was left before achieving our cherished goal... Next thing we knew was one of our lads walking behind gave a shout to Tosh, who was much further ahead, in broken English that I even can't put down, but it sounded something like *"Todar, comoun!"* You can just imagine how everybody turned around to see where that shout came from and the Old Bill guarding the gate recognised right there on the spot that we were all Bulgarians.

Our group split as some of us had already entered the ground together with the English, while the rest of us remained in the nearby home support section. Our plan had come unstuck just because of two words! Unfortunately, I and several other lads were left in the section with the Bulgarian fans. We tried to break through the buffer zone separating the two sets of supporters, but we were driven back by the police. I was furious, and could not put up with that disappointment. I felt like an utter fool! There was nothing I could do but watch, my eyes filled with tears and at the same time I felt helplessly angry. The ground was filled to capacity, but all the time I could only hear the voices of those 3000 Englishmen having flown thousands of miles to support their country. Before them there were hundreds of flags with the names of various clubs or their hooligan firms. Hands held high, they wouldn't stop clapping and cheering their team. I felt like being at Wembley and not at a Bulgarian ground. Their voices must have been heard for miles across Sofia throughout all those 90 minutes.

The game finished in a 1-1 draw thanks to goals scored by Stoichkov and Shearer. By the way that was Stoichkov's last game for Bulgaria. I was very happy for Tosh... He had been planning that for so long and nobody was willing to believe that he was going to succeed.

Here is how he saw the events from his perspective:

We had bought tickets for Section V (at the border with the away support section) of *Bulgarska Armia* **8** Stadium. The game was to be played there since *Vasil Levski* National Stadium was under repairs at that time.

Both grounds are located literally within yards and amidst a huge park called Borisova Garden. In most cases, when we had tried to sneak in the national stadium away support sector we had come unstuck and so prior to kick-off nobody believed that we would make it on that day. However, I had different intentions and I was fully determined and convinced that I would not fail this time.

Following my club, I had already specialised in making such cunning plans for infiltrating in sections occupied by rival mobs with the purpose of confronting them and I was damn sure that my experience in that field, though not very great, would help me this time, and I strongly hoped to fulfil my plans. I was well familiar with the approach to the ground and definitely thought that this time things would be different since the *"Army"* (as we called CSKA ground), the further one goes into the huge park, the more it resembles a maze of alleys and small thickly afforested areas. The venue itself has always facilitated fights and clashes and quite often it used to become the arena of battles between rivalry fans of Sofia big clubs and other teams. The problem is that it is extremely difficult to separate fans there and one could always find a loophole to sneak through.

Ahead of kick-off we gathered around some benches and discussed the possibilities clarifying our plan to perfection, but I could still see uncertainty and doubt in the eyes of some of our lads. I was sure someone would fuck up and eventually I turned out to be right. We agreed to mix with groups of English fans right from the ground's outer parameter and walk right beside them along the alleys and, most importantly, keep silent and not talk to each other in order not to be recognised by our accent. Several times we were on the brink of being asked by the cops to show our tickets. We had agreed to shrug our shoulders as a gesture of not understanding and not provide any tickets as the OB were going to turn us back straight away. We passed the police line, the plan was still working and we were extremely close to achieving our goal… when I heard someone call my name!

God Almighty, I didn't turn around… I just kept on walking. I was certain that something had gone wrong behind me as I saw the cops head that way, but I was inches away from my target and contrary to all unwritten fandom rules (which I knew to perfection) I just didn't stop and I even didn't turn around (sorry, lads!). I was obsessed with a fixed idea that I had pursued for so long that I would not let anything get in my way and stop me from fulfilling my dream. I knew nothing serious was going to happen to my mates, most probably the cops were going to turn them back to the home support sections, so I made several brave steps further and there I was in front of the away end gates. The only thing left to do was go through the last obstacle, the check at the turnstiles, which seemed to me as a piece of cake. Security checks were sloppy, no one even made an effort to ask for my ticket and the very strip search was not that meticulous.

I climbed the last step leading to the stand when some dumb cop grabbed my hand. *"Where do you think you're going?"*, he roared out angrily. For a brief moment I shuddered and then thought to myself, *"Fuck me! Is it written on my forehead that I am Bulgarian?!"* I was puzzled but managed to shrug my shoulders pretending not to understand. His colleagues urged him to let me in so that the inflow of people is not stopped, to which he reacted with colossal nonsense, *"I say, how come these Englishmen smoke Victory (a brand of Bulgarian cigarettes)!?"* Obviously, the poor bloke had always thought up to then that all British smoke Pall Mall, eh? I looked down to my jeans pocket and saw the tip of my box of cigarettes slightly sticking out of it. I silently cursed myself for making such a small but stupid mistake that could have ruined my perfect plan. I immediately ran the risk and started speaking in the best English accent I was able to speak and felt how he loosened his grip on my hand and ultimately let me go. I made a few more step and I was in!

Some things can't be described with words, they just have to be experienced, but if I have to describe how I felt at that moment in one sentence only, then it must be as follows - I was walking on air! As if flying in a dream! I saw that some ten lads from our firm didn't make it and so we instantly made sure we were stood along the same row at least. To the right, I could see Gilly and the rest of our lads who had remained in the adjacent section and were desperately trying to break through the police line, unfortunately to no success. I don't remember anything from the very game since I just felt like being in a fairy tale. I chanted and clapped with thousands of my role models and absolutely nothing else mattered...

After the final whistle we filed out downtown as darkness had already descended on Sofia. We decided to make one final search for groups of fans that were surely going on the piss in the local pubs and possibly join them. We were not scattered any more like before the game, we were walking side by side and constantly looking around. In one of the boozers we came across some Wolves and West Ham. They were sitting at the outdoor tables, talking loud and sometimes chanting *"England, England"*. We stood beside them, naturally after getting their permission, and without being intrusive we struck up a conversation. They started asking us about our firm, club and the town we came from. Every one of us was talking to somebody and I personally got introduced to an English (a Wolves fan) named Andy Whitehouse, who I exchanged addresses with. We used to write to each other for some time, but afterwards I lost his contact details. Andy, if you are reading this book, I would be greatly honoured to see you again someday!

We spent several hours in that boozer and we drank some huge amounts of alcohol, even mixing whiskey and beer in tankards. We felt our legs failing us as the exhaustion from that long and exciting day was beginning to take its toll, but still we just didn't feel like going home. Then we heard sirens wail and the word went out that this time it was Stoke hooligans having a go at CSKA, but actually we didn't know whether it was true or not and there was no way for us to walk around every street in Sofia after having so much to drink. The WestHam fans suggested that we joined them to another Irish pub nearby. We agreed, of course, and started trudging to that place. Upon entry I took a look around and I immediately saw that we had found the English hooligans core.

The pub consisted of two terraces, the first one being occupied by a mixture of firms, while on the second one stood some 30 lads and they were hooligans notorious not only nationwide, but worldwide. They were Millwall. None of them was wearing their club's jersey or an England shirt; they all had designer clothes on. They had those fierce looking faces and they peered at us and at our West Ham mates with contempt. We knew about the hatred between the London Hammers and Lions and we became aware that things were beginning to get rough. We saw them exchange offensive gestures and verbal abuse. We and our English friends moved away to the bar and went on to have some more beer.

We started singing along with everybody, completely drowning the music coming from the speakers around us. Millwall kept on staring at us and at West Ham, they were talking to each other and occasionally shouted something out loud. Then they started off some songs against the Hammers and the others in the boozer went silent so one could hear only the Millwall lads' voices. I had the feeling that if this wasn't an England game, but a local East London derby, the entire pub would be wrecked. We were immensely pleased by that encounter, even though at times it was a rather hostile one. We had finally met the people we had been looking for and so it was really worthy, even if it would cost us a punch or two. In an hour, the English Dockers became even louder (apparently the alcohol had taken its toll on them) and started literally yelling at us from above in their dialect that was already impossible to understand. Some of them (in particular their ringleaders) even started making Nazi salutes and all that verbal abuse meant one thing only – they wanted us to leave. They kept on saying *"Fuck off"* or *"Get out"*! There was nothing left for us to do but part with the rest of the English at the bar since we wouldn't welcome any complications. Besides, it was their own business and their own territory that night. They were celebrating in their own way and surely were not pleased with people like us spoiling their party. They didn't know who we were and what we had had in our hearts for years. And even if they had known they wouldn't have understood. For them we were just some blokes… or to be more precise… we were nobody. However, we were well aware of that and there was no room for resentment. We took it like men, we had our honour and dignity and so we left. We said goodbye to everybody and hit the streets still discussing the events in the pub. It was already midnight and as we were knackered after so much beer and whiskey, we decided to take taxis to the student quarter, where we were going to spend the rest of the night before going back to Gorna Oryahovitsa.

Quite understandably, there was silence in the taxi as we felt some kind of bitterness. We arrived at our destination and being so exhausted from all those emotions, we went off right away. On the next morning the hot rays of the sun once again came through the windows of the room where we were lying over one another on the dormitory floor and beds. Imagine this: a 4-bed room occupied by 30 drunken louts vomit and empty bottles all over the floor! We were woken up by the loud noise of a door being knocked down with a mighty kick and there in the doorframe stood a friend of ours (a Chelsea fan) who had been partying elsewhere. He dropped down heavily on one of the beds and we stared at him in surprise open-mouthed. Finally he stood up swaying and as he was taking off his jeans he suddenly freaked out, *"Holy fuck! Where are my boxer shorts?!"* He had left them behind somewhere and only God knew what happened to him that night. We all burst out laughing and the poor fella lay down ass naked, his jeans half down, and instantly crashed out.

We had just been cheered up by that joke when Tosh rushed in the room and he was enraged as one of the rolls of film from the cameras (we still had film cameras then) we had been taking pictures with for the last few days had been exposed to light and ruined. They were arguing with another fella about who exactly was the one to blame, as Tosh had accidentally opened the camera rear cover and entered the dark toilet in order to rewind the film and save what could still be saved from the exposures. At that very moment the other lad, still drowsy, entered the lavatory and screwed up his plan!

So that was our Jolly Roger Firm at its finest – always together and always arguing about something. We were really sorry about the ruined pictures, some of which could have been included in this book, but anyway, we got over that disappointment. The events from those exhilarating and unbelievable few days will always stay in our hearts and memories since we felt as if being in seventh heaven, experiencing for the first time in our lives that kind of captivating mood and satisfaction aroused by the incredible atmosphere of being among English fans.

8 Bulgarian Army (translation)

Macedonia – England 1-2, 06.09.2003

The next England game we watched in the flesh was a European Championship qualifier in Macedonia four years later. In comparison to 9th June 1999, that day was the icing on the cake, the cherry on the pie, because it was our first England away game and our firm for the first time actually mixed with their fans and hooligans.

It was early September 2003, but summer was still at its height not only in Macedonia, but also on the rest of the Balkans. Since it was an abroad trip, we had bought tickets for a coach from Sofia to Skopje. The distance between the two capitals is about 150 miles, which meant an almost 4-hour drive. Macedonia, which neighbours Bulgaria to the east, used to be part of our country, but after World War I it got separated and became a former Yugoslavia republic. There is a lot of controversy and a number of changes have happened in that country throughout the years, but I will leave that to historian. I only know that Macedonians, as well as Serbs, strongly dislike us, Bulgarians, and the population of Macedonia even says they speak their own language, but actually it is just a linguistic norm of Bulgarian language (South Slavic norm). Their language is not recognised officially by Bulgaria and Greece and it is also called "Skopje language" or "Bulgarian dialect". Anyway, we didn't care about that! We were just interested in meeting the English once again.

The evening before our departure to Skopje we gathered in the Domino Bar to clarify the last details of our trip and in general our plans for our stay in the Macedonian capital. Among other things, let me just mention that the day before we were off, I met the eyes of my future wife. It was just for a brief moment in *Bulgaria* restaurant, where we were having some beers, and we even did not get introduced to each other, but only exchanged glances. It was a love at first sight for me and afterwards, in April 2005, we got married.

The morning of 6th September 2003 was sunny and warm and it looked like it was going to be a pretty long, emotional and eventful day. After having several cups of early morning coffee, at 5:30 am I put on my usual casual clothes (Boss jeans, Burberry shirt and Adidas trainers), left home and headed for the train station to meet most of the Jolly Roger hardcore. We had to catch the early train from Gorna Oryahovitsa to Sofia as our plan was to arrive in the capital slightly before noon. There we were to meet the other lads who were in charge of sorting the coach.

We were already 25–26 years old, men in the prime of life. Our group looked quite strong and cohesive and we already had some 40 lads. Everybody would wear designer clothes and we looked like casual elite. The train journey went on as usual, we took over almost half a carriage (several compartments), we went on the piss-up with whiskey or beer, we smoked weed and sang England songs. We must have been quite loud cause at some point two coppers turned up and asked us what game we were going to as they knew no football was to be played in Sofia. In fits of laughter we told them we were going to Skopje to support England in their game against Macedonia. They just shrugged shoulders, looked at each other and called us crazy. It was their first time hearing Bulgarian fans were to support the national team of England. After they left, we burst out laughing and started chanting *"England, England, England..."* even louder. Some of the younger lads had already had too much to drink and could barely stand on their feet.

Our banter about English football went on throughout our journey and at times we were trying to out-voice each other. The craze about the game had taken its toll on all of us. It was just a few hours and we were going to meet the English elite, their most notorious hooligans.

We arrived in Sofia just before noon and going through the railway station subway we kept on singing English songs, which made the people turn around in fright and stare at us wondering what the hell was going on. They could have even thought we were English, especially as we were flying the British flag with the Jolly Roger badge, and as I already said the summer season was still at its height and it was normal to meet English holidaymakers spending their holidays at the Bulgarian Black Sea coast here and there. We met the others from the firm by the coach at the central coach station situated right next to the train station. We bought some more alcohol from the nearby store and set off for Skopje.

It was already scorching hot and some of us had stripped to their waists. The coach was far from luxurious, but at least it was air-conditioned and we were on our own, 40 hoolies pursuing their goal, i.e. mixing with the English supporters. We were praying to God to arrive on time in Macedonia safe and sound as the driver was driving way too fast. Here and there we would hit a pothole and we really hoped that nothing serious would happen. Having a flat tyre would have been our smallest problem in view of the speed at which we were heading for Skopje. We had draped the flag across the rear window just like the Chelsea fans on route to Liverpool in the Football Factory film that came out a year later. We kept on drinking beer, chanting and bantering and we even made the coach driver put on some hard rock after asking him to do so a few times. The atmosphere was unbelievable; I dare say it was one of our firm's best away days ever.

Several times we stopped to have a pee and in the towns of Kyustendil and Kumanovo- to replenish our stock of beer. The scorching rays of the sun were coming through the coach windows, making us increasingly thirsty and in need of more beer. At one of our stops the coach braked sharply and one of the lads, who was rather pissed and the youngest of all, lurched forward to the front door, which opened and he rolled down the steps and fell out of the bus right into the road ditch. We all burst out laughing and the poor geezer seemed to even not know where he was and what was happening. A few times he fell down to the floor swaying and ignored our pleas to have a nap until we arrive. Besides, we were approaching the border and, given the condition he was in, there was a clear danger of him being nicked and not allowed to continue his journey.

As we were getting closer to the checkpoints before entering Macedonia we saw something that made us delirious and immediately the entire coach went into an ecstasy. Right beside us we saw 6 or 7 coaches waiting and they were all full of English fans (most of whom seemed proper lads). We recognised some notorious faces that we had seen in the papers or on TV news reporting football violence in the UK. They had also put up their flags and banners on the side windows of their coaches and there were some lads that put aside those flags and started greeting us. We started chanting *"England, England…"* banging and kicking the sides of the coach. Our driver panicked and started shouting in the loudspeaker pleading us to calm down as we were approaching the border checkpoints. We went through the customary border passport and luggage checks, the police focused on looking for drugs and other illegal substances. The coaches with the English passed us by while we were being checked and the lads were pointing in the direction of Skopje, where we were supposed to meet. Once the boring customs control was over we set off for the capital of Macedonia.

The coach was driving at the same high speed but upon reaching our final destination it started swaying due to the poor road surface condition, raising dust all around. The driver lost his way and we started wandering about some neighbourhoods inhabited by Muslims. By the way, about 30% of the Macedonian population follows Islam and you can imagine what sights we came across. I remember going through some market surrounded by mosques and hearing the sounds of their afternoon prayers. Men were wearing turbans and the women's heads were covered in veils. We got the feeling we were not in Skopje, but in Damascus. After asking the way several times we left that different kind of world and headed downtown.

The central part of the city looked like any other place and had nothing to do with what we had just seen. Some two hours remained before kick-off time and we were in desperate need of food and beer. We told our driver to wait for us near the football ground after the game as we had to set off back to Bulgaria immediately. We found some stalls selling huge Serbian *pljeskavica* burgers and a local brand of beer and we fell on them like wolves. We pushed aside the people in the queue and they would just look at us in bewilderment and we could surely see the fear in their eyes. They wouldn't dare to make a stand. Having eaten and drunk more than enough, we headed for the Skopje Stadium, home of the local *Vardar* football club, a member of the Macedonian football league. We walked along the streets singing England songs and our chants echoed all around as we were looking for the English we'd seen in the coaches earlier. However, we didn't find any of them either downtown or in the park we passed by. Some of us started peeing by the nearby trees and causing couples in love who were passing by wonder what kind of people we actually were.

Obviously the coach loads of English and all those who had flown in with charter planes had been directly escorted to the ground. We had some skirmishes with local fans who challenged us by throwing bottles and stones at us so we had to charge at them using our fists and boots to disperse them. Several coppers intervened and got things under control before they could escalate. The Old Bill escorted us to the ground, where we were met by a veritable army of cops, gendarmerie and special police forces. Believe me, never before had I seen such level of security for a football game! All of them were heavily armed with machine guns and shields; there were even armoured military vehicles and those police buses for taking prisoners commonly seen in American action films! Other coppers assisted by police dogs were also patrolling the area. It's a pity we don't have pictures of those scenes, but everybody who was present could verify my words. We were wondering whether we were going to a football game or it was just that Skopje was under martial law! I am not sure about the exact number of security inside and outside the ground, but they must have been more than a thousand.

While buying our tickets outside we could hear the English songs and chants and we guessed they had once again turned up in huge numbers. Upon entering one of the English sectors we understood we were right. Some of our lads were again stopped and prevented from entering the away sections, but this time I was not among them. I had done it! I was over the moon and my ears were ringing not only because of all that noise around me, but also due to the adrenaline rushing to my head. There were more than 3000 English supporters, a mixture of rank-and-file and hardcore fans. Two thirds of the ground was occupied by their flags draped all over the fences, running track and stands. I had the feeling that every single English football club was represented, judging by the names of teams and firms written on their Saint George flags.We could see the likes of Peterborough, Leicester, Barnsley, Middlesbrough, Notts County, Wigan, Millwall and many others. I just cannot list all of them. Some English were wearing the colours of their team and looked like an army of crusaders, others were dressed in their usual designer clothes and still others were stripped to their waists enjoying the last sun-rays for the day.

We found ourselves among West Ham, Forest and Boro fans. The whole place simply erupted at the national anthem of England! It was priceless seeing all of them raise their arms, or hands upon their chests, sing in unison *"God Save The Queen"*. We also joined, feeling part of that English army. We introduced ourselves to some of the hooligans from Forest Executive Crew and The Frontline. Though we were having a chat, we wouldn't stop singing along with them. Once they knew we were Bulgarians who had come to support their national team, they also started wondering what the hell we were doing there. They had never seen or heard of anyone like us so obsessed with English football and English clubs in general. We might have been the first Bulgarians mixing with their crowd and maybe the only ones supporting a foreign national team with such passion that was typical of the English only.

This time it was Tosh who was one of those that couldn't make it to the away end and after the game was over he told me that he ended up at the opposite end of the ground (behind one of the goals) together with some other lads of ours and a small contingent of English supporters among a hostile Macedonian crowd. Here is what he has to tell:

I have never understood what kind of problems Macedonians have with us, Bulgarians. From a merely historical point of view, we should even belong to one whole and a number of historical sources prove our common origins.I won't go into any details so that not to get our readers bored, but I really find Macedonian psychology quite interesting. Quite a lot of Macedonians keep on coming to study in Bulgaria, and judging by my Macedonian friends and acquaintances (most of them students in Sofia), they feel quite comfortable in our country as they study, work and take advantage of all benefits just like the way any Bulgarian does! A number of them have dual citizenship, we speak one and the same language (with slight dialect differences) and I really can't name a single reason for them to hate us, Bulgarians! I don't really know why they are so rude to us as to even defame us! Although my country has suffered damages and has been literally deprived of some territories in this particular case, we have never provoked any conflicts with them whatsoever... there have been no ethnic tensions, assassinations, wars or any other signs so typical of territorial and racial redistribution or conflicts! We all know what our modern-day world is and how many stupid wars are going on exactly due to the reasons mentioned above. I dare say that Bulgaria has very rarely entered such conflicts with its Balkan neighbours despite its considerable military strength and capabilities.In the past we seldom invaded a country in order to annex its territories or following an autonomy demand. On the contrary, in our history we have had many occasions of irrevocable seizure of our lands by simple verification of an agreement with a signature and seal and with no retaliation whatsoever, not to speak of any kind of bloodsheds! And the examples that can be found all around us are numerous. We only have to take a look at what happened in neighbouring Serbia. That's why things like that should be remembered well! It is as if moving my back garden fence six feet further encroaching on your land and then getting angry with you for that! In the minds of the so called Macedonians we simply don't exist and have never existed, while all kings and rulers, even worldwide, have been pure-blooded Macedonians.

After all that has been said so far, you can imagine their faces when I and several lads from our firm found ourselves among them during the Macedonia vs England game in the autumn of 2003. Their eyes would have popped out of their heads from rage. They circled round us like hyenas waiting for the larger beasts of prey to get their fill in order to have a go at us and pick what's left. I had felt their arrogance throughout the day - wherever we went and whenever they found out we were Bulgarians. Even when we would buy beer and kindly thank them in Bulgarian, they had that peculiar look in their eyes saying *"You are not welcome here!"*

This time my plan for infiltration in the English section came unstuck right in the beginning, as in the vicinity of the ground I had a row with exactly that type of local moron, who, having found out what our nationality was, started cursing like a sailor trying to explain to me how matters stood. My response was shutting his filthy mouth with a single punch but I got nicked by the Old Bill for an ID check and questioning. The goddamn coppers also loathed us. I bet they did cause they were Macedonians, weren't they!? The very moment I took my passport out their behaviour became brutal and they started pushing me back and forth. I just don't know how lucky I got when they let me watch the game, but as if on purpose they pushed us into the beast's lair, where, fortunately, there were some BirminghamCity lads, who we made contact with and as far as I know still keep in touch with to this day.

At half time we noticed some disorder in the main stand. Ever since kick-off a Grimsby flag had been put up there and things must have got out of control as we could see some kind of stampede and we definitely saw a bloke get pushed and fall down the steep stairs! The flag was gone and the English around us bristled, rose to their feet and started singing. We, of course, joined their song. I remember that there was some kind of a scoreboard behind us and some of them climbed up that structure in an effort to drape their flags there. This made the locals even madder and what we had now in the section was a kind of circle with us (and the English) and them, the pissed-up ones, at its opposite ends.

With every minute gone, tension was rising up to its boiling point facilitated by the events on the pitch. It seemed only a matter of time before I was to be involved in my first fight wearing the Three lions on my shirt, and believe me, I could and I would defend myself! What followed was an exchange of insults and abuse, to which we quite instinctively responded in Bulgarian because apart from the standard *"Fuck you!"* the Macedonians would abuse and swear in a dialect that only we could perfectly understand. You should have seen all those ugly faces after we responded the way we are used to with our typical mean and cruel insults and swears. Nothing could be worse for them than a Bulgarian supporting their rival team at their own territory. Their expressions were a mixture of anger, rage, bafflement and to some extent helplessness as it was the OB that stepped up, segregated the section, setting us apart, and ultimately established order. Of course, the insults and swears didn't stop flying and I could more and more clearly see their genuine hatred for us. Come to think of it now, it was a rather dangerous trip in general that could have had much more serious consequences for our lot. At places like this you could always expect the unexpected. These are the so called "mean" venues, where absolutely anything could happen. This is definitely one of the few destinations (along with Turkey) to which I would travel to support the Bulgarian national team. Naturally, armed from top to toe. You can't allow for any underestimation in such regions and a lot of those who underrated them got into some serious trouble!

England did well on the pitch, playing with passion and enthusiasm. Every time they touched the ball, every single dribble, got applauded by their fans. Under the constant chant of *"Come on England"* the English players seemed to be flying high and their raids to the opponent's goal would never seem to stop. England won 2-1 thanks to goals scored by Rooney and Beckham and when the second goal was scored the ground simply exploded with the English roar just like a time bomb! We hugged each other screaming at the top of our voices as if we were English and not foreigners.

I can't get into words how I felt at that point; it was simply my best football related experience. You've got to be there to get that feeling. And all that respect we had for those hooligans standing next to us. You don't forget moments like those. They are these parts of your life that remain in your mind forever. Something that you'll tell your sons or the younger generations of fans. The dream we had been following for so long had finally come true. We had got in touch with the ones we had been only reading about or watching on Youtube. That day was one of the most exciting days in my life. It was as if being on another planet. Jolly Roger Firm was now deep into the drug called English football. After the game was over we bid farewell with our newly made friends (as it would almost always happen) knowing that we would hardly ever meet again, and intoxicated with joy we slipped away in the direction of our coach that was waiting for us near the ground. We had a long way to travel back home, but we could get a good night sleep now because in spite of our exhaustion from the long and exciting day, we were on cloud nine. We had taken the enormous pleasure of having the sweetest part of the pie!

England – Bulgaria 4-0, 03.09.2010

After the Fulham– CSKA club level game that I already told you about in this chapter and that I was able to watch in the flesh here in England, it was time for our two national teams to meet again.

A lot had changed after that momentous game in 1999 (12 years ago) and it was, let's say, like the end of a kind of a (20-year) cycle in our history of pursuing our ideal. Looking back now, I see that more than a quarter of a century had passed since the start of those ideas that we had been trying to follow and establish through all those years. For us, it had not been an easy and short period of time, while for others it had turned out to be huge and things in life had become insurmountable when they tried to combine family life with friends from the past, etc. Some members of the firm had almost gone without a trace, while others would very rarely appear due to our scattering to all corners of the world, and there were still others who repented everything they used to swear by before, people who had drastically changed the path of their lives and had given up everything created and done before. We still keep in touch with some of them, while others we just can't stand due to the huge differences that had the upper hand and resulted in painful partings.

Anyway, if that was what the phrase *"life has taken its toll"* meant, then Life had surely taken us all and using all of its might had swirled and hurled us like a storm does to a pirate shipwreck on a solitary island. The economic situation in Bulgaria may have actually also contributed to the events that followed, but I don't fully agree with that and I have never considered such reasons as justified. However, out there somewhere, the core of almost the same people that started everything had remained, as life had not taken its toll on them that much. Nowadays these people have felt mature and wise enough to tell the story to you, our readers.

The 2010 England vs Bulgaria game at Wembley turned out to be a cornerstone for all of us and a last game for a number of lads who had devoted a part of their lives to the terraces. We decided to mark the occasion in an appropriate way and gather before the game in London Hyde Park, from where we were to set off for Wembley Park. Loads of people turned up, having travelled great distances, like America for example, but the majority came from Bulgaria, of course. Our group here put great efforts to take care of our guests and make sure they were properly accommodated and made themselves at home.

This time we had decided to buy tickets for the away end as it was allocated for the Bulgarian travelling fans. Even the usually gloomy and miserable weather seemed to be on our side that day as the clouds had cleared offering us a bright sky and plenty of sunshine to enjoy. We got together early in the park and had a great picnic. A lot of lads living in London had brought along their wives and kids. It was a really wonderful day, which unfortunately was a farewell party for many of us.

We headed for the majestic Wembley, where we were met by several thousands of Bulgarians. We sang together our national anthem and the atmosphere was more than brilliant. Our mood remained festive till the very end of the game as we enjoyed every single minute of it as if knowing that for some of us it would really be the last game to attend and that our Jolly Roger Firm would never be in its full, original strength anymore. On that day we proved that primarily we were football supporters and not slaves to prejudice and other people's opinions and that hardly anyone could place us into a certain group or frame. We supported Bulgaria in the homeland of football and hooliganism and after the game we went to have some more drinks in a pub near the ground. Traditionally, we finished by having a wild party till the break of dawn in one of the most famous London clubs – Ministry of Sound.

The score of that game did not matter at all. Bulgaria got heavily beaten 0-4 and at the return leg played in Sofia on 02.09.2011 England won easily again 3-0.

Meet the Chelsea Headhunters
Chelsea – Levski (Sofia) 3-0, 20.09.2001
Return leg, Levski – Chelsea 0-2, UEFA CUP, 27.09.2001

Once again I'm going back in time in order to tell you about probably the peak, the climax in our meets with fans from the United Kingdom. Two years after the memorable game England played in Sofia, the UEFA Cup draw sent Chelsea to the Bulgarian capital. The London Blues were quite an interesting team then, but they hadn't made all their modern-day achievements yet. So they were drawn the play the Sofia Blues. After their comfortable 3-0 win in the first leg, played in London earlier in September 2001, Chelsea saw the return leg as just a formality.

Our target, naturally, was not related to the football pitch, but that didn't mean I wouldn't set off for Sofia several days before the game, together with our autograph hunters. Our route was the usual one, a train journey to the capital and staying with friends in Sofia student quarter. Of course, the evenings passed in plenty of parties hitting on female students at night clubs and discos, which one could find literally at every corner in that area. Our major goal in the days preceding the game was the airport and the hotels where football teams used to stay at. Those were usually Hilton, Radisson, Kempinski Zografski, etc.

I was accompanied by two close friends of mine, both proper Chelsea fans, though one of them was also a die-hard Levski supporter and that game was like standing at a crossroads for him. The other one, however, would enjoy every single picture, autograph, and generally even the slightest contact with his London idols, just like a little kid would enjoy his new toys (though he was several years older than me)!

From the media we learnt the time Chelsea were to arrive in Sofia, so early on the following day we got dressed, picked up our cameras and armed ourselves with patience. We headed for the airport Terminal 1, where I was expected to take loads of high quality pictures, at the same time having been warned by my mates to make sure not to expose the film to light like I did 2 years before (something that had brought me a lot of notoriety). I remember the airport was full of people and some were taking pictures with digital cameras! Obviously, at the dawn of XXI century, modern technologies had finally arrived in our country, too. I thought to myself how nice it would be to have such a camera as I was still afraid of making another mistake and losing once again such valuable photos.

Chelsea landed led by Claudio Ranieri and they also had a number of supporters travelling with them. Among the welcoming party I spotted Moon, a notorious Bulgarian hooligan and an absolute maniac when it came to pursuing the idea of meeting British fans. He was an expert in that field and even I, who had also become quite skilful, could only learn from him. I bravely dare say Moon was like an encyclopaedia when it came to hooliganism related topics and I know that afterwards he made and kept a number of good connections with hooligans all over the world.

So when he saw me there he approached and whispered in my ear, *"Some are already here, but the core is about to arrive! Well-known top faces from the Headhunters have decided to make the trip..."*

To be honest, I was a little surprised so I didn't believe him at first. I just wondered why they would come here when the tie was clear and there was no serious opposition from local fans. I simply didn't see any other reason except the cheap booze and beautiful Bulgarian women, of course. Through all those years, a good number of all those people we have met on the terraces have unambiguously acknowledged that and the sold-out Sunny Beach hotels in summer definitely proved it! No matter what some people say, no matter what bollocks the media comes up with and TV stations (like BBC for instance) broadcast, those two things are the major decisive factors and the magnets for the more hardcore lads and not only... Alcohol, women and the freedom to do whatever you like, what else would a football hooligan really need... we're only humans after all, aren't we?

Sofia Airport arrival gates started sliding to let out Chelsea football players one by one. Though the team didn't feature so many great stars then, the occasion was of great importance for the average Bulgarian fan. Total chaos ensued! Fans and journalists mixed and started pushing each other in their quest for interviews, photos and autographs. I wanted to stay away from this madness but I had to take pictures of my mates, who were running about like crazy! *"Frankie, Frankie... Can I have a picture taken with you!?"*, my mate, who I already said was behaving like a little kid, asked shaking with excitement. I had already seen Lampard in the flesh when he came to Sofia with the English national team and was still a rising star playing for West Ham. Just a few weeks later he signed for Chelsea and made his debut at the beginning of the season and so the expectations and the enthusiasm surrounding him were really great.

"Take my photo! Take my photo!", my mate kept on screaming while he was dodging the journalists (who were trying to take their interviews) from all possible sides in order to get a chance to have an autograph and his picture taken. So at one point everybody was already outside, where a huge coach was waiting for the team and the players, one after another, started getting on. Naturally, the fans started to surround the already full of stars vehicle, greeting on, frantically gesticulating and waving at the footballers. The journalists, in turn, held their breaths in front of the doors, turning their cameras in the direction of Ranieri, who gave his formal interview. One of the journalists aroused the anger of everybody else with his ignorance or, more probably with a slip of his tongue, but he addressed Ranieri with the name Ravanelli and my mates just went mad and immediately sent him to learn his lesson in football.

The coach set off for the hotel, where we were going later for our next autograph and photo sessions, and I decided to have my pictures taken with some of the Chelsea fans that had arrived with their team and were waiting to be transported to their hotels. I remember a minibus full of fat elderly men who poked fun of me and our Firm's British Jolly Roger flag. They asked me if I was a real pirate and my reply was a loud *"Yes, I am"*. Upon hearing that, they all, laughing out loud, jumped out of the minibus and had their pictures taken with me and the flag as if I was the last pirate standing (you will see some of those photos published in this book). That's the kind of people they are, always in high spirits, and one definitely has to take a joke or two in order to deserve their respect!

Analysing their behaviour through all those years, I got the impression that by doing this they put people around them (especially strangers) to a sort of test and if one passed, they would turn exceptionally friendly and amicable and even make great friends, which I was to ultimately understand in just a few hours. It applied to all of them, even the most die-hard ones, the ones that the British media had long stigmatised as mindless thugs! Nothing of the kind and so far from the truth.

I decided to hang about the airport for a little while and take a look around and to some extent I got my reward for being so patient and assiduous on that day. My mates wholeheartedly thanked me for all my help and opted for following the coach-load of players in their car all the way to the hotel. I wished them luck and went back to the arrivals lounge. Now it was only me and Moon – two maniacs and hunters, not autograph hunters but hooligan hunters, in the good sense of the word, of course. What was bizarre in our case was that we really hoped to meet the London headhunters!

At that very moment, as if by magic, the sliding doors opened and a group of 6 or 7 lads came out. Right away I was impressed by their attire, which I'd rather describe as sportswear than as "smart casual". At first I thought they were some kind of athletes. If I was right, then the kind of sport they practiced must have been triathlon, wrestling or rugby. They simply were enormous men, very well-built but not possessing that model or fitness looks.

They were tough lads. Some of them were wearing Fila and Hackett clothes while others, quite surprisingly I would say, Hockey Jerseys. They really looked like strength sport athletes. I was also impressed by the fact that they arrived on a flight from Germany, via Frankfurt I believe. One man in particular made the greatest impression. Shaved head, goatee ... probably a slight resemblance to "Stone Cold" Steve Austin... I even thought for a second that they were professional wrestlers! Suddenly Moon poked me in the ribs and said, "*You see that? I told you Chelsea Headhunters are here, didn't I?*", and he went to speak to them.

I am not a nosy type of man so I decided to stand by. They exchanged a few words and the huge blokes headed for the side exit in the direction of the cabs waiting outside. Upon passing me by, the man with the goatee smiled and said, "*See you soon, mate*", and I was left there stunned. I noticed he had something like a dental crown on one of his front teeth and it shone when he put that smile on his face. He also had an earring. The very figure of that man was somewhat different and so was the expression on his face and eventually I was to realise that my sixth sense was right! I had just met an unbelievable fan and a guy that was to leave a lasting mark in my life.

Moon said he had arranged to meet them later in one of the usual Sofia pubs, but I still did not believe him as he was fond of exaggerating and besides I just knew what I had seen – that was the special group I had been looking for for 10 years. They were another kind of fans, they travelled incognito and as a tight group trying hard not to attract attention and I really would not believe they were going to waste their time with us. But still, I chose to have a try so I went along. To tell you the truth, I was slightly disappointed after we popped round to all the pubs to see not even a trace of them. We got knackered so we went to bed. The following day was match day.

I remember that morning as if it was yesterday. Getting out of bed, I saw that the weather was vile. It was as if that year winter had descended upon Sofia in early September. It was freezing cold and to top it all I only had my cargo pants and an Adidas top. It was going to be a long day and we were going to try again to infiltrate the away end and, respectively, mix with the English fans.

Later, at about noon, we were joined by some other lads from our firm. We met them at the station and headed for the ground, where we met my Bulgarian Chelsea mates, who had spent the night outside going round hotels and pubs. We found them going round the stadium stalking for more pictures. They were rather disappointed cause they hadn't let them take photos in the hotel and one of them was showing his dissatisfaction by turning his camera round his finger as if he had nothing else to do. The weather was ghastly, the rain wouldn't stop and so we chose to find shelter somewhere and ponder on our tactics for infiltrating the visiting fans' section. In such cases our first priority had always been the visiting team supporters and looking at their disappointed faces I understood how important it would be for them to watch the game amidst the Chelsea fans.

The moment of truth came so we finished our beers and headed for the ground. This time the game was to be played at Levski club stadium. It is named *Georgi Asparouhov* after the greatest Bulgarian player from the past and it is located in *Gerena* quarter, which is far from being the nicest part of Sofia and that mattered a lot to us at that point.

I already mentioned that our National Stadium was the most difficult for us in terms of facilitating the achievement of our goals, while club grounds were easier to access, but in that particular case it turned out quite the opposite. The very approaches to the ground were heavily guarded by police cordons and the OB was ready to do anything in order to protect the law and order before, during and after the game. The separation lines they had formed were so far away from one another that there was simply no way for us to go undetected as a whole group without being asked to show them our IDs and match tickets.

We decided to split in groups of two or three and to try our luck everywhere we could. I went with the two Chelsea fans and I was ready to do any sacrifice to get them in, no matter whether I myself was going to watch the game or not. A cop noticed us and began to approach us. We were so close and yet so far from the away end gate, which looked like an impregnable fortress due to the fencing they had encircled it with. I decided to hustle and long before the copper could say anything I stepped up and told him that the two lads behind me were my guests from England and that I would like to watch the game with them in the Chelsea fans section. We had agreed on not uttering a single word in Bulgarian in order not to give ourselves away as we had done previously before the national teams' game. The two lads in questions arrived after me wearing Chelsea jerseys and doing their best to look as foolish as they could and showing a total lack of comprehension. In all honesty, they really looked like morons (sorry, mates), but at that very moment it was all irrelevant. The copper eyed them quickly and then his eyes returned to me, *"You want to watch the game for free, don't you? Get lost!"* At the same time he beckoned the two lads and they followed him to his colleagues at the gate who were supposed to frisk them.

Once again I could not believe I had such bad luck. Apparently, I always managed somehow to come across half-witted coppers, but this one was particularly dumb. Given the circumstances, he must have been a complete idiot to think I was playing the fool just in order to watch the game for free with some random Chelsea supporters! What a damn asshole! Surely the two lads, having already passed through the gate, must have been quite grateful to him. One of them then turned around and, with a sinking heart, I was expecting to hear the familiar *"Todar c'moun!"*, but this time the other one managed to pull him aside just on time and they disappeared from sight. Mission completed again! I remember jumping for joy as I was heading for the place we had arranged to meet, all of us who had not managed to sneak through. It turned out that hardly anyone had succeeded. I met the other lads, we chose one of the neutral sections and we were in. I enthusiastically told them what had happened and we all burst out with laughter.

Chelsea fans were sat at the borderline (curve) between sectors A and G and we stood at the border between sectors G and V **9** (as in most cases). No one else was around us; we were the only spectators in our section. We thought we were early and as kick-off time approached more people were to appear, but we were wrong. The Chelsea fans had taken the seats they had been allocated and were putting up their numerous flags and banners. Some were so drunk that it took them half an hour to do so, hanging on the fences. Among them, far in the distance, I could see our mates and I got the feeling I had done my duty. They had also seen us and thanked us for our assistance by bowing down and raising their hands in a gesture of appreciation and gratitude. It was a great moment for us as a firm. Even now, when I recall that moment, I just get goose bumps! Never again we were going to feel greater respect for each other. I felt extremely proud of our achievement and those two lads were absolutely grateful (at least until recently). The most interesting, however, was yet to come...

The game got underway and so the well-oiled throats started chanting out loud. In the middle of the second half, cops carrying shields and batons and wearing helmets and all their standard riot gear turned up in our section as if out of nowhere. We began to look around asking ourselves, *"Are these motherfuckers nuts!?"*, when at the top of our section we caught a glimpse of that very group we saw at the airport the previous day, maybe joined by several others. We were in the middle of the section, but no matter how far from us they were, I was dead sure those were the Headhunters. We asked a cop what was going on and who those people were and he hold us those were Irish who would like to watch the football sat in a neutral section since they couldn't stand either among the English or the Bulgarians and our sector was the least attended. I almost laughed out loud, Irishmen, eh? You just can't believe how dumb coppers can get!

The Headhunters approached being guarded like real terrorists and sat beside us, the coppers forming a huge cordon along the entire width of the stand standing in full riot gear on the steps dividing the stand into two sections. Although what they had on both sides were two sets of no more than 15 fans each! What a waste of security budget, isn't it?! Besides, the Old Bill thought those were Irishmen and we had told them we were neutral fans who supported another Bulgarian team, so no one should believe that there would be any trouble between our two groups whatsoever. I took a good look at that "Irish" crew and I met the eyes of the lad I had seen at the airport, who in turn winked at me and beckoned me to go to them. I set off in a somewhat abrupt manner, which made the cops immediately stop me. What followed was a quarrel with the police that lasted until half time, and from its beginning till its end the Headhunters tried to tell the coppers to let us come nearer, while we, in pure Bulgarian did our best to assure them nothing wrong would happen.

Finally they agreed to let us go and I approached, holding out my hand literally across the police line. I strong hand grabbed mine and I once again saw that friendly smile and the shiny dental crown. *"I told you we'll see each other again, mate!"* I was speechless; words just escaped me when I tried to speak! It was as if God had sent them as a reward for my sacrifice ahead of the game. We had definitely chosen the right section and I really couldn't believe that the dream

I had been pursuing for years had finally come true. At half time, the cops softened down, having seen the friendly conversation our both parties were having, so they took down the barriers. My mates joined in and we all started chatting to each other. The Headhunters were surprised at our fluency in English and I finally got to know my interlocutor's name. *"Nice to meet you, mate! Pat, they called me Fat Pat."* However, it wasn't until a year later that I really understood who actually I had had the honour to meet. I was absolutely thrilled by the encounter and then a mate came over and bragged like a small child that he got introduced to Stuart Glass, who we had only heard about in documentaries until then.

In the second half the rain finally stopped and our conversation got even livelier, while the coppers put their shields, helmets and the like down to the ground. They were probably wondering whether we had come to watch football or to chat. Pat went into details about their trip and told me that certain lads were prevented from travelling (The Sims brothers), finally getting to the coppers' "Irishmen" deceit, at which point we all burst out with laughter. I was fascinated by his diction and his ability to tell stories. Stories that I would later listen to for hours on end!

I managed to briefly introduce him to our story and tell him what we were doing at the ground. We exchanged contact details and went on chitchatting, when in the middle of the second half, I saw two photographers, a man and a woman, approach our end from the tartan track, adjust their lenses and, without warning, start taking pictures of us. Our companions immediately put their hoods up to cover their faces and turned hostile, waving their arms and spitting out insults at the people on the track. I thought those were either investigative journalists or plain clothes officers whose task was to take photos of notorious hooligans and document their activities, but I didn't have the time to ask cause Pat growled, *"It's time to go for us, mate! See you next time..."* We shook hands, hugged like brothers or like people that had known each other for years, and they were gone in the fog in seconds, just like the way they had appeared, leaving us speechless. I didn't even have the opportunity to ask them where they were staying (I stood there bemoaning), but at least I had some address that I could write to him at. I carefully folded the small sheet of paper and thrust it in the dryness of my pocket. Not a single soul of ours was following the game, we didn't care about the score and so we decided to leave the ground and have a few drinks as we had had enough of cold weather for the day. And who the fuck cared about football after such an encounter!

* Those two teams played each other again in the CL group stage on 27.09.2006 (Levski 1 Chelsea 3) and on 05.12.2006 (Chelsea 2 Levski 0), but those were games we did not attend.

---

6 CHORBARI (LITERALLY TRANSLATED AS "SOUP EATERS") – A BULGARIAN FOOTBALL DEROGATIVE SLANG WORD FOR CSKA FANS THAT ORIGINATES FROM THE CLUB'S CONNECTION WITH THE COMMUNIST ARMY, WHERE SOUP WAS THE USUAL MEAL FOR CONSCRIPT TROOPS

7 BOYARS – MEMBERS OF THE HIGHEST RANK OF FEUDAL BULGARIAN ARISTOCRACY DURING THE SECOND BULGARIAN KINGDOM WHEN VELIKO TARNOVO WAS THE CAPITAL. HENCE, THE NICKNAME OF THE FOOTBALL CLUB FROM VELIKO TARNOVO, ETAR, AND ITS SUPPORTERS

8 BULGARIAN ARMY (TRANSLATION)

9 USUALLY BULGARIAN STADIA CONSIST OF 4 SECTORS NAMED A, B, V AND G AS THIS IS THE TICAL ORDER OF THE FIRST FOUR LETTERS IN BULGARIAN LANGUAGE, SECTOR A BEING THE ALPHABE MAIN STAND, SECTOR V BEING OPPOSITE SECTOR A AND SECTORS B AND G BEING THE ONES BEHIND THE GOALS, WHERE USUALLY THE HARDCORE, ULTRAS FANS ARE SAT.

FOUR

PAT DOLAN (RIP)

After we met the Chelsea Headhunters in 2001 I tried to get in touch with Pat, but all I had was a wrinkled folded piece of paper with his address on and I didn't even know if it was correctly written as it all happened so fast and he had put it down in haste. When I look back I realise it was 15 years ago... Damn! How fast time flies, doesn't it!? Come to think of how many things have changed since then, like the means of communication, for example. I remember that when I finally set down to write to him I had lost all hope to get his answer. However, shortly afterwards I not only got a reply, but I found my first hooligan book attached as a gift to the letter. I naturally read it in a day as it was an absolute masterpiece, namely

Hoolifan by one of the genre founders Martin King. Here is what Martin himself has to say about Pat:

"I first met Pat I the early 80's when he was a skinny kid even then he had a great sense of humour and was keen to get involved in any terrace action. Over the years he matured in stature and ended up doing door work in the pubs and clubs of London, which he did in his own unique style. He would rather put his arm around someone and talk to them rather than throw them head first out onto the street. He just had a way of talking to people, a great personality that shone through.

Besides watching his beloved team Chelsea, he followed the England Team and got to know many well-known faces from clubs across the country, like Middlesbrough, Forest, Newcastle, Birmingham, Wolves, Cardiff, Glasgow Rangers to name but just a few.

He was a great organiser of meets for the big games and with a few phone calls he'd get all the boys together. He also had mates from Holland, Germany, France and Bulgaria who would often come over and meet up with him for the big Chelsea games.

Pat was a legend at football and I never heard anyone say a bad word about him. I classed him as a real good friend, who'd often phone me up and give me a bollocking and a telling off if he felt I had done something he didn't agree with. Other times he'd laugh at my exploits.

Sadly Pat died in 2015 and the turnout for his funeral showed just how much love and respect people had for him. They came from far and wide in their hundreds and I've never seen so many grown men openly crying!

He is still spoken about and his name lives on, he will never be forgotten.

R.I.P. my friend until we meet on the other side. God bless x

Martin King, author of *Hoolifan*

I still didn't have many direct impressions and I went on writing to him. The letters gradually became longer and longer until they finally transformed into parcels and I started getting gifts such as Lacoste trainers, a Stone Island shirt, a Burberry cap, etc. Generally Pat made sure I was not only well educated and informed of the scene, but also trendy and fashion conscious, in spite of the fact that we still didn't know each other actually! More books followed that I, naturally, would willingly read and learn and then meticulously arrange on the shelves at home. I set up a kind of home library with more than 20 books of the same genre.

In each book I would also find a recently taken photo or two as those were the times when we hadn't started to take advantage of the Internet for transferring digital files (I believe he didn't use this means of communication until his very end). I remember him sending me an album of pictures (some of them you will find published in this book) taken in Thailand, where he was quite fond of going. Here is what another great mate of his, Gary "Boatsy" Clarke, remembers of one of those visits and of him in general:

"Big Pat Dolan, I first came across Fat Pat in Thailand around 2002-3 although I had heard of him over the years. Around 18 of us had decided to have an end of season blow out in Pattaya for 3 weeks (mainly the younger active Forest lads at the time). I'd been friends with Chris "Chubby" Henderson since the mid 80's from the England scene, he had a bar in Pattaya for a number of years with another Chelsea boy I knew Steve 'Hicky' Hickmott. I first visited Thai in 99 but didn't manage to make it down there from Bangkok. So this time I was determined to visit the bar The Dogs Bollocks bar, and that's where I first met Fat Pat on our first night in Pattaya. On our first night we went in search of the famous hooligan bar, all 18 of us. We came across it on Soi 13/2 Soi Yamato. It looked fairly busy but smaller than we expected, so we walked in and stood at the bar and a voice behind me in a deep Cockney accent said "Where you boys from? Bit of a firm I turned and said "Nottingham" to Pat and shook his hand. I said I was looking for "Chubby" Chris, Pat said he is at the back over there, and that was the start of a long

friendship that spanned many years. I had many a long top night in the Dog Bar with him in years to come; he was an absolute gentleman and a hardman who run doors in his time and was respected by football lads and people from all over the world. I think I know a lot of people but Pat took some beating. We had some cracking nights over the years at various book launches and events the length of Britain. I had the privilege of him attending my own book launch in Nottingham. I was gutted when my good Boro friend Craig rang to tell me the bad news of his untimely death. I couldn't make his funeral unfortunately, but sent a Forest wreath down. I will never forget the man! RIP Pat, my friend. Respected and loved by so many. A true terrace legend."

Gary 'Boatsy' Clarke, Forest Executive Crew

Another mate of his from those parties in Thailand:

"Got to know Pat through holidays in Pattaya, where would turn out to be the place I live now in the end. I always knew his name to be associated with the Chelsea Headhunters who I knew well off through my going to England matches. However it was in Pattaya where we bonded, having met in the infamous Dogs Bollocks bar founded by General Hicky and Chubby Henderson, RIP. We get right on it drinking through the night into the next day talking about football violence war stories, probably repeating the same stories all the time, hahaha. He was a big unit, a right friendly giant who be polite to anyone in his company, however he wasn't to be crossed, a genuine football lad who sadly is no longer here but to his credit his name will be talked about for future years around Chelsea and beyond."

Lee Spence, Oldham Athletic

In 2002 my wife gave birth to our gorgeous daughter and as it often happens, I temporarily withdrew from fandom, of course, not for long. I kept up the correspondence with Pat, but gradually the letters got fewer due to my family obligations. I know it sounds trivial, but I really had some great financial difficulties so I had to work almost 24 hours per day. Some of my mates had already migrated to the UK, but for me, at least at that stage, the long-year dream seemed rather like a chimera.

The economic situation in Bulgaria was getting worse every day and after another 5 years of hardship, I was increasingly thinking of moving to England. I turned to Pat for advice, explaining him my kind of situation and he immediately encouraged me by giving some particular suggestions. That's the kind of guy my London acquaintance (at that point) was... responsive, dedicated, helpful ... and he also had a number of other merits that it will take more than a page if I am to list all of them here. I dare say that no one in my life had helped me before the way he did!

At the beginning of 2007 I decided to take the plunge and arrived in England with some mates of mine and most of them started working in the construction business.

Quite normally, at first I started working the same jobs, too. I worked for about a year and then for 6 months I found a job working in a kitchen. During my first meets with Pat he explained in details the ins and outs of the security business (where he used to work) and he suggested that I should do a course and train for a doorman and he also recommended several companies to work for afterwards. So that's how I ended up on Tattershall Castle (a ship on the River Thames), where I did my courses and was awarded the necessary certificates.

So after 9 years of experience as an electrician in Bulgaria I got my bouncer license here. At first it was rather difficult and I found Pat's advice simply priceless. As time went by, I managed to get back on my feet again and settle with my family here, and I am absolutely positive that the major credit goes to Pat. Besides, he was extremely hospitable (which is not so typical of people's mentality here). Me and my mates would frequently pay him a visit. I don't know why, but in terms of personality he somewhat weirdly resembled my father, who I learned so much about football from.

In the first chapters of this book we touched on the topic of idols and rode models on the pitch and of mentors on the terraces, who, no matter what we say, everybody had looked up to and undoubtedly learned from. I also used to have a lot of those in the past, but if we have to take into account the present, then it is definitely Pat who I would constantly be willing to learn something from. The other thing that reminded me of my old man was the pair of boxing gloves I saw hanging in one of his rooms during one of my first visits there. Actually it was the first thing I noticed and was most impressed by when I first entered his house. *"You want some mate...!?"*, he asked me putting on one glove. It just sent shivers down my spine as I felt déjà vu. One of those moments when you feel as if you know it has happened before, you have already experienced it; and in that particular case I remembered very well where, when and who with I had had such an experience.

Apart from my father, who I already told you about how he made me hit the pillows at home till I dropped with exhaustion, I also had another mentor from whom I learned a lot about football hooliganism and who also used to invite me quite often to a boxing sparring. He was the leader of our mob then. He was much older than me and, accordingly, much stronger and fitter. I remember him phoning me one afternoon to invite me to his place. He met me in the same way, putting on his boxing gloves and handing me another pair. In an instant the living room would be cleared up to make space in the middle and we even didn't need a bell as the training would usually begin with a heavy punch in my face (to make me feel welcome). Each and every punch that would follow would blow my head off. It was as if I was taking off on a jet plane.

I remember once, after I had had such a sparring with him, I had continuous headaches for whole two weeks and, mind you, he did limit the strength of his punches and wouldn't let go of his fist the way he really could. I really wouldn't like to think what would happen if such a man hit you with all of his might! Of course, in that case at Pat's place, our boxing enthusiasm was quickly overcome by the excitement and joy of our second meeting, this time on English soil. I noticed he had put on a lot of weight, but I've never had the habit of making such comments and besides, I had also put on weight, which he didn't fail to mention with that peculiar sense of humour he had. We hugged each other like brothers, just like the way we had done in Sofia some 6 or 7 years before, and we started a long conversation as if we had known each other for 30 years and had been meeting every day. At least I had that feeling, since Pat would always make his company feel themselves at home. He just knew how to do it.

After a brief summary of the situation in my life and job in the English capital, the time came for my first "lesson" (something like an introduction) "in the big game". I looked around the room for a second time and with the approval of my host I took a closer look at the stuff put on a small souvenir shelf, as well as at the pictures on the wall. He then joined me and started explaining in details as if we were at an exhibition in a London picture gallery or museum. First I as deeply impressed by a framed photograph of a hollow-cheeked teenage boy and before even asking a question, I heard, *"Oh, yeah by the way that's me on that picture there if you wonder..."* Greatly surprised, I glanced at him and he just laughed out loud with that specific full-toned and soft voice he had, which made him such a charming narrator. More jokes followed regarding us both being overweight, and there we were, Fat Pat and Fat Tosh, sitting opposite each other in two armchairs in Shepherd's Bush, just like Sherlock Holmes and Doctor Watson at 221B Baker Street, discussing yet another important deductive investigation.

My first lesson in "hooliganism" was about to begin in a few minutes, hearing all that stuff straight from the horse's mouth. We were sat so comfortably in our cozy deep armchairs that we had to lend each other a hand in order to stand up and then another burst of laughter and self-criticism by two fat boys would follow! Pat was a really fascinating storyteller (I have no idea whether he had inherited that trait), but what he had stacked in that room made him a true encyclopaedia. As expected, he had a bookcase full of books and a striking number of video cassettes that he kept on inserting in and ejecting from the VCR in order for his stories not to be unfounded. I remember crystal clear the first video he played. It was of a street fight between Hearts (*Casual Soccer Firm* – CSF) and Hibs (*Capital City Service* – CCS), which he would relentlessly wind and rewind and pause in order to explain in details what was going on and who was who. Until then I had always considered myself a collector and an absolute maniac for football and football fandom, and as I said in the previous chapter, a "hunter" of anything that's football related. Starting from newspaper cuttings that I used to collect, read and arrange in a most scrupulous manner (sometimes even a magnifying glass in hand) and finishing with the football posters on the walls of my room that looked more like photo wallpaper. But for the love of Mike, never before had I seen a man explaining everything the VCR was playing with such genuine passion! The fascinating stories would go on for hours and quite often I ended up sent to get "refreshments" from the nearby shop.

I remember once taking a friend of mine to Pat's place and we were talking not only about football violence, but rather about more general but still related stuff. On that particular occasion Pat was playing a video of a bare knuckle fight between Lenny McLean (RIP) and RoyShaw and was going into ecstasies after Lenny's powerful strings of blows like, *"Look at that, chaps....Now this is the Guv'nor!"* And he would raise a toast for him... That's the kind of guy Pat was in his stories, pure old school and authentic. My mate (being the youngest in the company) who came with me that evening had to make several trips to the shop to replenish our stock of drinks and menthol cigarettes, which Pat was fond of smoking every now and then. In fact, come to think of it, my mate had no time to even sit down since he was either gone to the shop or looking at the real exhibition arranged along the room walls, where, besides all the other staff, there were all kinds of proudly hanging Chelsea vintage souvenirs and memorabilia.

During our meets, which followed one after another and had become much more frequent, Pat would introduce me to some other top faces and, though indirectly, to the stories of some Headhunters. When I wasn't his guest, we used to meet at Belushi's in Shepherd's

Bush, one of his favourite places to go to. There Pat would proudly introduce me to his mates, which I found rather embarrassing at times, if I had to be honest. I felt like some kind of star, *"Hello lads... This is my new matey Tosh from Bulgaria and those are his mates..!"* Once, we had arranged to meet in that same pub and we turned up with our entire firm (G.O. London Firm) plus several other lads from our black-and-white Plovdiv alliance **10**. The particular occasion was a game between Q.P.R and Boro and our crew on that day amounted to 20 lads! Pat had a lot of friends supporting Rangers and Loftus Road was near his place. In some of the books he's featured he says that Q.P.R. should have been his "home team" and if I'm not mistaken, it is the Rangers that his close relatives supported.

We went to the pub as early as an hour before noon and the moment it opened we got our first beers. We were so enthusiastic; we felt like having been unchained. Pat himself got rather surprised by our early gathering and when I knocked on his door to pick him up he opened it, still sleepy, *"For fuck sake, mate! I thought it must be the fucking Old Bill... You were knocking like them, mate... Come in!"* I went in, a little bit embarrassed, and waited for him to get dressed. He had already started having his health problems and had lost a lot of weight. We went out almost immediately because all my mates were waiting for us in the pub and since some of them were meeting him for the very first time, naturally, they were quite eager. In just a single minute he managed to shake hands with and hug them all and in what seemed about five minutes he was already chatting to everybody and joking the way he always did. We posed together for some photos and went on with our even livelier discussion. Here is what a very good mate of Pat's from Barnsley says about this feature of his character:

"Pat was true old school, a man who could hold a crowd with his stories, a man who was a diamond, a true gentleman respected by all from Barnsley 'Five-O' Firm. God bless you Pat!"

Mark Fisher (Barnsley "Five-O")

Our meet was attended by several Q.P.R top faces (featured in the book of the same name) and some Dutch fellas, as far as I remember Feyenoord fans that he also used to keep in touch with. Pat left us with them and we went together to the game. I was looking forward to seeing what the away Boro supporters had to show, as they also had a reputation of having a tough and serious firm. However, on that day they didn't have their best turnout and the game itself wasn't much attractive. What mattered to us was that we had had another wonderful day in the company of Pat and his mates and had made a number of new friends and acquaintances. In the years to follow I followed the same routine for several times and was a regular at Loftus Road, but to my great regret I never ever managed to attend a Chelsea game in the company of Pat. This is something I will really regret for the rest of my life.

It is always extremely painful to recollect that period of my otherwise great friendship with my wonderful mate Pat Dolan due to his health deterioration.

I remember him calling me one day to ask me to pop round to his place. He sounded somewhat different, something in his voice had changed and I felt really worried about him. I went to his place and found out that things were rather serious. He told me how, on his flight back from Thailand, he suddenly had some health complications and so he only just made it back. Doctors told him he had to go to hospital and I accompanied him there. I remember that quite well. I felt like my entire world was on the verge of collapsing. In about two weeks, Pat called me again to say that he had had abdominal surgery. His voice sounded a bit better and I promised him to visit him in the hospital together with my little girl (my daughter who was 7–8 years old then) since he had long wanted to meet her. She would also frequently ask about Pat as she had only heard about him in my stories.

I will never forget the moment we entered the hospital room and she jumped on him to hug him and his joy seemed simply infinite. I almost shed tears of joy and then I saw that crystal sparkling look in his blue eyes, the same look I had seen almost 10 years before at the stadium in Sofia… *"I thanked God that everything was all right with him!"* It was almost lunchtime and he had to have his lunch. He was served a plate full of vegetables frowned upon by him. I excused and said we were about to leave him to have his meal, to which he responded, *"You call this lunch… As far as I can see I don't have a nice steak in my plate... isn't it Tosh mate!?"* These words made us both burst laughing out loud and my daughter just looked at me puzzled and innocently asked what was going on and why we were laughing. *"Tell your Daddy to be really careful with the stakes, darling"*, he replied, still laughing. A piece of advice she still remembers well to this day and whenever I have too many steaks she reminds me what Pat had said that day.

After two more weeks he called me again and said that since everything was just fine, he was about to be discharged. He asked me to go and take him home. Without even waiting for him to hang up, I got dressed as quickly as I could and, in turn, rang a mate to take me there faster in his car. There, Pat was already all set and waiting and apparently eager to go back to his normal way of life. I signed at the hospital reception as a companion and we plunged into the West London traffic. *"Let's take a walk, mate"*, he proposed and though it came as a bit of a surprise for me (but taking into account his condition, I immediately said yes), we started walking slowly along the pavement. Even a regular walk with him could teach you so many things. He seemed exhausted, but he just wouldn't stop talking and joking.

We took a shortcut through some back streets leading to his home and while walking, he told me a lot of stories about his childhood. He would always have a topic to talk about and when he was around boredom just went away. Even at such times, when, I'm sure, pain was unendurable he would find the powers to laugh genuinely using his internal strength. As we approached his house we dropped in the shop where we used to buy beverages and cigarettes when we were his guests. The shop assistant asked him if

he would buy the regular stuff, but Pat replied, *"Not this time, mate...*
Not this time" and the menthol cigarettes and wine were replaced
with orange juice. As we would always do, we sat in his armchairs,
he poured himself a glass of juice and opened a can of Stella for
me. Each took a sip of his drink and Pat pulled such a face that one
would think it was the first time in his life he had drunk orange
juice. *'Fucking hell, mate. I'd drunk probably tons of beers in my life and now I
can't drink a whole glass of juice... can you imagine!?"* And once again his
started laughing with all of his might. I was laughing too, but deep
inside, I had the feeling that things would never be the same again.
It was one of my last lessons in "hooliganism."

I wouldn't like to go into details of the events that followed as I
know I would meddle in the hearts and souls of a number of people
who knew Pat much better than me and still know what kind of
person he really was. Of course, we all will preserve the wonderful
impressions and the memorable track he left by living his more than
note worthy life. People like me, for example, are definitely likely to
follow the advice of that dignified, wise and loyal true gentleman
since people like him are extremely hard to meet these days.Yes, I
can boldly say that Pat was my real mentor here, in the UK, and I
do take real pride in the fact that I had the honour and the chance
to know him and listen to his stories and advice. These are all things
I would be glad to pass on to future generations before I take them
out there, somewhere, where I will hopefully meet bit Pat Dolan
again.

I really hope that by publishing this book, the idea for which was
born exactly in my meets with him, and he was, I dare say, our
major inspiration and motivation to write it, we will manage to
contribute to the common struggle led by all hooligan scene players
against the system and the misconceptions of hooliganism in
general. I know that our book won't put an end to the out-of-date
and retrogressive way of thinking of all those narrow-minded and
prejudiced at the higher levels of power and of those who imposed
such policy against all of us, shaping and distorting the public
opinion to such an extent that nowadays even a pedophile is
considered a better person than a football hooligan. I won't resort to

plagiarism as I know that much better and more prominent authors (than us) in this genre have tried (a number of times) to research and explain things in depth from various perspectives, like another of my favourite authors, Dougie Brimson, who in his works quite skilfully studies the issue from all of its aspects.

However, I would like to add something and say to all critics and those considering themselves as "big heads" from the football authorities (FIFA, UEFA) and any other politically and economically dependent organisations, who stigmatised the people on the terraces calling them names such as "thugs, scum of society, mindless minority, yobs, degenerates, hooligan disease, etc."

The same people who regularly boast in all media that they care about this magnificent sport and its fans and that, fancy that, have coped with hooliganism imposing harsh rules against the more hardcore lads on the terraces. Dear great philosophers and leaders, let me tell you something. I have been working in the CCTV surveillance field of security business for five years now and I am well familiar with the video surveillance capacities. A rather large percentage of all security cameras installed are just fake, the so called "dummies", so that money could be saved from the construction of the entire surveillance network, which in most cases is ineffective when used against real criminals and if someone has decided to perform any illegal act, he will simply put on a balaclava or put his hood up, eliminating that entire system, on which millions have been spent after being taken from ordinary taxpayers and not from you! Having saved money from dummy security cameras, you didn't invest it to facilitate services and supports for people with disabilities or people in need, did you? We all witness what's going on in the streets around us and we see how people are getting poorer and live in even greater poverty (many of them living rough).

You don't pay for that, either and your huge bank accounts don't get thinner. On the contrary, it is us who pay and what is more, that money seems to go directly to your huge pockets. Most fans in the so called Eastern bloc have long been using the above mentioned means of disguise, more typical of the ultra style supporters, but when I play on the FA Cup Chelsea vs Cardiff clash in New Kings

Road in February 2010 for instance, I only see faces of middle-aged men, some of them having already been punished severely, banned and sentenced only because they want to fight other like-minded fellas! Here what a participant in those events, Andy "Nightmare" Frain, says about Pat:

"I knew Pat for around 25 years, he was a proper character and a gentleman, we always had a laugh at the football especially travelling abroad, also with his work as a West End doorman, sometimes I would not see him for a couple of years thanks to the Old Bill locking me up (cunts) but he would always greet me with that funny old grin of his and a firm handshake, he was like a fountain of knowledge on the whereabouts of different firms, where they were, how many they had etc, well handy when we were hunting around looking for them. I have not met anyone with a bad word to say about him and as the amount of representatives from other firms present at his funeral shows others thought the same, he will never be forgotten and we will always raise our glasses to him. Remembering him as one of the best and one of our own.

RIP, Pat, your old pal."

Andy "Nightmare" Frain,

Chelsea Headhunters

OK, I could do with fines for charges with affray, but being sentenced for more years in prison than a notorious pedophile… I can't really understand that and I don't see any reason in such judgments. It's high time some people realised that those lads consider it as a kind of sports. Yeah, maybe it's a little bit aggressive, but it is just their way of expressing themselves, and the streets and terraces are their stage, where they would like to show their attitudes and views in front of society. For them it is just a hobby, a habit, a fad. They all have kids and families and, believe me, they are fully aware of what they are doing in any particular moment, what they are fighting for and what they stand up for, as well as what consequences they are to face. That's why their faces are not disguised or covered and once and for all it should be made clear and understood that for them it is a matter of huge honour and pride.

Well, just think about that. otherwise, would they risk their lives, jobs and future of their families!? Quite a few of them say in their stories, interviews and books that they see it as a kind of bug, an obsession, a drug, and they put quite a lot of effort to give it up though some never succeed. All of this does not make those men mindless yobs. Quite the opposite, it makes them even more honourable!

I won't give you many examples of really dishonourable men sitting in their comfortable chairs at the football authorities higher levels showing off about all of that in the falsest manner possible. They are already infamous for being nothing more but thieving bastards and people have started throwing wads of fake money during their even faker press conferences they organise with the aim of convincing us that they have eradicated this and that in the name of the greatest game… bollocks! As people here like to say. And from where I come from, we have a lot of sayings that perfectly apply to cases like this.

For example, *"Water will run wherever it has always run"*; *"No one can extinguish what cannot be extinguished…"* and many others. You haven't eradicated anything and you will never eradicate it because it lives within us and is not a temporary phenomenon. Sometimes it calms down as if after a storm, but in time it rises again. The only thing you do is take money (from us). Usually you take billions, you keep half of them and the rest you invest in yet another useless thing just to wash your hands and blur people's eyes looking for the next scapegoats to be blamed for everything, including your own failures and misunderstanding of the issue… As a song goes, *"You can take me out of the streets, but you can't take the "streets" out of me!"* This is what I've learned from my mate's lessons in hooliganism.

One Nil to the hooligans!

Many a time have I thought what those people would say if they knew at least a single person from the real scene and terraces. Erudite, knowledgeable, true experts in their field. The truly honourable men of our time… Men like our great mate Pat Dolan, about whom even those who didn't know him well will say:

"I didn't know Pat Dolan that well all I can say I heard he was a top fella and got respect from Bristol City (City Service Crew) in the 80's."

Angus Nutt (Bristol City)

And there's more:

"Although I could never claim to be a close friend of Pat, I encountered him many times on my travels both with Chelsea & Rangers. I had heard the name many times through regular Chelsea attendees Carrick, Ecky & Browny. I first met Pat in the early 90's and liked the big guy straight away despite his Irish sounding name. He was well respected by fellow Rangers lads and that was good enough for me. Amongst Chelsea lads like Frainy, Liam, Marriner etc. he was very warmly thought of. I'm sure that's the same for lads of the many lads from mobs throughout Europe Pat acquainted. My abiding memory of Pat is Rangers steaming in versus PSG in a UEFA Cup 2nd leg tie in Paris in the early 90's. This dash would rank in the top three results "off the field" our Firm (Rangers ICF) gained on European travels. The death of Pat was very sad news to ALL his friends from Glasgow Rangers ICF. Gone but not forgotten Pat. God bless."

Sandy Chugg, Glasgow Rangers ICF

I really hope that this book of ours will help lift the unnaturally dropped curtain between fans from the two blocs called Eastern and Western. I believe we share a common cause and have a common struggle, no matter where we come from. The first steps have been made and friendships like the one between me and Pat come to prove it. I am particularly sorry that while he was alive he wasn't able to introduce me to all of his mates, which could have been a mission impossible anyway, but I do believe that things could be sorted with the release of this book. We have already invited a decent number of them and they have agreed to take part in this project. Their interviews were already included above as their approval to publish all our materials has been given.

We intend to end this chapter and the first part of our book with two more opinions of Pat and an idea of ours that will use an already paraphrased nickname in order to pay tribute to this great man. We publish this memorial banner (in the form of a candle) with Big Pat Dolan's face and we will also make a flag of it to leave as a keepsake with his *Headhunters* mates. I think you will all agree that he does deserve the nickname *"The Hooligent"*.

Annis Abraham Jr.

"I am the Author of 7 Football/Lads books. Fifty years old and a Cardiff City fan.

I met my old friend Pat 34 years ago at a Leeds v Chelsea game, and boy, that was some game to be at. Chelsea that day had a firm of lads that I have never seen again by any club in the UK or Europe. In those days Pat was young like me, but well known by all the main faces of Chelsea. As the years went by, Pat became one of the big names and was *known as Chelsea Fat Pat, a game lad, organiser, but one of the funniest lads I've ever met.*

Pat also came along to a lot of Cardiff games and everyone liked him, who could not. A pub would go silent when Pat would tell one of his many, many tales of either a fight, a fruit machine being robbed or of a full day out with the lads, but it was the way he told these stories that would have everyone listening and in laughter.

I invited Pat to my wedding and even then he was the star of the day.

As the years went on and Pat pulled away from football violence etc. he became a friend to every lad in the country and abroad. You only had to attend his funeral last year and see how everyone from all over had come to pay their respects.

As well a terrace legend, a lot of people did not see the side I knew, Pat was also a true Gent and would do any favour for anyone and even never forgot my daughter's birthdays.

Pat will be truly missed by everyone and God bless his soul, Pat will never be forgotten."

Rob Sanders, ex S.C.F. (Feyenoord's firm)

"I was honoured when I was asked to write a few words on my best friend Pat or Fat Pat as he is known to most people. My name is Rob, ex S.C.F (Feyenoord's firm) and since my childhood (12) also hooked on Chelsea. Must have been the violence of Chelsea firm that attracted me as their results in the league were always poor in that period and they always had a fall down around Christmas.

As I loved following Feyenoord, I also wanted to go to London and see the mighty Blues play their games. I think I was about 27 in 1993 when I met Pat in a London bar and we got talking to each other. And as most of you will know, the man could tell a few stories. The beers came in and we spent the whole evening together telling each other firms "war stories". When we left we exchanged numbers and promised to meet up soon. Not for long his first letter came in about what happened to Chelsea and the firm and soon the phone rang.

This was the beginning of a friendship and soon we became best mates. Every Sunday evening the phone would ring and Pat got me updated on all that happened that weekend on the terraces in England. Through following England, Pat made many friends and he knows all the faces from all the clubs up and down the country. He is a gentleman and would talk to anyone, something which I wouldn't do.

He's funny as f**k and soon I would spend weekends at his house in Shepherd's Bush and Pat introduced me to Chelsea's firm. Still remember the first time he couldn't come with me to a meet as Chelsea played Man Utd. in the FA Cup Final at Wembley. The Old Bill told him to stay put at Waxy O'Connors, where he was working as a doorman and he told me to go alone. There were major meets and he told them he would inform the boys I was coming. Got off in Kilburn as I saw many hooligans leaving the train and it was one of the meets Pat mentioned to me. Followed them into a bar and had a lovely day with the boys. Although I hardly knew anyone they were all nice to me and the beers got in before we went off to Wembley.

I got back at about 8 in the evening at Waxy's and when Pat saw me he was furious. Not of anger, but he got himself worried that something must have happened to me as the boys I was supposed to meet came back to him before and after the game telling Pat they hadn't seen me or heard from me. I just told him I was OK, made a lot of new friends and laughed at him for being so worried. He hugged me in front of a large queue at the door of the Irish pub and then said his famous words which I'll never forget… "Never make me worry about you again, stupid f**k or I'll kill you". He must have loved me then!

Our friendship kept on growing till we were best mates and told each other anything... in good and bad times we were there for each other. A lifelong friendship started!

In March 1997 Pat was invited to a Feyenoord away game, never thinking it would be the most violent away match he ever watched. On our way to Alkmaar the S.C.F ran into their most hated rivals of Ajax

Amsterdam. We were travelling in a convoy of cars when suddenly we pulled over at the motorway. Everybody got out of their cars and through the mist and drizzle came 300 Ajax fans.

It was like Braveheart as the two firms tore into one another with baseball bats, knives, etc. It went toe to toe for a moment and the bulk of Ajax retreated, leaving a handful of them getting a serious beating. The Feyenoord firm climbed back into their cars, covered in mud, to carry on to the game. Although I got Pat a ticket, he refused to go in, as rumours started that a man had been killed in the field. While Pat got himself a few drinks I went into the game. He always blamed me for that... the most stupid thing to do. As he then saw our firm in action, Pat and most of Chelsea's firm had a massive respect for Feyenoord. And only Pat and a German lad really know what happened that day... although a well-known prick who writes books has cast a few times his thoughts and views on what happened that day. As I told him many times, "You know f**k all, so keep your big mouth shut. You've only spoken to clowns like yourself who know nothing!"

Pat and me experienced so many things that I could fill a whole book on Pat alone. But I never met a man who had so much time for everyone who wanted to talk to him and always he behaved like a gentleman. Pat was even liked by Millwall, West Ham and Spurs, ha-ha-ha, that was Pat for you.

Pat lightened up a room, many would love just to listen to his stories and his stories were the best.

I got married on 9th December 2004 (the day my dad died in 1965) in the stadium of Feyenoord and of course Pat was my best man. He also did me the honours to become a godfather to my daughters Amber and Robin.

By Pat I got to hang around with some famous faces as Tony C., Chris C., Kevin W., Hickey, Mark A, Stuart Glass, Black Willy, Babsy, Andy F., Martin K. and Mickey H. But also met top lads from other firms like Andy, Mickey and Chris F. (Man. City), Davie C and Sandy C (Glasgow Rangers), Baz (Birmingham City), Ginger Bob and his brother Terry (Millwall), Cass (West Ham), Rob S (Portsmouth) and Annis, Mac and Tony R from Cardiff City.

This turned out in famous drinking nights and loyal friendships till this day. Pat and me shared joys and sorrows together and I can express how hurt I was when he forgot to live himself the last two years of his life. He had a heart for anyone else except for himself. We argued a lot about it as he was my best friend and I didn't want to see him this way but always loved each other at the end of our regular visits or phone calls. He never forgot the birthdays of my daughters and my wife!

I will never forget the morning of 29th April, Wednesday, when I started up my phone and saw the numerous phone calls I missed from Chris and immediately felt that something was wrong with Pat. I called Chris straight away and when he told me that Pat had died the day before I couldn't stop crying. The gentleman had left us...

I felt very proud to be asked to be one of the guys to carry his coffin, but was also glad Chris had my back that day as I felt so empty! Thanks Chris! Couldn't have done it without you! Also brought my wife and daughter Amber to the funeral and his brother John made sure that all my daughter's drawings she ever made for him were in his pocket. Also got Pat a signed Feyenoord shirt by our firm and a signed shirt by Frank Lampard. So pleased with the huge crowd gathering to say the last farewells!

There is not a day passing that I'm not thinking about Pat... never his phone calls again when he said he was George Clooney as my wife answered ... never all the stories about what happened in England during the weekends... never sharing a drink together.

I'm sure at this moment he's sitting next to God telling him and other loved ones we lost his war stories and looking down at all of us with a smile. My dad will love him over there and I'm sure there sitting next to each other laughing at me. Rest in peace Pat.... glad to may have called you my best friend!"

10 Lokomotiv Plovdiv fans living in London

GALLERY

JRF in Domino Bar during one of the numerous meets to watch an England national team games

In the picture Tosh in front, Gilly and the owner of the boozer Milen dressed in white

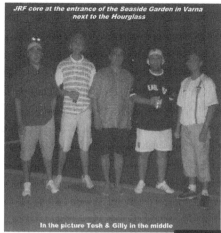

JRF core at the entrance of the Seaside Garden in Varna next to the Hourglass

In the picture Tosh & Gilly in the middle

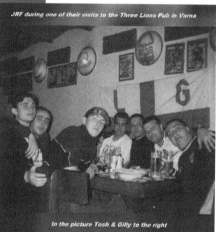

JRF during one of their visits to the Three Lions Pub in Varna

In the picture Tosh & Gilly to the right

JRF carrying a Loko Gorna Football Club flag beside the Drazki torpedo boat in front of the Maritime Museum in Varna Seaside Garden

In the picture Tosh & Gilly in the middle

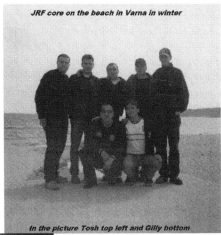

JRF core on the beach in Varna in winter

In the picture Tosh top left and Gilly bottom

JRF playing football on the central beach in Varna

In the picture Gilly front left

1999 -some JRF together with Leeds fans in Sofia

ahead of the Leeds vs Spartak Moscow game

Some JRF together with Leeds fans in front of the National Palace of Culture in Sofia

ahead of the UEFA Cup Third Round game played on 02.12.1999

In front of the Ministry of Interior in Sofia ahead of the UEFA Cup First Round CSKA Sofia vs Blackburn Rovers game

played on 03.10.2002 (In the picture JRF core as youngsters, Tosh top right)

Vasil Levski Stadium, segregation of different sets of supporters during the UEFA Cup Third Round Levski vs Liverpool game played on 03.03.2004

In the picture Tosh & Gilly in the bottom of the fence surrounded by CSKA fans and facing the English supporters

JRF drinking beer with English fans

relaxing in parks and gardens in Sofia

Some JRF chatting with English fans ahead of the important 2000

European championship qualifier played at Bulgarian Army Stadium

JRF having close encounters with English supporters

ahead of the 1999 Bulgaria vs England game

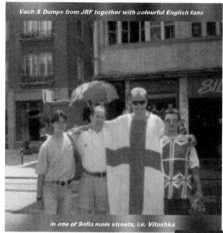

Vach & Dumps from JRF together with colourful English fans

In one of Sofia main streets, i.e. Vitoshka

Amidst English fans in front of CSKA ground ahead of the 2000 European championship

qualifier played on 09.06.1999 (In the picture Tosh & Gilly and some other JRF)

Minutes before meeting Pat (Fat Pat) Dolan (RIP) & Chelsea Headhunters at Georgi Asparouhov Stadium in Sofia

In the picture Tosh to the left and some other JRF

Tosh with some Chelsea fans at Sofia Airport, Terminal 1

Several days ahead of the UEFA Cup tie between Levski Sofia and Chelsea in 2001

Rego (JRF) & Stuart (Headhunters). Standing beside them is one of the policemen (in riot gear) sent to guard the two firms

the empty stands of the stadium in Poduene quarter

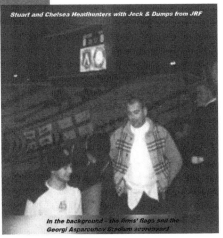

Stuart and Chelsea Headhunters with Jeck & Dumps from JRF

In the background - the firms' flags and the Georgi Asparouhov Stadium scoreboard

Pat (RIP) & Stuart and Chelsea Headhunters with Jeck from JRF

during Levski vs Chelsea game played at Gerena ground

One of the pictures of Pat (RIP) in The Dogs Bollocks Bar in Pattaya, Thailand

together with Chubby Henderson (RIP) and other terrace legends

JRF & Lauta Hools with Pat (RIP) at Belushi's in Shepherd's Bush

London, ahead of the QPR – Boro game

Pat (RIP), Tosh & Komi at Belushi's

in Shepherd's Bush, London

Our mates Pat (Fat Pat) Dolan (RIP) from Chelsea Headhunters

& Rob Sanders ex-S.C.F. (Feyenoord's Firm) featured in this book

"Old School" brawl deep in enemy territory

In the picture JRF & G.O. Boys having a go at the "violets" behind Ivaylo Stadium main stand in Veliko Tarnovo ahead of the 2004 local derby

11.09.2004. Seconds before kicking off behind Ivaylo Stadium main stand in Veliko Tarnovo ahead of the derby between

Loko GO and Etar (in the picture some Boyars after the fight and the consequences of it)

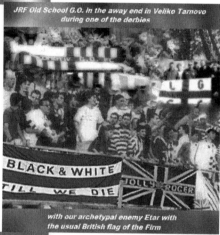

JRF Old School G.O. in the away end in Veliko Tarnovo during one of the derbies

with our archetypal enemy Etar with the usual British flag of the Firm

18.09.2004 "Old School" pitch invasion at Lokomotiv ground in Gorna Oryahovitsa

In the picture JRF & G.O. Boys in the foreground having a go at the Bultras (Botev Plovdiv fans)

JRF & G.O. Boys taking over the town of Mezdra

hours before invading the pitch in 2004

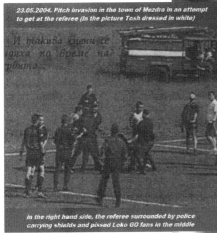

23.05.2004. Pitch invasion in the town of Mezdra in an attempt to get at the referee (In the picture Tosh dressed in white)

In the right hand side, the referee surrounded by police carrying shields and pissed Loko GO fans in the middle

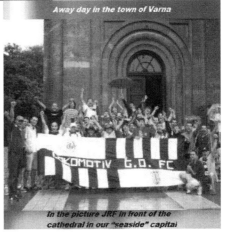

Away day in the town of Varna

In the picture JRF in front of the cathedral in our "seaside" capital

JRF warming up ahead of another game of their beloved Lokomotiv in the seaside town of

In the picture Gilly in the middle of Varna beach with the water slide in the background

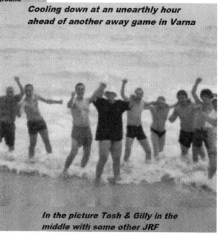

Cooling down at an unearthly hour ahead of another away game in Varna

In the picture Tosh & Gilly in the middle with some other JRF

The usual sight before a JRF away game at the seaside

Beach and parasols taken over by their flags

Legitimized alliance between the oldest club in the world Notts County and Lokomotiv G.O.

In the picture joint black-and-white flags at Meadow Lane in Nottingham

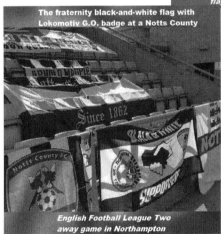

The fraternity black-and-white flag with Lokomotiv G.O. badge at a Notts County

English Football League Two away game in Northampton

Putting up joint flags of fraternized clubs Notts County and Lokomotiv G.O. along the fence at Gorna

In the picture, wearing white in the middle, Anto Platt, featured in this book

JRF Youths & G.O. Boys together with Notts County Anto Platt during another away game in Bulgaria

In the picture the joint flag with the badges of both teams

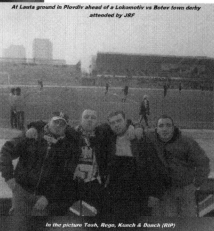

At Lauta ground in Plovdiv ahead of a Lokomotiv vs Botev town derby attended by JRF

In the picture Tosh, Rego, Kunch & Donch (RIP)

After another Plovdiv derby between Lokomotiv and Botev in the Gondola Bar

In the picture Tosh & Donch (RIP) dressed in orange together with NUP & GMU lads

G.O. Boys (Youth Firm) celebrating in Barabina Bar

after their beloved club's winning game

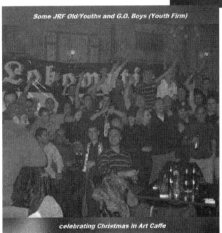

Some JRF Old/Youths and G.O. Boys (Youth Firm)

celebrating Christmas in Art Caffe

20.09.2001. JRF meets Chelsea Headhunters at the UEFA Cup Levski Sofia vs Chelsea game

In the picture Par, Stuart & Toch in the middle together with Stoby, Vach, Dumpa, Simo, Jack, Rego, Mitko

PART TWO

FIVE

7 MILES

It all started in the hard rock and heavy metal era, when we used to have long hair and wear tight jeans, military boots and badges.

We would spend all day listening to our favourite style of music and having a good time in the company of young ladies and lots of booze. In a few words − a picture portraying a kind of mild debauchery. I think there was the same phenomenon in England, when in the ecstasy pills era, the most notorious English hooligans replaced football grounds with music clubs for quite a long period of time. It was a *"Make love, not war"* between the violet and black-and-white fans. Gorna Oryahovitsalads would fuck the rivals' birds, on much rarer occasions some of them would chat up our local girls. Apart from some drunken rows, both camps would get off lightly, being involved in minor accidents only, something like a fist or two from the one side or the other.

Things were even more different and peaceful back in the hippie years. Then the black-and-whites used to be friends with the "Boyars" (the nickname of the citizens of Veliko Tarnovo, our rival). There were joint trips to the Black Sea beaches and music concerts, so generally it was a period of blissful peace between the two towns. Here is what the long-lasting leader of the Boyar firm nicknamed the Pedagogue, has to say about it:

"Ever since I remember, I have been cradled in football passion on the terraces. I used to be an Etar FC top boy and also a leading figure in the heavy metal movement and other subcultures that originated in the early 1980s (at least in our region and area).

Those years were more easy-going, somewhat natural, free and more genuine. Things would come and go so spontaneously that some of us did not have the time to analyse what was going on. Simply because events would follow one another and our lives were quite dynamic.

Some of my best mates would be precisely from our neighbouring town. On a number of occasions we would throw parties together in both towns. Those parties came with our mutual love for football and music, which went hand in hand in those days (people from other towns in the region would sometimes join, too), and would often spread to concerts all over the country and, most naturally, along the Black Sea beaches.

I remember being one summer in Sozopol resort near Burgas, where we used to have a lot of conflicts with the locals as they found it difficult to understand people like us who were different from their lot… The way we dressed, our 24-hour parties including beach binges accompanied by screams, loud music and campfires. We even set on fire one of the nearby groves where our camp was (unintentionally, of course) and not that it matters much, but it was through Gorna Oryahovitsa boys' fault. As you could guess, the entire town was mad at us and in the mass brawls that followed we stood side by side with them like brothers! After returning from our seaside holidays, our teams would often play against each other at the very start of the season so we would stand in the opposite ends, but somehow we managed to keep on good terms with them. "

Maybe the seven miles of picturesque scenery separating the two towns facilitated such meetings.

The area between our two towns is called Arbanasi, a small tourist village and practically no man's land. In terms of geography, the area is a hill, and, believe me, it is one of the most beautiful and enchanting places in our country! It was there where the house of my best mates was situated and it was exactly in that house that some of the parties in questions were thrown. The very structure looked like a castle and was quite spacious. Inside I would meet crowds of people, not only from the two towns, but also from the nearby towns of Gabrovo and Lovech. Sometimes I would get the feeling that there were more than 100 people there partying and if any problems were to arise among them even Stephen King would have found it hard to put the stories into words.

Nowadays it would be unimaginable, impossible, something close to insanity. It would be a disastrous occasion with sinister consequences for the people and totally destructive for the very place. Not that Adrian's Castle (as we used to call it) was not dilapidated by those constant parties and poor maintenance as time went by.

I dare say that probably from the time when our fathers chased theirs up to the Arbanasi Ridge, where not long ago the Boyars took the liberty to write "Death to G.O. Pechenegs", to the time we became active, there were no serious troubles between the two warring camps.

The very facts that the two towns are so close and that Veliko Tarnovo is a former Bulgarian capital have more or less always made us feel as people living in one of their town quarters. You know how bigger towns assimilate everything around and drain all resources they need from their surrounding smaller towns and villages. Years ago, there even used to be a project for merging three towns into one. Thanks God, that project failed. The very thought that I could be now called a "Boyar" and wear a violet shirt instead of a black-and-white one makes me sick. I am glad my place of birth has survived and preserved its identity as it has the charm of being independent. Our town's good infrastructure and industry must have been tempting for the culturally developed historical capital. I really don't know how exactly we have managed to survive under the pressure of the bigger town.

All of this fully applies to football in the two towns. They were the bigger club, champions of Bulgaria, a much more successful team. Quite often they would turn to our footballers in order to keep playing at their top level. We were always in their shadow and whatever player we created would go and play for them. Naturally, it was pretty reasonable in view of all those things that happen now in the world of football. Money took over the game and all small clubs are subject to robbery. However, I think that all these things have an opposite effect on the fans supporting the weaker side. They firm up, get used to adversities and become die-hard and devoted supporters. They believe in what they pursue. They have strong feelings of love and hate, while those who only hunt glory become choosy and spoilt. The latter disunite; start to have increasing demands from their team and when they do not get it they began to insult and offend their club. It happened just like that in our case. Our love would grow even stronger and we would become more and more dedicated, while at the same time our hatred for our enemy would be even more vicious and uncontrollable.

I know a lot about hatred between supporters of rivalry clubs all over the globe, I also have some close range observation, but I'll tell you what, the hatred between us and them was so intense that if we were at one and the same place together, I bet you could cut the atmosphere with a knife. With the lines to follow I will try to plunge you into the sea of hatred.

"Boyars", as they like to call themselves, are rather cheeky bastards. They have huge self-confidence as inhabitants of a former capital and they believe they are descendants of the great Bulgarian kings. The town of Veliko Tarnovo is situated along the Yantra River amidst its picturesque gorges and the landscape is various: there are plains and hills, mounts, rocks and landslips. It is naturally protected by the river and the rocky hills that surround it.

Its original name Tarnovgrad was derived from the Old Bulgarian words "tranov" meaning "thorny" and "grad" meaning "an enclosed space, fortress, stronghold" and further developed into the different names of the town. Veliko Tarnovo is an ancient town featuring a fortress called Tsarevets, where the throne of the kings during the Second Bulgarian Kingdom used to be. It is famous for a number of monuments of culture and a university where thousands of students come to study each year. Probably this is what makes it attractive for people. We also loved going there, stroll down the streets, drink in the local pubs and chat up the female students, however, always hoping to come across their fans and settle our scores. Gorna Oryahovitsa boys adored being in the heart of the enemy's land and sing their songs deep into their rivals' territory. I remember an occasion when a lot of us had gathered in front of Tequila Bar. The pub itself, like most of the buildings in the town, had a huge terrace, which enabled us to have a view from above and made our voices echo loud and be heard in one half of the town.

After consuming plenty of alcohol, we marched through the town as if on parade looking for trouble and confrontation with the locals and, as in most cases, we ended up in the police precinct where we were fined for affray. On another occasion I recall we went to Spider Club, which was one of the most popular clubs in town. We would always end up fighting the club bouncers in the street and then having noisy quarrels with and hurling verbal abuse at cab drivers who would naturally refuse to take us back to Gorna Oryahovitsa.

Those were all occasions on days with no derby games between our two clubs. It was just that we used to have fun at weekends at their expense and on their ground with not a single case of resistance from their lot. Their fans would never turn up, even in their own town. If their ancestors, the genuine Boyars, had protected the town from invaders the way they did, then the majestic fortress of Tsarevets would have been completely useless. You just let the enemies in, hide and let them go on a rampage. To say nothing of derby days. Anyway, we will try and recreate some of those derbies from the past. We will go back in time so that you can see where the rivalry between the two clubs and the hatred between the two sets of fans stem from.

Here is what my long-standing and like-minded friend and co-author has to say about them:

_____

Our arch-enemies are the supporters of Etar, the club from Veliko Tarnovo and their bastards calling themselves the "Boyars" or the "violets". We loathe them! We have always been at war with them. We have never liked them and we shall never have any respect for them. I will try and summarise our hatred for those tossers. The rivalry between Lokomotiv GO and Etar dates back to the early 20th century. Our derbies have always been rather tough games full of riots and fights. Both towns are divided by only 7 miles across the Arbanasi Ridge and they were some of the founders of football game in Northern Bulgaria along with two other famous local rivals, i.e. Spartak from the town of Pleven and Yantra from the town of Gabrovo. Our hatred for the Boyars has always been strong and we have never felt any sympathy for them. We hate them and we hate their team. What is the reason for that? Political and social life has always been a top priority for the town of Tarnovo. We are working class people living in an industrial town and they are former capital citizens relying on material goods mainly coming from us. They have always believed they belonged to the upper class in society and considered us as "some railwaymen" (due to the great percentage of people employed by the railways). Our football backgrounds have always been different – they were champions of Bulgaria, most of the seasons they played in the top flight and they would always find ways to save their asses even when they were on the verge of relegation down to the Amateur League. For them we were just a small town club as we had only several seasons in the top league and most of the time we would play in the lower echelons. Besides, we could not boast of huge financial resources and we had never been champions. What we had was courageous players and extremely loyal supporters. Whenever a star player would appear from our academy, they would find a way to sign him and it would always be a good bargain for them. Dislikes were manifested during the games we would play against each other as it would be most intense and tough games featuring sent-off players almost every time. It is around those derbies that the seeds of hatred were sown.

Here is what those derbies meant according to the ringleader of Tarnovo supporters, the Pedagogue:

"In our region the most appealing events still remain the derbies between Etar and Lokomotiv GO. They are full of passion, tension and, especially in recent years, extreme hatred between the supporters of those two teams. However, it was different in the past and I can share a few words about that:

In 1987 I was doing my military service (in those times it was mandatory) a long way from my home in the seaside town of Shabla, where the Danube meets the Black Sea. A derby was to be played in Veliko Tarnovo and it was much anticipated because Lokomotiv GO had just been promoted to the top flight and they brought a huge number of fans to our former capital. The day was fast approaching but I just didn't see how I could go on a leave in order to attend the game. And I had to!

As the days went by my patience wore thin and my desire to watch the game in flesh reached its height, but still there was no chance to be let on a leave. So I decided to run away from the barracks, which was considered as a rather serious crime in those days, but who cared. I had to go to that derby game and I didn't give a fuck about the consequences. And so I did, I ran away from my military unit, I changed trains several times and I travelled for hours until I finally reached my native town. The derby met everybody's expectations and was a unique game. A genuine football clash full of rough tackles and it ended in a breathtaking 1-1 draw.

On going back to my unit I was given a 10-day detention, which actually equaled imprisonment."

We have always found a way to meet them face to face on the terraces and in the streets, to challenge them and get what we all wanted and that was to kick a Boyar's ass or two, to smash their faces in, to shed their blood on the pavement, to stamp them out like the animals they were. There were occasions on which we would beat the shit out of them in their very den, but they just wouldn't admit defeat. Now, as we are writing this book, they are in the second division and their fans are gone. They are gone because they betrayed their club and they have never really loved football. They will always be violet cunts, while our club has always enjoyed a real and constant support, even when it played in the lower divisions in the last 15 years. The difference between us and them is that we are proper fans and we will always be, no matter which division our team plays in, while they will always be pathetic wankers and glory hunters.

I started loathing them in my very freshman year at high school in Veliko Tarnovo. It was full of Etar fans and among them there was this notorious group of 6-7 boys led by their ringleader B. (I won't say their names, they know who they are). He was a short and robust fella with an ugly spotty face. His mates were skinny, long-haired tossers. They would follow their leader everywhere and would not leave him alone for a single second (probably a sign of weakness). As they knew I supported their rival team, they would always find a way to meet me where our classmates could not see us. They would threaten me that I would take a good hiding because of the black-and-white scarf I used to always wear. There were times that I would come home with a bleeding nose or torn clothes. I was just fourteen and they were in their last school year. I got systematically bullied on a daily basis. I kept silent, I would lie to my parents that I had no troubles. I was planning my vengeance and I was ready to do anything to see his face covered in blood, crushed down on the pavement. I loathed his dumb expression and the way he used to treat the others. I had been suppressing my anger for far too long, the venomous hatred had been building up in my heard and I had been looking forward to the day I was going to make him suffer.

It all erupted shortly before Christmas. It was a gloomy, chilly day. Classes finished in the late afternoon and I was off to the railway station to catch my train to Gorna Oryahovitsa. The road passed through the school backyard. It was almost dark. B. and his crew were waiting for me in the schoolyard (where the football pitches were), away from the eyes of the other students. They were wearing bomber jackets and military boots; their faces were grim and fierce. I was alone among a pack of wolves.

One of them went behind my back and the rest, with their leader at the head, stood in front of me. *"The time has come for you to take a hood hiding, you fucking railwayman!"*, *"Do you think you're gonna get away with it?"*, they said. They pulled my black-and-white scarf and tore a piece off my jacket. I clenched my fist and hit one of them, but unfortunately my punch was not strong enough to knock him down. Then he head-butted me in the nose and the rest rained blows down on me so I fell down to the ground. Afterwards they started kicking me, tugging at my clothes and hitting me wherever they could. I huddled up to protect my face. However, B. managed to kick me in the face with all of his might and then he bent down and spat at me. Some blokes in the neighbouring street saw what was going on and started shouting. My attackers ran away. I was left lying on the ground until I came round. My jeans and jacket were torn and my scarf was gone. I gathered up enough strength to try and stand up. An elderly passerby asked me if I would like to call the police but I said no. Wiping the blood off my face, I went on my way. I was sorry I could not resist, but they outnumbered me. My head was now full of ideas for revenge and retribution. I just had to do it. I got home dirty, clothes torn and nose bleeding. Thank goodness, my parents did not get the real picture. I hid my clothes and I explained my nose injury with stumbling and tripping on my way out of school. They must have had their doubts, but actually there was no way for them to understand what had really happened. I went to bed brewing my evil plots.

The following day was a Friday as far as I can remember. I put on my military boots imagining how hard I would kick him in the fucking head, smearing his face with blood. School over, I followed B. until he was alone. He loved working out at the gymnastics bars next to the playground. I started slowly walking behind him determined to pay him back and I kept looking around to make sure there was no one else. I had to gather a hell of courage as he was fitter and stronger than me. Walking down the path to the playground I bent over, picked up a stone and held it tight in my hand. I decisively approached him from behind. He sharply turned and asked me, *"So, you didn't have enough of it yesterday, did you? You want some more?"* I didn't answer back. I just came closer to him until we were face to face. We looked at each other's eyes wildly. He didn't suspect what was lying in wait for him.

He had just opened his mouth to say something when, using all the might and anger I had accumulated, I punched him with my hand carrying the stone right in his jaw. I heard the sound of chattering teeth and blood spurted out of his mouth. B. crouched down in pains and then I hit him in the head with the stone. He collapsed, blood pouring down all over his face. He was screaming in pain and he looked like a pig that had just been slaughtered. Having completely lost my mind, I started kicking him all over. He had rolled himself into a ball and was begging for mercy. I didn't give a shit about him as rage has taken over me. I bent down and hissed, *"Try and tell anyone about me and you are dead, you fucking violet scumbag"*. I didn't care if I had done any serious damage to that bastard. I just wanted to see him down with a face covered in his fucking blood. Oh, yes! I was somewhat filled with pride. I breathed in the fresh air and was so self-satisfied.

Suddenly becoming aware that someone might see me, I started running. I ran to the train station happy that I had taken my revenge after all those days and weeks of being bullied. I didn't care what was going to happen next. I only got slightly worried about having him killed. I hoped someone would find him soon. A lot of things crossed my mind, but ultimately I was happy with what I had done. The weekend gone, I found out that he was taken to hospital as he had several teeth missing and he needed to have several stitches in his fucking head. His mates found him lying in a pool of blood. Since that day I have never crossed paths with B. and his crew.

Season 1994/95 was full of exciting games and experiences, but in particular it brought that bitterness we feel every time we recall it. It was then that our team got relegated from the top flight and since that season we have not been able to come back to where we belong. We will remember the season not only with remarkable victories against reigning and former champions, but also with our two clashes with our much hated rivals, the Boyars. In the autumn of 1994 we played away to Etar FC. A train trip was organised, though the distance between the two towns is just a few miles. Our meeting point was prearranged by my friend and co-author Tosh, the place was the railway station and the time – early morning. We wanted to avoid the coach and car ride because of the coppers. By the way, as always, the game was to be attended by a huge number of our supporters, but our top crew consisted of some 100 lads. No doubt we were loaded with alcohol, flares, and mostly determination to smash them on their territory.

Our trip naturally involved a lot of songs, empty bottles thrown out of the train, seats turned inside out and upside down, ashtrays ripped off and windows broken. The rest of the passengers found themselves among a pack of beasts and were too terrified to say anything to us. As we always did, we travelled without any tickets. Any ticket collector would not have stood a chance against such unruly tempers, noise and roar anyway.

Upon getting off the train in Tarnovo, we lit up several smoke canisters and the locals standing on the platform in wait of other trains dispersed in seconds. There were a few cops who decided to escort us and so stood on both sides of our cavalcade. Nothing of importance happened on our way to the ground, apart from the arrival of gendarmerie to back up the few coppers. So we arrived at the ground heavily guarded by police and gendarmerie. We were sat in the away end opposite the main stand.

As I already said, there were more supporters from Gorna Oryahovitsa, but they were just ordinary football fans. While waiting for the game to start, we put up our flags across our entire end, we chanted the name of our beloved club and we lit up several smoke bombs and flares. Opposite us (diagonally) were the Boyars, approximately 50 of them. The ground was full to capacity, but their fans do not have the reputation of being among the top hooligan firms in our country. In the first half nothing happened, not counting the efforts to out-sing each other and the exchange of insults and offending gestures. There were no signs of what was about to happen at half time. The end we were stood was close to their main stand and there were only some 100 yards between us. Moreover, the area around the main stand was hardly ever guarded by cops as it included the main entrance to the ground and no one would ever suspect that anyone could dare to break into.

At the gate of our section there was only one police patrol car and the other cops were stood all over the running track. We decided to try what seemed impossible by making our way through to the main entrance and climbing a few steps on the terraces to get closer to the opposite and where the Boyars were. A mob of ours broke through the police lines and headed towards our rivals' end. Those of us who were at the back couldn't make it due to the police response, but those in our front lines had already attacked their supporters. Chaos ensued as the exchange of punches and kicks started. Our lads were right amidst them and they had never believed it would happen. It was hell of a fun to see our boys knock them down between the rows of seats. The OB intervened and a great melee began. You could not tell who was punching who, you could only see batons, boots and fists flying in the air and you could hear the victims groan. The rest of us started hurling ripped off seats at them and we got hold of some of their flags. We didn't care what was going on around us and what was going to happen. What mattered was that we were right amidst them and we were crushing them down.

They were totally confused as they hadn't assumed we would get at them so fast and the hail of punches made them even more disoriented. Using their best efforts, the OB managed to set us apart. Some of us got nicked and ejected from the ground. The others remained under heavy police escort and there was not much to be done any more apart from the exchange of jibe and abuse that continued until the end of the game. We watched it until the final whistle and though we lost 2-1, we were satisfied with our off the pitch victory at their ground and at their very sector. We had to walk from the ground to the centre of town under heavy police presence.

They had decided to get us on some coaches in order to prevent any further trouble. There was no way we could be squeezed in a single coach as we were too many. Some of us (about 20 lads) stayed on to wait for the last coach. The cops had already started pulling out. It was now more than an hour after the game was over. We got on the coach and after it drove off several stones hit the side windows and smashed them. It was the Boyars, some fifteen of them, who had gathered courage to revenge. The coach driver would not open the doors as there were other passengers on board. Some of us were injured from the shattered glass. We started kicking at the doors in order to open them and make our way out. Fists cut by the fragments of smashed glass, we started throwing the remains of the panes outside. The passengers were screaming as they didn't want to get off. We were pushing them in order to make way and the driver got scared, left his vehicle to the mercy of fate and ran to the nearby building. Finally the doors yielded to our kicks and we were out getting at them.

Our first ranks got under a shower of punches, but when gradually all of us got off a bloody brawl started at the bus stop. Some shop windows next to it got smashed and everywhere there were people running in panic. We started throwing debris and dust bins at them or anything we could lay our hands on and one of them threw back a shoe that flew over and landed on the coach roof! Some of them were down and we started kicking them all over. The rest of them fled while the fallen ones remained on the ground injured. The cops arrived, but it was too late. We had defeated our enemies at their ground for a second time in one day. Of course, we also had casualties, but elated with our triumph we just didn't pay attention to our wounds and injuries. OK, we lost on the pitch, but we won off the pitch and we did it twice!

The spring of 1995 was as exciting as the autumn of 1994. We were walking on the razor's edge in the lower part of the table winning this week and losing the next one. We had some impressive wins against the leaders, but we lost 1-2 at home to our bitter rivals Etar. After what we had done in their town, we expected a strong support of theirs to arrive at our ground. Some of our lads got in touch with their ringleaders and we did expect a huge turnout. This time we knew they had organised a coach trip, which in a way facilitated our job as we didn't have to wait for them at the train station like we had done in the past. We also anticipated an enormous crowd of home supporters not only because we were hosting our archenemy, but also because we had beaten the leaders in the table Levski two weeks before.

All day long we prepared for the event, discussed where and how it would be best to have a go at them before and after the match, though we knew it would be extremely hard to break through the police escort and get at their coaches before kick-off time. Furthermore, the Boyars were expected to arrive right before the game in order to avoid any trouble and confrontation. This time the police had been well prepared in view of what happened in Tarnovo in the autumn. However, hardly anyone had the illusion that the day would end with no violence and riots whatsoever. We mobbed up downtown several hours before kick-off time.

Naturally, we needed to oil our throats with alcohol. There were also those of us who could barely stand on their feet as they were properly pissed by then. Anyway, our mob was just huge, about 150 lads. It was all white and blue flags and scarves. The entire centre of the town was flooded with fans and their songs echoed all around. Some were singing, other were blowing up bombs or lighting up smoke canisters, while still others were lying on the pavements weary of the amounts of booze they had devoured. A huge sea of fans. This was probably one of our best turnouts. We were watched by the Old Bill but there were no grounds for serious trouble. We set off for the stadium. The streets were echoing with our songs and chants. We saw some elderly people and mothers with their children look for shelter in their homes as no one could be sure what could happen at any time. Everybody was well aware of what the unpredictable Gorna Oryahovitsa mob was capable of doing and everybody was familiar with their history of numerous outrages. On approaching the ground we could hear the crowd shouting and we also recognised the much loathed songs sung by the Boyars. They had already arrived and had stood in the away end. Our info was that there were two coach loads of theirs carrying some 80 more hardcore fans. The ground was full, even more than usual. There were probably about 15 000 people who had come to watch the big regional derby.

While getting escorted to the section we always used to gather we challenged the violets with insulting gestures and stones thrown in their direction. The first whistle almost made the ground erupt. Everybody jumped to their feet and we started singing out loud, throwing bombs and lighting smoke bombs and flares. Flags were flying high across the entire ground. The Boyars hit back by lighting up their sector with pyro. It looked like it was gonna be a memorable day and an unbelievable support by both sides.

During the game we made plans how to get at them after the final whistle. No one thought it would be easy due to the massive police presence. Nothing remarkable happened till the end of the game, apart from the ejection of some of our lads due to being drunk and disorderly. Well, it was inevitable as some went on drinking even during the game. After Etar scored their second goal in the 90th minute, led by our anger and disappointment, we stormed the fence and it simply collapsed under our weight. The metal railings looked like just a useless pile of iron. We tried to jump over the debris and some of us even went closer to the pitch. The cops were doing their best to restore the order and they would tug away our boys and hit them on their heads with their batons. The Boyars were madly celebrating their victory, but at the same time they were busy collecting their flags with the intention of sneaking out of the stadium. We waited for some time until the ground was empty and their fans were gone along with the OB. We regrouped into smaller mobs in order to move faster, catch up with and have a go at them. They were heading for the bus station where their coaches were.

We followed them at some distance. At one of the bus stops along the way we saw a group of Boyars surrounded by cops.Our mobs reunited and a mighty black-and-white wave of tough lads went towards them. However, we couldn't get at them immediately due to the heavy police presence. The distance between the two mobs was no more than 100 yards. A large part of our mob split off and headed for the main road leading to Tarnovo in the vicinity of the local hospital. Our idea was to attack their coaches with bottles and stones in order to challenge them. The area was suitable for battles as there were some narrow streets and places where you could easily get lost. If our plan worked, the rest of us had to back up our first line. A wall of police shields was protecting the violets. We were challenging them and the cops were keeping us apart with great difficulties. Stones and debris were flying at the Boyars from our rear lines. The entire bus station was taken over by our lads. At one point their coaches arrived and they started getting on, hurling insults and obscene gestures at us. We were wondering how to get through the police barrier and get at them since we couldn't let them leave just like that, with no consequences. One by one their coaches were off to Tarnovo escorted by two patrol cars. We ran after them sticking to the plan to back up our mates who were already waiting at the fork before the main road to Tarnovo.

While we were running to our destination we heard sirens wail and saw the people from the neighbourhood hide in their homes, startled by the noise made by the hundred or so irate fans running. One of our lads waiting for us at the road split told us that they had managed to smash the windows of the two coaches and the Boyars had got off and had a go at our mob. We quickened our pace and when we got nearer we saw the violets running in all directions. We started chasing them, scattering in the small streets, and it kicked off everywhere. I was with some ten other lads and we had a go at 4 or 5 of their mob. We exchanged punches and I got blood all over my clothes as my head was busted open (probably with brass knuckles).

The cops appeared and went at us in a baton charge so we dispersed into the narrow side streets. While running, we saw another mob of ours fighting some Boyars. We ran over to help them and readily joined the fight. You could hear the sounds of punches hitting jaws and heads. Couples were fighting all around, some were already down wrestling on the ground and others were using Kung Fu style kicks. One or two of them were lying on the pavement and the others fled in the direction of their coaches. We saw more cops coming our way and a police patrol car was about to cut off our way. We scattered with the aim of hiding around the nearby residential buildings and evading the coppers. One could still hear screams and shouts and siren wails. In a while there was complete silence. Dusk had started to descend upon the town and I headed for our pub, meeting some of my mates on the way there. I was told that there were lads nicked both from our mob and the Boyars. The rest of the away fans had boarded their coaches and were off to Tarnovo heavily escorted by the police.

In the pub everyone was telling about our great experience, i.e. how we defeated them, how they ran away in fright and how several of them had their asses kicked hard. It was clear that we defeated them for a second time, now at our territory, and although we were slightly chaotic (we didn't get the chance to act in a more organised manner), we had another victory over our arch enemy.

Here is the occasion seen through the eyes of my friend and co-author Tosh:

_____

Our main mob consisted of some 150 lads. We were enraged as we had lost the game and we just wanted to hunt violets. We tried to get at their coaches but were surprised to find out that they had been one-way only and that the Boyars would be escorted to the bus station where some other coaches were waiting for them. The prospects for laying an ambush made us regroup. The Boyars were still inside the ground so we had to get a move on. We decided to split into smaller mobs. We knew that the train station is also an option (though not highly likely) for some of them, but we decided that the distance and the number of open spaces along the way to the bus station were just fine for our plans. The cops also knew very well that those areas would be used by us for possible raids. About 40 of us separated to head for the railway station. Our worries that our numbers would be reduced vanished as we saw that the desire to hunt violets was also seen in most of the ordinary supporters, who would otherwise just go home right after low-risk games. But it was different that day. I had the feeling that something similar to the past events our fathers had told us many times about was going to happen. Back then they were led by the same desire to get at the enemy and they chased them up the hill all the way to Arbanasialong the short way between our two towns! Of course, it was going to be different now as the woodlands along the way to Arbanasi suited us just fine and facilitated our evil plans. Our rivals left the safety of the ground. Mayhem ensued. Several bombs exploded to welcome the violets out of the ground. We chased them like hounds trying to break through the massive police convoy at the nearby crossroads. The group of 40 who had been off to the train station returned as they had found out that the Boyars were to be escorted out via a different route and, in turn, attacked the away fans from their flank, hurling stones and bottles at them. There was utter panic. More and more people were joining our mob. There were even folks coming out of the nearby houses and others who were helping us find arms. To my surprise I saw a middle-aged woman hand out something that looked like a picket to someone in the mob.

Now I was damn sure that this day was going to be talked about for many years to come and there would be legends about it. We could see the bus station through the thick smoke from the explosions of the many bombs made of red lead and bronze. We could unmistakably see some objects being hurled at the Boyars from the top floors of the residential buildings around us.

What followed was 15 minutes of extreme hostility before the coaches came to their rescue. I could clearly see their terrified faces. The first arrests were made. I saw several lads being nicked and taken to the nearby police station. It was becoming increasingly impossible to complete our punitive mission. A group of about 20 of us decided to follow the routes of the coaches past the town hospital towards the town of Lyaskovets.

We went past the town park and Pirot street, running like hell. On our way we saw small groups of strangers, no scarves or shirts, some of them suspiciously seeking shelter in the nearby shops. We didn't have the time for that and besides, it was not our style as they were just ordinary violet fans. Our targets were the two approaching coaches. We could see the distant smoke accompanied by wailing sirens. We started looking for "ammo" so we overturned several dustbins. We were now desperate in our efforts to hurt them. The coaches passed by followed by a volley of stones and other debris as we were running after them almost to the road sign designating the end of our town.I turned around and saw the "Welcome to Gorna Oryahovitsa"sign across the road. The lads coming from below had run all the way from the bus station to the end of town pursuing the coaches and now were throwing their stones almost at us! We had no strength left, but there was more to come. It was time for the organized police mission aimed at dispersing us.

I ran for my life taking the side streets back to the town. That was my only chance to avoid being nicked. Having reached some crossing, I looked back and saw that a police car was in pursuit of me. I ran as fast as I could again and at the next turning I noticed a house with a low fence garden. Without thinking twice I jumped over the fence, landed in the garden, lay on my back and then heard the engine roar passing by. Lying in the tall grass and watching the sky, I tried to calm down my breathing. My heart was beating wild and I could feel my head pounding. After my breathing was back to normal, I burst out laughing as probably I had reached the height of my adrenaline rush. I decided to wait and since I must have been pretty exhausted I dropped off to sleep. I woke up at dusk, looked around and then jumped over the fence again to happily head back home.

We had been waiting for that day for too long. It was our first derby in the Amateur League after our unfortunate relegation from the top flight in 1994/95 and our gradual fall to the amateur division. We were about to host our much hated rivals Etar.

It was the spring of 2000/2001, a campaign we will remember only with the massive fight we had with their fans around Lokomotiv stadium. The events about to happen were going to stay forever in our memories as one of the best fights we have ever had. There was a change of generations and most lads were some 15–17 years of age. Nevertheless, our core was well preserved though some of us were already living in other towns. Especially for that day we made a massive turnout. It was a warm and sunny morning, as if a sign of a long and eventful day.

The derby was scheduled for the late afternoon and we had the time to organise and meet our rivals on our ground. I hadn't felt so alive, energetic and eager for the big clash for a long time. It was only their fans that could make us, even without any challenge, resort to violence. They were also few in numbers following their relegation to the amateur division, no matter that they won the championship way back in 1991. I left home early in the morning to meet some mates from the neighbourhood to agree on a meeting point ahead of the game and possibly get some news of their fans' trip. We expected them to arrive from Veliko Tarnovo by train at noon. As we lived in different parts of town, we decided to meet up near the railway station. We didn't expect any massive police presence as we played in the Amateur League, which was not supposed to engage large numbers of coppers in those days. There were about ten of us.

We had a few beers in the pub nearby and at noon we headed for our meeting point where the Boyars were supposed to pass by. Twenty more lads led by Tosh came from the other side of town. So there we were, a relatively decent mob, though not in the numbers we used to be before. We waited for a whole hour and there was no trace of them although there were only three hours left before kick-off time.

We waited until the last midday train from Tarnovo arrived to find out we had been misled by our spy. We got disappointed and were on the brink of giving up as we thought they would not turn up when one of our youngsters called us to inform us that they had arrived by coach and were hanging around in the park in the vicinity of the stadium as if they owned it. We quickened up our pace, satisfied that our day was not wasted after all. We walked the distance of a mile and a half in several minutes only. We were so fast when driven by the desire to get at them. As we approached the ground we slowed down since we weren't sure where exactly they were. To our great surprise, they were sat in the nearby park on the north side of the ground. There were about twenty, lying on the grass and peacefully enjoying their drinks with their backs to us. We saw a few cops and other people around the stadium, but they would not be an obstacle.

We ran towards the Boyars shouting our battle cries. Tosh, I and several other lads were in the front and the rest were following us. We went straight at them kicking and punching them all over. Fists and boots were hitting their heads. Some of them couldn't even stand up due to the shower of blows while others were trying to put up some resistance. The passersby were watching us in horror and the few cops (not more than 3-4) didn't dare to interfere. One of the violet top boys ran off in the direction of the main street hoping to get some kind of help. However, there was no help around. Tosh and I ran after him. We reached him, my mate kicked him from behind and he was down right in the middle of the road. I started punching him hard in the head and face. Tosh was kicking him all over his body. The wanker was screaming for help, blood all over his face. Cars were stopping as we were blocking the road. Our other lads were fighting on the other side and soon they made Etar fans run for their lives. Having made sure the fan we had beaten up was out of the game, we ran after his fellas. Police backups had arrived and so they put up a blockade and didn't let us come closer to the ground until kick-off time. The Boyars were escorted to the away sector where they waited for the game to begin. We found a way through, jumping over the fencing at the eastern end. The rest of us had already made their way inside the eastern stand.

During the game, we teased them about the fight they had lost again, although the distance between us and them was great and we were separated by a massive police line. Tension was rising increasingly higher and we wanted to have another go at them.

At half time some Etar lads broke through the police convoy and headed towards us. We didn't hesitate at all and immediately rushed in their direction. The coppers went at us with shields and batons. It kicked off between the hooligans and cops. I had parts of my clothes torn and got hit hard on the head with a baton. More police backups arrived from the other side of the ground, trying to restore order. Finally they stopped the fight and set us apart. It rarely happened so well at our ground, in front of our crowd. We were so pleased with all those clashes throughout the day. I got nicked with several other lads and we were kept in custody until the end of the game. We won (1-0, I think) and it was a great day for us. We had our chances and we took them. I'll never forget that day though I got hit on the head several times and afterwards nicked. In the evening we ended up in the local pub celebrating our victory and our great day out.

I already told you about the times when our fathers used to chase theirs up to the Arbanasi Ridgedue to the sign placed there and so, before the mid-1990s, there were only minor clashes between our two sets of supporters! It would end with only a couple of punches, and in most cases it would be a personal thing. Taking into account the friendships we also told you about before, the parties at the Castle and at the seaside, I really understand that for long periods of time there was no such bad blood between us. Anyway, we should keep in mind that our two clubs played in different divisions for quite a long time. However, come to think of it, both teams played in the top flight from the late 1980s to the mid-1990s.

I really don't have a clue how older fans managed to keep on such friendly terms when they played all those derby games.Obviously the hippie era and mood had alleviated the year-long hatred. I remember a party we threw together and that boys of ours started arguing with one of their lot regarding team support. The argument went on to include serious questions like *"If Etar (who had become champions the previous season) play Arsenal (also champions), who are you going to support!?"* Our lad said, *"Arsenal, of course!"*, and they ended up on the floor rolling over and exchanging some innocent blows. Next thing I saw was both of them, nose bleeding, sitting next to each other and drinking their beers! If I have to speak for myself, as I already said, only one of them (i.e. the Pedagogue) gets my full respect and admiration as he is a real role model for any football fan with self-esteem.

It all started deep into their territory after one of the most humiliating defeats they have made us suffer. Most of our older lads, disappointed from the 5-2 score, left the ground several minutes before the final whistle, hopped in their cars and went back home.

After the game was over, the rest of us decided to take a bus from the centre of Tarnovo. We were aged between 20 and 25, and I can't deny that all those who later on formed the core of Jolly Roger Firm were present. I remember we went as if on parade through half of their town and nothing happened apart from the usual banter. Naturally, we were on the alert as we always kept in mind that something may happen and they may appear out of somewhere. We knew what those mean bastards were capable of, especially on their own ground. We were walking together, as we would always do, and we were distinctly feeling the need to take it out on some Boyar wanker. We reached the bus stop and thought that nothing was going to happen again. We started waiting for our bus in silence.What followed was going to open a new page in our history of hostility and after that incident we understood that in the future we would have to show no mercy at all for them on every possible occasion.

That moment arrived when I turned left and saw probably the ugliest human face on this earth. His hair was straw blond and his eyes the brightest blue (as if white) I had ever seen. For a brief moment I even thought he had white eyeballs and they were so huge as if ready to pop out. Besides, his hideous face was twisted and malicious. I knew very well who that scarecrow was and what was about to happen.The interesting thing was that the previous year the same scumbag was for a while at the same place, but then he must have realised that it was not wise at all to try and have a go, as on that day we were untouchable with all our older lads in the firm. I saw his crew in the distance behind him. They had definitely caught us off guard, judging by their numbers and the age of the blokes approaching. I tried to estimate our chances for a few seconds, but I just failed because at that very moment our eyes met and after that we were like hypnotised and set to have a go at each other.

Thinking about it afterwards, I realised he had passed by 4 or 5 of our lads in order to get at me because they came from one side and I was standing in the middle of our group. *"Let's have it, you twat"*, was heard from his twisted mouth and then he reached out and grabbed my black-and-white scarf trying to pull it and kick me in the groin at the same time. I immediately hit back and after we exchanged several punches, the wanker fell down and I started kicking his ribs using all my strength. Then it kicked off everywhere as his mates joined. I saw one of them take out a knife and come at me in order to rescue the bastard.

On such occasions time just stops and a second seems like an hour. You focus on the blade and you do your best to keep it away from you and your mates. It was that split second the tosser took advantage of in order to rise up and slip off running like hell into a side street. My attention was thoroughly drawn to the cunt with the knife and all I was thinking about was how to disarm him. Then, out of the blue, I saw a foot fly up and kick the wanker straight in his chest. He collapsed and dropped the blade, which was picked up by one of our lads and, mind you, was not used in the fight any more. I turned around and saw how one of my mates (a quite tall fella) just went on kicking them around, which was his trademark. It was him who had kicked the bastard in the chest, probably saving my life! It was then that I really understood why we used to call him the Horse. Having never wondered before, now it was all clear – it was his great height and strong legs that had earned him such a nickname. Can you imagine being kicked by a man with such a nickname?

Going back to the scuffle, I immediately followed my protagonist in a small dead-end alley behind the bus stop, which was probably my biggest mistake. I knew well that on such occasions, when you split from the main group, you take much bigger risks, but my desire to beat that bloody bastard got the better of me so I ran after him. I managed to catch up with him and then I tripped him up, he fell to the floor again and I started kicking him madly. In just a few seconds 4 or 5 of them pounced on me and this time I was down on the floor. It was then I realised how stupid it was to have long hair when you want to take part in such actions. I had the feeling that 4 or 5 pairs of hands had grabbed my hair and the same numbers of feet were kicking me all over. I'm really glad my mates didn't let me down and came to rescue me and I'm particularly thankful to the Horse, who saved me twice on that day. Thank you, bro! You deserve my full respect, mates, you know who you are!

After I was back to the main street it seemed it was all over. I was stupid enough to have taken my girlfriend to the game and there she was waiting for me at the bus stop. I took her hand and we crossed the street. I looked back to see the battle field and I saw them lined up along the pavement hurling the usual verbal abuse and showing obscene gestures. I no longer wanted to go back, I had my girlfriend with me and we had all dispersed. The police had also arrived. I checked my face for blood, but surprisingly I had none. Instead, I had a lot of hair ripped out; hairs were falling down all over my face. I don't know if you have ever felt such kind of pain!? Your very scalp hurts! The damage was rather mental than physical, my self-esteem being hurt the most. Anyway, having made so many mistakes like wearing my hair long, the scarf that they got hold of and pulled me by and the girl waiting for me at the bus stop, what else could I have expected? That incident was to entirely change my views on a football hooligan's appearance in general. Moreover, we promised ourselves from then on to be much more organised and accurate in what we were going to do and be totally obsessed by.

I couldn't wait for our next game against Etar to come. I was toying with plenty of ideas of taking my revenge. I thought to myself that if that game was to be played within several days, some of them would be even killed for sure! Time heals, they say, but definitely not in my case as the more time went by, the closer we were to the day they were going to come to our manor. The very thought of it made me feel full of anger and malevolence. Considering with my mates our possible ways of seeking revenge, we decided to go for an ambush. We wanted to do them as much damage as possible without using blades and other weapons, things that, unlike them, we have never used, by the way. We decided to use old wooden table and chair legs. I remember we even went to a factory where we found a lot of old wooden stuff meant for recycling. We took all legs, some of which were made of quite solid and heavy wood and had various ornaments. For me, I chose some square shaped, i.e. four sided legs that would perfectly suit our purpose! I think that for a man who had so much spite built up inside that was nothing else but a deadly weapon. I imagined how the solid edges of the legs would crush their bones one by one, turning us into a real *Boyar* grinder. It was everything I and we all wanted – to leave them lying on the floor in complete mess.

The memory of having my hair ripped out was still painful, but I just couldn't find the guts to have it cut. At the same time, I wouldn't let it be my weak spot again so I decided to put on a stocking, just like bank robbers do. A lot of you are now probably laughing out loud, but only if you could really see the way we looked on that day! We made no compromise regarding our attire as no one wanted to have his best clothes torn or tattered. We decided to put on some ordinary work dungarees and, naturally, the usual for those days military boots.

The moment we had all been waiting for finally arrived and there we were almost in the centre of our town. We looked like ordinary construction workers on their lunch break, so nobody really paid attention to us. However, in our jacket sleeves, we all had the table and chair legs in question. We had shortened them so that they wouldn't stick out and make us look suspicious. When we arrived at the place we had chosen for our ambush we put the stockings on our heads, took out our tools and had the appearance of real terrorists. I think Gilly already described the very location.

There was a huge number of stairs leading from the train station to the town. Someone had even decided to count them as their exact number, believe me, was of great importance for the visiting fans, who were brave enough to take that steep and dangerous roundabout way. That was why our town was not a dream destination for many of them and on a number of occasions they would end up in an endless maze leading to safety. Due to its major railway hub and strategic central location in the country, our town is an important railway centre and a crossing point of trains going in all directions both across Bulgaria and the Balkan Peninsula. Therefore, it was easily accessible for anyone who had decided to travel by rail. A coach is also an option, but then one would risk being properly escorted passing through the town centre. The same goes for the public transport to the station and so most visiting fans would use those steps as an entrance to the town. Having overtaken that obstacle, they would find themselves in a vast open field with no structures on that went for half a mile and greatly facilitated toe-to-toe fights like in Russia and Poland. It was right there where we stood going through the last details of the ambush we were about to lay in a few minutes.

We had checked the train timetable and had sent a spotter to watch the station and inform us of their arrival. We got a message that they had arrived and that there were not many of them. We outnumbered them by two to one. I have never been fond of unequal fights. It simply isn't fair when three people have a go at one, but after what happened on the previous derby day there was no place for mercy anymore. We hid in the bushes on both sides of the steps deploying all the way down so that we could close the circle. When their first boys had climbed the top step it was our turn to close the circle and intercept their last ones at the bottom and the first ones at the top.

Our plan was meticulously drawn to the tiniest detail and everybody knew what they had to do. It was a fine example of military precision as we had prepared for a real war. I felt like a predator lying in wait, stalking his prey. I was breathing heavily and I felt my heartbeat getting faster as my temples were pulsating. On top of it, we all had those outbursts of laughter while waiting in ambush in the bushes. I could hear the other lads' distinct snigger coming from all directions although they were doing their best to stifle it in order not to be overheard by the enemy. There was no more time for jokes as I could clearly see our opponents approaching. They were there and they were about to fall into our trap any minute now. I felt wonderful and was the first to go out of my hiding place giving out a loud cry that sounded more like a battle cry you'd hear watching Brave Heart, or probably like a roar of a starving beast that had been stalking its prey for far too long. I heard my mates roar and then the sound of chair and table legs hitting wildly our victims' heads.

Truth to tell, I didn't see anything but red and I didn't care that someone might get seriously hurt. Anyone who has felt that raging fury mixed with the satisfaction brought by revenge knows what I am talking about. I simply didn't know who to hit first, but then I just couldn't reach at them as the hail of punches raining all over them was simply amazing. I remember some of them tried to escape jumping over the solid iron railings on both sides of the steps, but our lads stopped them using the railings in question as a support and a place to climb onto and with their mighty kicks turned the Boyars back into the trap. Their next attempt to get away was back downhill, but it was there where we had concentrated our forces. Our lads did a really good job blocking their way and preventing them from running away. Many a time through all those years I have witnessed and taken part in similar scenes on those steps and only once those who were climbing them got the upper hand. I will keep this story for the next chapter and now let me go back to the top of the hill where the wooden legs kept on beating flesh.

It is really hard when you're tired after going up all those steps to walk into an ambush and fall into a trap from which there is practically no way out. You are surrounded by people in masks who have enough spite and urge to kill you. The last thing I felt for them was pity, though! I couldn't stop seeing red and then I heard a familiar voice crying, *"Stop it! You're gonna fucking kill him!"* It was as if time had stopped for a second and it made me really see what had happened. I looked around and saw plenty of them lying on the floor, one of them in a complete mess.

Later, during the game, we even started wondering whether we had not pulled one of his eyes out and that thought really terrified me. I don't know if you would call it fate, but that same guy was also hurt in another fight we had that Gilly already told you about. For me the fight was over, especially as after having a good look at them I didn't see the ugly bastard's stare, which meant that I would have to wait for some more time to get my personal revenge. If I have to be honest, I even knew where he lived since, as you already know, our towns are neighbouring and not that big so I had my ways of getting information about him. I even had that crazy idea to break into his house at night and beat the shit out of him while he was sleeping. But no, as a man with principles I wanted to have it the proper way. I backed off from the battle field in order to take another look at the scene. It was a really horrible sight. I could see something more than fear in the eyes of many of them while others were lying on the ground agonising. I saw our most merciless lads went on throwing punches at those who could still stand on their feet. I climbed a few steps to get to the meadow where I sat down and took a deep breath letting some adrenaline out of my body. I looked down at the wooden legs I had in my hands and they were all covered in blood.

There was another weird and somewhat funny encounter with them Boyars in a little village called Resen, where on an ordinary day (no football involved), some 10 of us and a little more of them were invited by some mutual friends to celebrate their village fest. So we were on one side of the village and they were on the other. We found out about them being there a little after midnight and, bellies full, we broke into a 200-yard sprint to get at them. We tried to exchange some punches, but soon after that both parties realised how drunk we all were so we just went back to our separate camps to finish our drinks.

By and large, such occasions are only a few and recently it has been very unusual to avoid serious incidents, not to speak of any friendships between our two parties. In bigger cities that have a number of football clubs one could come across, let's say, brothers supporting different clubs. This could hardly happen with us not only because we come from different towns. Never mind our towns are so close to each other! Though we may seem to belong to one and the same community, actually we do not!

Naturally, many of us live, work and study in their town, but few would say "I come from Tarnovo". I have always found it extremely irritating to hear a Gorna Oryahovitsa citizen say he was born in Tarnovo. I find this absolutely inadmissible!

Of course, there is an exception to every rule, especially to those unwritten ones, and my relationship with the Pedagogue from Tarnovo just comes to prove that.

Here is what he has to add about us:

"I knew some of the older boys from Gorna Oryahovitsa quite well and despite our football related differences we managed to be on good terms and respect each other. I have always enjoyed their good reception (something few Boyarscan boast of) even now, when generations have changed. I remember one night in the legendary hard-rock boozer called "The Street", which was visited on a weekly basis by not only students from all over Bulgaria, but also people from neighbouring towns and most of all from Gorna Oryahovitsa. In the natural course of events, fights would often break out between our two camps in the early hours when both sides would have had too much to drink. So on that night in question I was approached by a group of young lads from Gorna

Oryahovitsa. Some of them I knew well since they grew up close to the older geezers who were my friends. At first I was a bit reserved as only a few weeks before, that very pub had witnessed a serious wrangle between blokes from the two towns, which I was not involved in. However, those lads showed their full respect and even invited me to a birthday party (on the following morning) of a very close friend of one of the authors of this book – Tosh.

As a fan of the English style of football and in general of their football fan culture that I was also fond of and willing to establish on the terraces of my beloved club's ground, I was surprised, impressed and amazed at their Pro-British organization they had set up locally and if I have to be honest, I was really sorry we didn't have. Their hospitality was way beyond what was considered kind and the very atmosphere at their parties with all those Union Jacks hanging from the wallswould send shivers down my spine! Talking about confessions, however, they are rare among fans of both clubs and the abuse and infinite hatred understandably prevail. In my particular case with Tosh, however, things were quite different... I mean that our relationships were and still are at a much higher level beyond what one is supposed to take for granted. And I think it is due to the fact that people like him don't forget where they started and they do remember and believe that football fandom is about respect and heritage as things should be passed on to future generations.

Years later we met again at a concert and, both of us having had a decent number of drinks, he told me, "Ventsi, you are my terrace and music mentor and if I ever have a son, I will name him after you". I am still waiting for him to have a son...

However, nothing prevented him from taking some 30-40 tough lads to our town the following year and before we knew it, they charged an unprecedented surprising attack behind the main stand of our Ivaylo Stadiumin Tarnovo. I had come back from a bikers rally especially for the game and upon approaching the ground I saw their group walking fast together... I was sure something was gonna happen and before I reached the stadium it already had. At some point we even faced each other at the front line and our eyes met for a brief moment amidst the rampaging crowd...

Well, a fan's life can be quite interesting, don't you think?"

It is really and I do remember that moment very well and all the preceding events…

We met up in Gorna Oryahovitsa early in the morning, probably at about 10:00, in a snack bar selling beer. It was the only place we could get beer that early and we needed it cause we had a hell of a job to do. So there we were, about 40 of us, lively discussing our forthcoming trip to Tarnovo and, in particular, any way that we could evade the cops' attention. Our aim was to get through to the centre of the enemy lines.

We decided to travel incognito in cabs without wearing any colours. We had some of our top boys back from abroad especially for that derby and some well-respected old faces. Our chances of success were beyond doubt. So, having arrived in about 10 cabs, our compact and elite firm of approximately 50 lads settled in a pub in Veliko Tarnovo, where we went on drinking. The night before we had tried to prearrange a fight and we had got our rivals' agreement. I decided to call them again to find out whether our agreement was still valid. After I told them our numbers, the Boyars started beating about the bush so I told the others that it wouldn't go as planned. It would have been a waste of quality and numbers, as well as energy and adrenaline we had that day so we all decided to go for their very heart, namely the home end of Ivaylo Stadium.

Now I have to make it clear that the allocation at their ground is as follows: even after its reconstruction the home supporters are stood at the main covered stand only (including their ultras) and the sectors behind the goals are usually empty (before the repairs they even didn't have any sectors there). The opposite stand is entirely allocated for away fans, regardless of their numbers, be it 50 or 500. I have seen that stand filled to its capacity on very rare occasions, but I'm going to tell you about that later in this story.

Let's go back to our well planned and organised raid, which became possible also thanks to the Old Bill's plain stupidity. We were walking in almost complete silence, split into groups of 4-5 boys, no one wearing any scarves or shirts. We were determined and focused and upon approaching our target we stepped up. The cops stopped our first group, including me, and without asking any questions directed us as if they were traffic controllers, *'Gorna Oryahovitsa fans proceed down, Tarnovo fans go up'.* We all went up, of course.

Upon approaching the main stand we sped up even more and I felt my heart began to beat faster. The ones behind caught up with us and seconds before the charge we were all together in a compact core. I just couldn't believe our luck and how easily they let us get there. There were violets all around. Our time had come and we went through like a hot knife in butter! We rammed through them in complete silence, no war cries and stuff. We just let our fists and boots do the talking. This was our second attempt to attack their main stand, but the first one, several years before (Gilly told you about it above) came from the inside of the ground, while this one came from the outside (something unheard of and unimaginable up to that moment). The Boyars couldn't believe their eyes and stood there in dismay. The element of surprise is always a benefit and once again we had taken advantage of it. Before they could get over it, organise and regroup, we hit them hard and there was this cacophony of police sirens, car alarms and shattering glass and all those scenes of chaos were shrouded in smoke. The violets were at a complete loss, crying *"Are you fucking crazy, what the hell are you doing here?!",* while we were kicking the shit out of them no matter that they outnumbered us 5 to 1 at least. Truth to tell, after the fight was over I took a good look around and I saw in the crowd a lot of officials, ex-players, official guests, managers, journalists, etc.

The funniest thing was (as seen on the pictures) that the cops intervened trying to stop the fight without any batons or other equipment and so they were caught up in a kind of a messy situation that we later called 'a rollercoaster train of horrors'. Since our main symbol is the locomotive, we still celebrate when our team scores in the same way. We call it "the train of triumph" and we also use this ritual to cheer up the crowd. What we do is stand behind one another and start running or jumping ahead in a row. Players have also picked it up and nowadays do it after they win a game.

7 Days of Sport Newspaper

Police detain four in Veliko Tarnovo: Police detain four in Veliko Tarnovo

---

Ahead of the derby game between local Etar and Lokomotiv (GO).

Later on they were released, but drawn statements of offence. The fans were involved in clashes during which the windows of two vehicles, a VW and a BMW, were smashed.

"Our colleagues' response was quite adequate as they put an end to the clashes around the football ground at their very beginning", commented the head of the Veliko Tarnovo police station, Colonel Yordan Doynov.

It is also reported that Etar FC players will receive for their 3-0 victory an additional bonus of 2000 BGN, granted by the local construction entrepreneur Doncho Karaivanov.

Correspondent Dimitar Nikolov

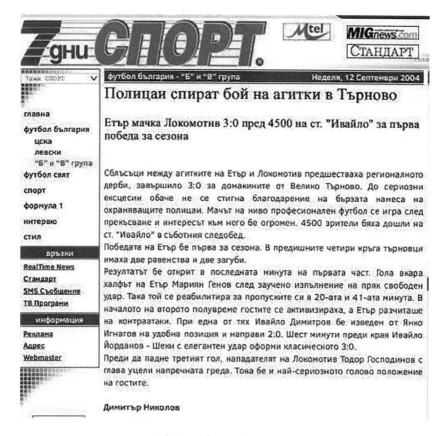

7 Days of Sport Newspaper

7 Days of Sport Newspaper

Police stop fight between mobs in Tarnovo

Etar FC crush down Lokomotiv 3-0 in front of a 4500 crowd at Ivaylo Stadium to win their first victory in the campaign

Clashes between mobs of Etar and Lokomotiv fans occurred ahead of the regional derby which was won 3-0 by the home team of Veliko Tarnovo. However, they couldn't evolve into any serious riots due to the timely intervention of the police securing the game. The professional division football match was played again after several years and attracted a huge number of spectators. A crowd of 4500 turned up at Ivaylo Stadium on the Saturday afternoon.

This was Etar's first victory in their campaign. The previous four games of the club from Tarnovo ended in two draws and two losses. The opener was scored in the last minute of the first half by Etar midfielder Marian Genov after a free kick set play. Thus, he made up for the opportunities he missed in the 20th and 41st minutes. Early into the second half, the away team was the active side while Etar relied on counterattacks. During one such episode Ivaylo Dimitrov was given the ball from Yanko Ignatov to score for 2-0. Six minutes before the final whistle Ivaylo Yprdanov-Sheki made it 3-0 with a precise shot. Before the third goal was scored, Lokomotiv striker Todor Gospodinov's header hit the crossbar. That was the visitors' biggest chance to score.

Correspondent Dimitar Nikolov

The last derby between our two rival teams in March 2014 showed that, like in nature and seasons, football also has its endless rotation. This time it was our turn to get promoted leaving our arch enemies (a renowned club) far behind. I am not a football expert so I will leave the analyses to those who really understand and comment on the game. I will pay attention to the fans' part and the issues I am actually familiar with. I am sure that the time will eventually come when some of them will read these lines and will just kick themselves, but those are facts that cannot be refuted. Lokomotiv brought to that game not just a mob, not only a big crowd, but dozens of black-and-white army squadrons (an absolute record for Bulgarian football standards, especially for its third division). Furthermore, it happened just a few days after the renovation of *Ivaylo* Stadium in Veliko Tarnovo was completed. It had the honour of welcoming its first visitors and finally seeing a capacity crowd. A fact that some people will have to accept, no matter how unpleasant it is for them.

The evening before the game we had a huge fan party that coincided with my name's day so I decided to combine the celebrations and invite everyone to join the party and treat them a few drinks (a tradition in my country). We had chosen the ridge separating our two towns that we already told you about at the beginning of the chapter, namely the Arbanasi area, to be the place for our party. In addition to its picturesque nature and amazing architecture, this place if famous for its traditional Bulgarian style taverns offering delicious meals and real homemade alcohol.

On the night in question, we had invited our habitual guests from our football alliances (Levski, Chernomorets and Spartak Varna), who were also represented at the party. To top it all, it was the International Women's Day (8ᵗʰ March), and about midnight, when we spread out our huge flags and banners (especially made for our choreo at the derby) and started singing our songs outside amidst the beauty of nature, we found out that actually there was also a ladies' party in the restaurant above us. So there were, approximately 40 drunken mad louts ready to tear apart our rivals on the following day, at a party together with loads of middle-aged women!

Some couldn't make it in the small hours and chose to end the night in the coziness of their soft pillows, but a good number of us decided not to go to bed at all and try to take by surprise our enemy. We tried to get in touch with the blokes beyond the hill and prearrange something in the early morning, preferably on the outskirts of their town, somewhere below the walls of the mighty fortress of Tsarevets.

Yeah, I know it may sound like a fairy tale or a film script, but that was exactly what we did! In the morning some of us took taxies and others (even crazier) walked the steep indirect path down the hill. Ultimately, at about noon, we were all at the gates of the former Bulgarian capital and we occupied the first pub, literally yards away from the entrance to the majestic citadel in Tarnovo.

The very place offers really imposing scenery that makes you shudder and get into a belligerent mood. Mobile phones started buzzing again as we once again tried to prearrange a fight before the cops smelt a rat, but then it was too late as the Old Bill arrived with their usual stupid requirements and regulations. They wanted to get us on some coaches and take us to the ground, but we refused to do so and decided to go for a corteo with our flags and banners across their town. After a brief quarrel, dissatisfied, they followed us as we had started to sneak away gradually (our standard tactics in such cases) and the last thing they wanted was a mob of Gorna Oryahiovitsa fans freely roaming in Tarnovo. The town was just waking up when our voices started echoing across the ancient buildings. We took out and held in front of us a huge banner reading "Pechenegs" to respond to their previous year insult in the form of banter in the streets of the former Bulgarian capital.

Going all that way (for some of us it was already full 7 miles after the morning walk), we didn't meet a single violet. It looked as if their town was not going to host a derby game on that day. We arrived at the ground too early and decided to hang around some crossroads in order to have a good view around. We got some beers and started singing our songs. All the time, cars decorated in black and white would pass by sounding their horns, to which we would respond with loud roars, while the town was still sleeping. In the late afternoon the black-and-white invasion got beyond control and the streets looked like the approach to Wembley ahead of an FA Cup final… More and more Lokomotiv supporters were coming for the big game.

Come the first whistle, both ends came up with great choreos. We displayed a 15-metre image of a "Demonic Locomotive", and they unfurled a painted mounted warrior. Security for the game was top level. After the Police Chief Secretary (by the way, a Lokomotiv supporter) had personally ordered his subordinates to send gendarmerie units, there was simply no way for us to even move an inch without being noticed. After the game we found out that a small mob of theirs ambushed the coach carrying our players and attacked it throwing stones, coming from behind some dust bins! As we sing in one of our songs, *"What a shame it is to be a Boyar"*, but courage, you Boyar boys, as this book will finally make you famous!

Meridian Match – Sports Newspaper

Bringing more than 2000 fans, the Northern Masters Clan broke a record at Ivaylo Stadium in Tarnovo

A game being attended by 6 or 7 thousand is already quite an extraordinary fact. Unfortunately, this is the reality and such numbers are actually unattainable by many top flight teams, including Litex, Slavia and Lokomotiv Sofia. However, when a crowd of that size goes to watch a third division game, we are talking of a real sensational event.

But when you get to know that we are talking about an Etar vs Lokomotiv (Gorna Oryahovitsa) match, you won't be that surprised anymore. The rivalry between the two neighbouring towns separated by the Arbanasi Ridge has a year-long history full of violent clashes both on and off the pitch. And after the last game from Northwest Division Three, despite the 1-1 draw, almost 2000 fans from Gorna Oryahovitsa felt like winners. To a large extent, it was them who should take credit for the magnificent atmosphere on the *Ivaylo* Stadium terraces, which reminded us of the times some 20 years ago when the "black-and-whites" were a notable side in the first division. "All our ticket allocation was sold out. We didn't turn out in such big numbers even when we played Etar in the top flight", Lokomotiv fans say. "In Veliko Tarnovo, we brought three times more fans than they did when they played in Gorna Oryahovitsa", the "railwaymen" are sure.

SIX

THE OTHERS

ONLINE INTERVIEW WITH **TOSH** ON THE *FANFACE* WEBSITE:

"We were definitely away days loving fans and we have always done our best to support our club. Naturally, away days in the towns of Gabrovo, Stara Zagora, Sliven and Tarnovo, where we would always take huge numbers, do stand out in terms of atmosphere because our team used to be famous for being a strong home side, but not an away one! Take this example – 20 men in the town of Dobrich on a 6-hour train journey. Or Kurdzhali – same number, 8-hour trip, etc."

Journalist: *Did you use any pyro and if yes, what was it?*

Tosh: *Regarding pyro, if you mean homemade red lead and bronze bombs, yes, we did, and we used them a lot. Making and carrying them were rather dangerous, but smuggling them into grounds was more than easy. We used to make smoke bombs out of ammonium nitrate and newspapers!*

Journalist: *Do you have any friendships and alliances with fans of other clubs and if yes, who with?*

Tosh: *We've got friends from Levski, Chernomorets Bourgas, Spartak Varna, i.e. the blue teams from the cities of Sofia, Bourgas and Varna,* as well as alliances with the "black-and-whites" from the town of Plovdiv, and last but not least (n.b.) with the oldest professional league club in the world Notts County FC, i.e. another black-and-white team from Nottingham. We got to know each other thanks mainly to mutual friends, students in Sofia, etc.

Journalist: *Now I'm gonna ask you a slightly embarrassing question whether you have been involved in any fights with rival fans!*

Tosh: *Embarrassing? Why? Some say fighting on the terraces is greater than having sex with any beauty, but this is not a question that could make me embarrassed in any way (laughing). Of course I have had such fights! Otherwise what are my words doing here (laughing again). I've been involved in a few brawls with Etar, 6 or 7 times, Gabrovo twice, Beroe twice, Shumen, Spartak Pleven, Dobrich, etc. Mostly on away games! You know, anyone can do it at home!*

SEVEN

ENEMIES

Botev Plovdiv

I REMEMBER BEING 12 WHEN I STARTED GOING TO FOOTBALL GAMES on my own to watch my beloved Lokomotiv (GO), who had been playing in the top flight for a few years after their promotion in 1987. Our team was doing relatively well at home, but it would ebb and flow away from home. That was why they couldn't make it higher than the middle of the table in the first division.

As we said in the previous chapters, we were a small club with no trophies, but we would boast of being a tough home side (having beaten a number of big clubs), having decent local players and passionate supporters.

On 26th March 1992 we were to host one of the biggest Bulgarian clubs, a team that had won a lot of trophies throughout its glorious history, namely Botev Plovdiv. They are nicknamed "the canaries" as they play in black and yellow striped shirts. Way back in 1963, when we first played in the top flight, we had battered them 5-2, a score to be long remembered. By the way, Lokomotiv (GO) had played quite a lot of successful games against them in the first division. Their fans had made a name for themselves as having one of the leading hooligan firms in the country and they would go on the rampage in every town their club would play. Even Sofia ultras were afraid of them, especially when travelling to their town of Plovdiv. The *Bultras* (that's how the other firms call them) were arch-enemies on and off the pitch with the fans of the other famous Plovdiv club, i.e. Lokomotiv Plovdiv, who, in turn, are friends of ours. Their rivalry can be compared to the one between Rangers and Celtic in Scotland, as their games are always preceded by fierce bloody street fights resulting in a huge number of arrests and a lot of material damage. Through all these years we have formed an alliance with Lokomotiv Plovdiv hooligans, which is still preserved nowadays, and so by default Botev are our enemies, too.

The long winter had been over, but it was still cold in late March and only a ray or two of sunshine would break through on that Saturday afternoon. The top division season was approaching its height and everybody expected a capacity crowd at Gorna Oryahovitsa stadium. As younger fans our job was to drape our flags along the fences of the Eastern stand, where we used to gather. I had had great respect for the lads from the future Jolly Roger Firm and our older supporters that I already told you about since the times I used to sit together with my father at the opposite stand during our home games. I think we were a mob of about 150–200 lads and Botev fans were, let's say, a hundred and they were sat at the Southern stand at approximately one hundred yards from us.

In those times stadia still had low fencing that was easy to jump over and that was the reason for the heavy police presence between and around the two rival sets of fans aimed at preventing a possible pitch invasion. The game was a nail-biter and both teams were on the attack and had a lot of opportunities to score so the crowd wouldn't stop cheering. I don't remember who scored for Lokomotiv, but the game ended in a 2-2 draw. We and the visiting supporters didn't stop supporting our team with songs and choreos including smoke bombs and red lead and bronze bombs, which made the atmosphere more than impressive. The verbal abuse and banter between us wouldn't stop, either. There were even those who tried to hurl ripped-off seats or other debris at their opponents, though it just didn't make sense due to the great distance separating us. The rest of our supporters would also boo and abuse the referee and Botev players, which is something usual for a football game of such importance and tension.

Shortly before the second half, at half time, a Botev couple (a boy and a girl) wearing black-and-yellow scarves, passed by our sector as if on parade. He was a skinny geezer with bushy hair and she was fat and wearing military boots. With an air of arrogance they made their way by pushing 2 or 3 younger kids who were straightening up our flags. The couple in question was then given some verbal abuse and after that a few of our lads literally threw them away onto the racing track. The cops had moved aside not assuming that something like that could ever happen. While the coppers were chatting and laughing out loud, they saw the couple being kicked out so they asked them what was going on. The two Botev fans complained of our offensive treatment. Meanwhile, a group of Botev supporters also saw the incident and headed to the area between the two stands, while we slowly dispersed and started walking towards them trying not to attract attention. There were no more than 10–15 of us because any large group of people separating from the others on the terraces immediately becomes suspicious. We covered about 100 yards regrouping and preparing for an attack.

We went for their first boys who were also heading towards us. Two cops saw us and tried to stop us, but we dodged them and we kicked the first line of Bultras the Kung Fu way. They just couldn't respond at first. We exchanged a few punches, but seconds later their other lads and more cops arrived. Absolute mayhem ensued as a great melee went on for a couple of minutes. A rain of kicks and fists showered all around. I was already down on the floor and our other lads were engaged with their lot. More cops intervened wielding their truncheons and hitting everyone in sight. Some were already arrested and were being dragged away by their feet. A cop hit me across my legs and truth to tell, it hurt like hell, especially when you're just a 12-year-old kid. A few of our lads had their heads cracked open or faces bruised while others were holding their ribs where obviously the truncheons had hit. Botev also had casualties so I can't say anyone got the upper hand, but definitely their lot was quite a decent one. The scuffle went on for no more than 3–4 minutes as huge police reinforcements arrived at the scene and restored order. So actually it was the police that finally got the upper hand and who could say what would have happened if everybody from the two mobs had joined the fight. They pushed us back to our sector while we kept on hurling abuse. Nobody got nicked and nothing else happened till the end of the game due to the increased security measures undertaken by the Old Bill.

We should definitely give respect to the Bultras, who in those years were probably the most proper football firm. Though their prevailing style was anarchistic and one could hardly speak of any organisation, they somehow managed to control all that chaos and were infamous as the greatest "destroyers" among football fans in Bulgaria. I knew well some of the faces in their front battle line and, mind you, they were not just anybody.

Several years before I had had the opportunity to watch them in action at the Cup final against Levski played in Tarnovo. The "cattle" probably outnumbered them 3 to 1 and had occupied the steps in front of the Tarnovo theatre. Two coaches with Botev fans passed by and the Levski boys threw a couple of bottles at them. Then the Bultras just had their coaches halted and got off without any hesitation, all primed for battle. Though in terms of colours they looked like a bunch of circus clowns (not only due to the prevailing yellow), as they had a lot of punks with gaily coloured crests, earrings everywhere, denim jackets and vests bearing the anarchy sign on their backs and other stuff typical of that subculture, they were well organised when it came to fights and, more importantly, they had people brave enough to fight.

So that was what they did then. Almost instantly and in an enviable speed they climbed up the steps in question and had the Levski fans dispersed in the nearby gardens. I could clearly see their ringleaders and, believe me, they were well-built middle-aged men who had tied bandanas round their heads and faces. They looked rough, extremely resolute and rather awe-inspiring for the "cattle" who just didn't wanna know anymore. Years later, I was going to meet those yellow Plovdiv anarchists a few more times, but generally speaking, despite the hostility, they deserved credit and respect for what they did in the past.

The next more serious clash between our two firms happened after 12 long years, on 18th September 2004, when Lokomotiv (GO) and Botev played against each other in the second division.

There were rumours that our mob would feature some Lokomotiv Plovdiv hooligans as we were on friendly terms with them. Probably that was the reason for the alleged threats of violence coming from the Bultras mainly on Internet forums that we cannot say were genuine, but videos of what happened after the game could be found on Youtube and I think they tell the whole story. Whatever the reason, we expected a huge turnout from them and JRF was also at its height and up for it. In those times Botev fans were also on the rise having one of the leading hooligan firms in Bulgaria that would go on a rampage unpunished in any town and stadium they played across the country turning them into real battle fields. That was part of the war they had declared against their club owner then. The club's financial instability and the club owner's attempt to sell the club resulted in acts of vandalism by their hooligans as they were trying to discredit and put additional pressure on him taking into account the considerable fines the club had to pay for those acts of violence and vandalism. There were also death threats against their club owner followed even by attempts made upon his life. Several games before, the owners of the club that hosted their away fixture threatened to electrify the away end fencing on their ground to prevent the Bultras from invading the pitch again! After that incident Botev fans must have taken themselves too serious and were probably looking forward to doing the same things in our town.

Whatever had happened before, we were ready and waiting for them on that autumn afternoon ahead of the game. We had taken about 50 lads in the park by the ground and were eagerly anticipating their coaches to arrive. However, they didn't turn up before kick-off time and we even began to doubt that they would arrive at all. Bitterly disappointed, we joined the rest of our crowd that had already taken out their arsenal of pyro and choreo stuff awaiting the first whistle. We already had the impressive for our standards mob of 300 fellas. Not many cops were around as security had been taken care of by private companies. Lokomotiv (GO) also experienced financial difficulties after their relegation from the top flight in 1994/95, alternating the second division and the Amateur league for some ten years, which resulted in the loss of interest in football for the majority of Gorna Oryahovitsa citizens. Probably that was the reason why the ground was not sold out for that game.

We stood there wondering why there weren't any Botev fans. We had read in the papers (including photos and a lot of info) that their fans were looking for a fight with some Plovdiv gangsters that had some tight connections with their club owner. We thought they were boycotting the game. A few minutes into the first half, however, we heard some bomb explosions and the roar of hundreds from behind the southern gates of the ground. For fuck's sake! Where the hell did they come from and why were they late? They stormed the gates spreading around beyond the area segregated for away fans and suddenly all hell seemed to break loose. They were more than 350 and like an avalanche they went down the steps of the southern stand onto the running track. The police escort hurriedly pushed them back into the away fans' pen. Most grounds had such types of fenced areas to prevent more serious aggro. They kept on throwing bombs and smoke canisters, gesturing and hurling abuse at us.

The police were finding it difficult to cope with them and the Bultras invaded the pitch a few times during the game. They tried to get into a fight with the security guards, but failed. The home fans' entire attention was directed at the away end rather than at the football though the game was quite interesting. We hit back by passionately supporting our team throughout the match, challenging our rival fans and throwing insults at them and their players. We also lit up a few smoke bombs and the atmosphere resembled a top flight game rather than a second division fixture. We really hoped something would happen come the end of the game. We hoped we could get into a fight with them as it was a matter of honour for us, · and besides, it was going to be a top football hooligan scene for

Bulgaria. We got even more irritated by the fact that Botev beat us 4-2. I can't remember any details of goal scorers and the like as my attention was more often drawn to the opposite end where the Bultras wouldn't stop making trouble for the Old Bill, who several times rammed through them using their shields and truncheons. A cop had got hit on the head with a stone and that actually escalated things. Their notorious hooligans did not fear the cops at all. On the contrary, they would fight them back with fists and boots. An angry mob of 350 brutal thugs against dozens of cops was a rather serious problem.

Tensions kept on rising with every minute gone and what everyone had expected actually happened just seconds after the final whistle. Some 100 of them invaded the pitch trying to get at us, but were challenged at the halfway line by several coppers and about 50 JRF. At first we were outnumbered, but still we engaged in a toe-to-toe fight throwing punches and kicks all around. There were fighting couples all around and a stunning brawl followed. One of them got knocked down and 5 or 6 of our lads started kicking him all over. Others were exchanging flying kicks. The Old Bill stepped in and tried to set us apart. A mate of ours, a Levski fan, was tussling with a Bultras bloke on the floor and had sunk his teeth into his throat just like a Pit bull would. The coppers were trying to pull him away, but he just wouldn't let go if his prey. I had never seen anything like that before. I felt like watching the *Hannibal* film sequence… Here is what he remembers of that incident:

"At a Levski vs CSKA derby, JRF lads invited me to a game in Gorna Oryahovitsa. The local Lokomotiv was playing at home against Botev Plovdiv. It didn't take them long to convince me as I have this certain aversion for that club and the majority of its fans. The reasons are quite clear: they are an ex-army club and good friends with their "big brother" CSKA, the primordial enemy of everything new and progressive. So there I was on that autumn day in 2004 attending a second division derby to support my mates' team from Gorna Oryahovitsa. Upon the very arrival I was able to feel the great football atmosphere, the enjoyment, emotions and anticipation of victory against the "canaries" from Plovdiv. On the

terraces there was real joy and excitement. Those are emotions that could be felt much better in smaller towns as they look forward to such big games all year long. For me the game itself didn't matter much, but it was different for my JRF mates. I was not the only Levski fan there. During the game I had this quarrel with a Lokomotiv (GO) fan, who also supported CSKA, but things didn't get out of control. After the final whistle and Botev 4-2 victory, the black and yellow mob invaded the pitch. This provoked us to do the same and to start a fight on the pitch, though we were heavily outnumbered at first. Once I was on the pitch I ran towards the halfway line to face two Botev blokes. I punched the first one and started wrestling with the second. My aggression and desire to go for a kill, as well as my adrenaline, were at their peak, and I just didn't notice the punches my body was taking. Time had stopped and it was only me and my victim. Later on, I realised how a man could murder another human being quite purposefully and cold-bloodedly. To understand my point better, I will now describe in details two of my actions then. First I stuck two fingers in his nose and ripped it. It felt like opening a beer. After that I sank my teeth into his throat and all the punches and attempts to separate me from him were in vain. Like I said, time was ticking away for me at a different speed. It had actually stopped and there was only silence.

After that game the press reports about us were, to put it mildly, rather negative, but for us, the ones involved in the action, it was a sheer victory or at least a kind of vengeance against the yellow scum."

The security guards could not handle it and more of their fans invaded the pitch steaming in at us. We could hear the shouts of the rest of the crowd encouraging the battle scenes. Several Botev had a go at one of our lads throwing loads of punches and tearing his clothes. Even the Gorna Oryahovitsa Chief of Police got hit in the melee.

More of our lads invaded the pitch hurling debris at our opponents while the cops were trying hard to push us back and restore order. However, it was all beyond anyone's control. The ground announcer went on pleading with both mobs to stop the violence, but no one paid any attention to him. Kicks and fists wouldn't stop flying, the players were running along the racetrack and some of their lot even urged people from the main stand to join the fight. I just can't imagine what could have happened if some men aged over 40 had joined the scuffle. More police carrying riot shields turned up, started dispersing us wielding their batons and eventually took control of the situation. Gradually pushing at the Bultras with their shields, they managed to drive them back to their end. Some got nicked and frogmarched out of the ground. The fight went on for no more than 5 or 6 minutes, but the scenes will remain in the history of football related-violence in Bulgaria forever.

The Old Bill got more backups and it was now hard getting through their lines. The two rivalry mobs went on exchanging insulting gestures and verbal abuse. The atmosphere remained tense after the skirmishes. The police started escorting the away fans to their coaches while we hurried out of the ground from its opposite end as we wanted to have another go at them. Nothing more happened around the stadium apart from them blowing up several bombs before leaving our town.

The game got extensive coverage in the press on the following day, videos were released in the social networks and it was top news for all hooligan circles in Bulgaria. It is still being talked about as our clubs did not play any official games against each other anymore as they got promoted back to the top flight and we remained in the second division. Lokomotiv (GO) actually played a friendly against them last year, but the game was uneventful, especially as Jolly Roger core scattered all around the world and our new generation is still "tempering the steel" as they say.

Here is the game account of one of our youngsters, a member of the G.O.Boys firm:

_____

"Playing Botev at home was one of the most significant games for us then. Besides, we had just climbed back to the second division after several hard years spent in the amateur leagues. It was the first time our ground was to welcome away supporters, particularly in such large

numbers, for a game in the second league. It was football day so I started drinking with a few mates of mine in the morning. We wanted to prepare well for the early afternoon game. I had this feeling that something big was going to happen and since I knew that Plovdiv hooligans were not always playing fair when it came to fights, I borrowed a knuckleduster just to be on the safe side. An hour before kick-off time the Bultras started coming to our ground on coaches and in cars. I was walking alone and I came across their column of vehicles.

Loads of them were leaning out of the side windows, showing indecent gestures and hurling abuse at random passersby. So I couldn't take their insults anymore and I grabbed the first big stone I saw, it was more like a cobblestone actually, and I hurled it at two skinheads sticking their heads out of the windows of their vehicle. My goal was to hit at least one of them but I missed as the car was moving and I just broke one of the side windows. The cops around saw me and started chasing me and I had to sprint really fast to get away. At half time, as we were drinking beer in front of the ground, I noticed a Botev fan at about 100 yards so I started walking hurriedly towards him. However, he saw me and took to his heels. I chased him all the way to the car park where they had left their cars and I was really on the brink of catching him when, unfortunately, I ended up nicked by the Old Bill. So that's how I missed the greatest pitch brawl in Gorna Oryahovitsa, all because of that stupid act of mine. Later, I even got a suspended sentence for the earlier accident when I threw the cobblestone at their car."

главна
футбол българия
    цска
    левски
    "Б" и "В" група
футбол свят
спорт
интервю
стил

връзки
RealTime News
Стандарт
SMS Съобщение
ТВ Програми

информация
Реклама
Адрес
Webmaster

футбол българия - "Б" и "В" група   Неделя, 19 Септември 2004

Агитки се млатят яко на Локо (Г0) - Ботев

Костадин Видолов вкарва два гола на края за гостите

Масов търкал заформиха феновете на Локомотив и Ботев след мача в Горна Оряховица. Двубоят завърши 4:2 за гостите от Пловдив. Фенове на двата отбора нахлуха на терена след последния съдийски сигнал. Близо 50 полицаи се наложи да ги усмиряват. На стадиона обаче са нанесени огромни щети, които са описани от длъжностните лица.

Ботев поведе с 2:0 след голове на Урумов в 22-ата и 38-ата минута. В 44-ата минута Кязимов върна домакините в мача, след като засече центриране на Бакърджиев. Петър Кънчев изравни 11 минути след подновяването на играта. Победата за гостите донесе Костадин Видолов, който нанесе прецизен удар от границата на наказателното поле 10 минути преди края. Отново той оформи крайното 2:4 от дузпа. За нарушението срещу Андонов съдията първоначално отсъди фаул, но след консултация с помощника си промени решението си.

ДИМИТЪР НИКОЛОВ

7 Days of Sports Newspaper

Mobs fight hard at Lokomotiv (GO) vs Botev game

Kostadin Vidolov scored 2 late goals for the final 4-2 for the visitors

---

Lokomotiv and Botel fans got into a massive fight after the game in Gorna Oryahovitsa that ended in a 4-2 victory for the away Plovdiv team. Supporters of both clubs invaded the pitch after the final whistle. It took about 50 policemen to restore order. However, the ground suffered great damage as game officials report.

Botev took a 2-0 lead after Urumov scored in 22nd and 38th minute. In 44th minute it was Kyazimov who scored one for the home team converting a good cross by Bakardzhiev. Petur Kunchev equalised 11 minutes into the second half. The visitors won the game thanks to Kostadin Vidolov who scored from the edge of the penalty area 10 minutes before the final whistle and then converted a penalty for the final 2-4. The referee first awarded a free kick for a foul against Andonov, but after consulting the linesman he changed his mind.

Correspondent Dimitar Nikolov

Dobrudzha (Dobrich)

This was probably one of our first coach trips away from the times we changed the railways for the allegedly more convenient but sometimes hard to organize coach journeys. The problem was that our first priority seemed to be the motto of ICJ (Inter City Jibbers & Grafters as described by another author in our genre, Colin Blaney), i.e. "To pay is to fail", and so the very organisers who took care of the trips would sometimes find it rather difficult and we would take fewer (than our usual) numbers to an away game. For a brief period it was me who dealt with trip organisation, and, believe me, I don't want to hear anything about such things anymore. We would resort to any methods to attract more people on the coaches so that they could be less expensive as a whole, ranging from free booze to girls on board, but I think coach away days continue to be a problem even nowadays. Second, it's the freedom you enjoy when you get on a train.

I remember a midnight trip to the town of Dobrich several years back in time, when absolutely spontaneously 15–20 of us got on the night train without buying a single ticket. We even didn't notice when we had arrived, but the most important of all was that we had evaded all kind of police supervision! Moreover, the trip itself was quite eventful as it featured what not, from vandalism to a fight in our own ranks.

I remember two of our lads starting a fight in the compartment and though they were completely pissed, they managed to demolish everything around and, to top it all, one of them literally lost his front teeth! He used to have such problems quite often as his real front teeth were long gone in a fight against the Old Bill and he had to wear implants but he didn't have them screwed, but glued instead. I will never forget the moment when, on my way to the toilet, I passed by the compartment in question and everything seemed fine and peaceful. The bloke smiled at me and his teeth were in his mouth. I went into the loo and all of a sudden I heard a thundering crash followed by that loud rumble. I went out to see what was going on and the geezer was already down on the floor looking for his teeth. He smiled at me again, but, naturally, without his front teeth this time. The light in the compartment was broken and they both had cuts and slashes on their heads and bodies.

On a number of occasions some would decide they had had enough so they would just get off at the next station and catch a train back home while others would have endless quarrels with the ticket collectors and would end up ejected from the train at some station where they would have to spend the night. Naturally, in the morning they would catch the next train without buying tickets again and that procedure would be repeated until they got to their final destination. The first to arrive would always wait for the others, which would sometimes mean waiting for hours. Taking into account that we would most often take night trains, in the mornings we would have enough time to wait for the others, organise and take advantage of the entire day ahead evading all police escorts and boring police instructions. Moreover, since train stations are generally located away from football grounds, we had a lot of time on our hands and the opportunity to do mischief marching through an entire town.

In the past the town of Dobrich was named after a Russian general Tolbuhin. It is situated in the northeastern part of Bulgaria near the Black Sea and the Danube (which is our natural border with Romania). The area is known for being the "granary of Bulgaria" due to the cereal crops grown there. Offensive or not, that was everybody's reason for calling their fans "straw boys". The town centre was full of marble-clad administrative buildings and morning walks there were a real pleasure, especially for classic intruders like us, sleepy, starving and ready to plunder.

But let's go back to our coach trip to the beautiful town in Northeast Bulgaria. The very trip turned out to be much more exciting than the forthcoming game and our encounter with the rival fans. In most cases no carrier would even like to hear about us and if they happened to agree to transport us, they would usually send their oldest and most dilapidated coaches for the simple reason that they were well aware of what the consequences might be. Those coaches were just going to be written off once the trip was over! In that particular case I was in charge of organising our trip and in order to avoid any responsibility I had got in touch with the father of a very good mate of mine who used to run such a coach carrier company. After a short conversation he reluctantly agreed and on match day he brought the weirdest vehicle I have ever seen in my whole life.

Generally the coach was in a good condition, but in order to prevent significant damage to the interior its owner had removed half of its seats. If only you had seen the big gap in the middle! Some would reasonably ask, *"Is that allowed by the road traffic regulations?"* Trust me, in those times anything was allowed in a country like ours and, believe me or not, we travelled some 300 miles on that coach and what happened on board was just difficult to describe. It was something one has to see as words are hard to find but still, I will try and describe it.

The very sight of the coach in question made the first who embarked it fall into ecstasy as they knew quite well what was going to happen on board. The missing seats had made really good room and it looked more like a moving party platform than anything else. To add to the "comfort" of the interior, there was this proper musical gear on board and once the first song started booming from the loudspeakers the lads were over the moon and simply went wild when that strange vehicle got going! I'll never forget the expression on the faces of all passersby who had the unique opportunity to see that vehicle rocking down the streets and heading out of town. You really can't see things like that every day! Our usual battle cries sliced through the air and, mouths wide open, people looked at us, probably wondering *"are those people inside or animals"*.

Right on the outskirts of our town, the Old Bill, having found out what was going on, immediately sent a patrol vehicle to escort us. On our way out of town we drove by some barracks still housing soldiers (In Bulgaria military service was still mandatory for all boys turning 18) and I'll never forget their sad faces, which, upon noticing the approaching coach, livened up for a while, probably seeing a kind of freedom bordering on anarchy passing by. Many of them smiled awkwardly and waved at us and our coach left Gorna Oryahovitsa rocking even more heavily.

Probably in an hour, our trip had turned into a kind of mobile party, a travelling disco club. It was a *"Let's go fucking mental!"* style revelry featuring abundant spraying and pouring huge amounts of beer under the sound of God knows what kind of music. When we first stopped to have a rest we had our first casualties as a few lads were carried out just like dead bodies in order to freshen up and continue the journey. I remember we even picked up two hitchhikers who we made friends with and we still keep in touch to this day. You understand that hardly anyone of us was going to have clear memories of whatever happened on the pitch that day..I remember we arrived late at the ground and the game was already underway. The moment we went in, we went straight for the home supporters end, which was not full anyway.

Adrenaline was running high and blurring our minds. We all had gone wild and into a drunken stupor. The cops pushed us back to the away end several times, trying to surround us as there were no special enclosures for away "animals" (fans) back in those times. We sure were wild animals on that day as we once again broke through the police line trying to have a go at the locals. After things had calmed down a bit, at half time I saw several of them approaching us so I said to myself, *"They must be out of their minds"*. We, in turn, also headed towards them. The coppers got busy again, but one of their lot relieved the tension as he took off his green-and-yellow (their club colours) scarf from his neck, waving hands, looking as if he was trying to give it to me, probably as a kind of gift, which in those times was simply unacceptable. I thought to myself, *"Are you being serious, mate?!"* I told him he was supposed to fight for the scarf, protect it with all his might, be brave and stand his ground. He was a young skinny lad, probably not aware yet of the value of what he was offering me so I gave him back his scarf and wished him good luck. A gesture that was also so unrepresentative of the times we used to live in and of our fan mentality, habits and disposition.

Maybe one could think that we got knackered and slept all the way back to our town! No, there was no way that could happen, mind you, we didn't have seats on the coach! The party went on in full swing! We blew up a smoke grenade on board and it started letting out orange smoke (we nearly suffocated) painting our clothes from head to toe. The coloured smoke went out through the open windows of the coach and all passersby were delighted that we were finally leaving their "marble" town.

Yantra (Gabrovo)

We are known to have a serious rivalry with another club from the region, i.e. Yantra (Gabrovo). Oh, what experiences we have had with the inhabitants of the town of Gabrovo. It was a great place to go to, if you're looking for aggro, although in those hippie years a major part of their hardcore was on friendly terms with both our lot and the Boyars. I also have a friend or two there and I think I have been on all our away days to Gabrovo. I dare say each of those days had the wonderful atmosphere of a regional derby. If I am not mistaken, in the year our club was officially established, i.e. 1932, the first game we ever played was against Chardafon (Gabrovo), which was the name they used to have in the nineties after their yet another change of names.

Yantra is a football club founded in 1919 in the town of Gabrovo, but in general their history is far from successful. During the nine seasons Lokomotiv (GO) played in the top flight we met them four times and in the autumn of 1993 their club was administratively suspended from playing in the top division. Their team plays in green and hosts its games at Hristo Botev Stadium having a capacity of 20 000. Most often our two clubs have played in the second division. Since Gabrovo is a town situated along the Yantra River on the northern foot of Stara Planina mountain, their fans were one of those so called "highlanders" who have always been tough to fight against both on and off the pitch and as such they were one of our great opponents and enemies.

Of course we didn't share such hatred as we did with Etar, but Yantra had a good number of proper lads that were always up for it. To be honest, they would usually put up a decent resistance against us. In particular, I think we had some tough times there in the early 1990s. I remember an away day there that saw some brawls inside the ground as a mob of theirs managed to make it through half of their sections, fighting the Old Bill, in order to get at us.

In the beginning I have to say that we would always travel to Gabrovo by rail, changing trains at some small station where we would get off to reload our booze supplies and wait for the change. The distance between our two towns is not so great and the train journey is relatively short, but still we somehow managed to get drunk even before changing trains. For that game some of our lads broke out of hospital where they had been hospitalised with alcohol intoxication. A few of them had escaped in their patient gowns and had to change clothes on the train.

We arrived at Gabrovo station and as tradition goes we sat down in the famous boozer right next to it. It only had a few tables and chairs in the open and our numbers on such away days there were simply beyond belief. We would usually take there between 150 and 200 tough lads and there would be serious trouble in the "town of humour and satire" (as Gabrovo is traditionally called in Bulgaria). In front of the railway station there was a small platform that would usually be used as the arena for our performances that used to include draping flags on the floor, pouring one another with beer, jostling (playing football with an old thrown out capor rugby with a rag ball).

Ahead of kick-off time we were all smashed and half of us were sleeping on our flags on the ground. Truth to tell, I could not see how those blokes would manage to get up and reach the stadium, but no matter how impossible it seemed to me, they actually did it! Then, we heard a loud roar coming from one of the side streets and there they were; the locals! At the same time, a bus stopped on our other side and out of it poured another mob of theirs, who blew up a couple of powerful homemade bombs. In seconds, everyone was up faster than soldiers on their routine morning exercise. It was now our turn to give out our mighty roar and have a go at them. The problem was we had to split in two to face them on our both sides. However, a third mob of theirs appeared in front, which meant that those blokes were not just anybody as they were well organised, had refined their tactics and were also good in one-to-one combat. Though our numbers were quite decent, at one point I thought they were going to do us. We were definitely caught off-guard and scattered in small groups all around. I got involved into a toe-to-toe with a thickset, strong boy (like me) and we were exchanging punches. What was going on behind me sounded like an apocalypse. Bottles, shop windows, car and bus windows were being smashed. In about five minutes, the sirens put an end to all that mayhem, and everyone was tired as if we had been fighting a nine-round professional boxing match. Everybody was moaning and cursing, some were spitting blood, but the majority just had their clothes torn and dirty due to rolling down on the street and pavement. None was seriously injured and the cops herded us like sheep walking all the way to the ground under a hell of an escort.

I already said that there were some serious clashes on the very terraces, but the icing on the cake was added after the final whistle.

I had the feeling that they were everywhere! I expected someone to appear from behind every corner and every bush and that was almost exactly what happened. As if their entire town had gone out to hunt us and our advantage in numbers was now gone. They even managed to nick one of our bigger flags and our older lads fought hell to take it back. Finally the Old Bill kept us all in the train station concourse for identification as there were some serious injuries, including stabbing wounds!

The funny thing was that when the injured lad was brought to identify who stabbed him, slightly bewildered and scared, he said that the perpetrator wore military boots. Then we each raised a foot and there was not a single different shoe. We all had military boots on! Naturally, we had made sure the perpetrator was hidden in a freight car outside (on the tracks) and the Gabrovo geezer obviously just played a trick on the cops and out of sheer fan solidarity he acted like a man and didn't reveal our lad.

During the years that followed, our away days in Gabrovo were just as exciting for us, but something happened with their lot maybe as a result of the change of generations. Later on, when we faced the same problems things started to get even, but despite both sides' fewer numbers, still we had good away days there. I remember more funny situations, as well as some not so pleasant incidents.

On one such occasion a good mate of mine got so drunk that he wouldn't stop throwing up in the coppers' feet during our usual escorted corteo from the station to the ground and he finally ended up not inside the police patrol vehicle but underneath it. It was raining and he slipped, lost his balance and after making a spectacular plunge ended up caught deep under the patrol vehicle. After the cops did even the impossible to take him out, he expressed his gratitude by puking again, but this time right in their faces! On the same away day, the heavy rain ahead of the game and the wretched condition of the away end benches almost involved me in an unpleasant accident as my foot got jammed in between and I nearly broke it.

On our last trip there we crossed the entire town as if on parade both ahead of and after the game and nothing happened, which was something unusual for Gabrovo! Our support there has always been proper and as far as its refined form we mentioned earlier in this book is concerned, we just showed an example how things should be done. For my part, it was my last away trip in that town and on that ground. It happened exactly in the height of our passion and unremitting terrace support as JRF members. I remember our core consisted of not more than 40 people, but the support we gave our club on that day will always be remembered by the locals. 2 or 3 years ago, there was this birthday party thrown by a close friend of mine in that town and I (not accidentally in any way) came across one or two lads from the past.

Actually, truth to tell, I asked about them and they were told to come and see me. We greeted each other, hugged like brothers after probably 20 years and found out that we had grown a little bit older and fatter, but that wasn't the point. We started looking back and one of them (nicknamed Joyce) immediately remembered the game in question and said, *"Hey, Tosh! You gave such an "English" support then that I just couldn't believe my eyes! I came to the segregation fence after the game to congratulate you, but the Old Bill didn't let me do it. So I do congratulate you now after all those long years"*. I also congratulate you, lads, and pay due respect (though we are enemies in terms of fandom) to you with these several lines. You know well who you are.

Probably the only, so to speak, disadvantage of theirs was the home game oriented nature of their support and their lack of proper turnouts at away games, but I definitely have great respect for them and place them among the top lads in Bulgaria in those times.

Spartak (Pleven)

It was September, 1995/1996 season, right before Lokomotiv (GO) got relegated from the first division. We were going to play away from home against Spartak FC from the town of Pleven.

In the "Why?" chapter we told you about our first away game experiences as kids, which were exactly in the town of Pleven. We consider this football rivalry as a derby since our first games against this opponent date way back to 1939.

Pleven is situated in Northern Bulgaria and with a population of over 100 000 it is the seventh biggest town in our country. It is has a central location between the Danube River and Stara Planina mountain. Their club has played 35 seasons in the top flight at their 25.000 capacity ground called Slavi Aleksiev. It was founded as early as 1919 and their team is known as the "white-and-blues". After the late 1980s changes (the fall of the communist regime) Spartak faced serious difficulties playing mainly in the second division. By 2001 they played three more seasons in League One but afterwards they settled down in the second league. The club relies on their own youngsters and talents just like our beloved Lokomotiv. Spartak Pleven is the first Bulgarian club to play in the Intertoto Cup tournament way back in 1964. In 1981 they played the Intertoto Cup for a second time in a group against the famous SV Werder Bremen, Malmo FF and Zurich FC. However, those "golden" years had long gone and so they were looking forward to playing the derby against our side.

During the season in question, Spartak had the Bulgarian waning star Plamen Getov playing for them. He was the idol of a whole generation of Spartak fans and Bulgarians. He is one of the players who have scored more than 100 goals in the first division. Their club had the reputation of a strong home side and they boasted of pretty passionate supporters. Our games against them have always been tough and full of clashes both on and off the pitch. That game did not make an exception...

The morning was bright and sunny. It looked like it was going to be a beautiful warm day promising a whole load of good emotions. The previous night in the Domino Bar we had made an arrangement to meet at the train station at 6:45 am as the train for Pleven was leaving at 7:30 am. The bar was our usual meeting point at weekends and on some weekday nights. It was in that bar that we drank till late the previous night (must have been Friday).

In the morning I found it kinda hard to get up as I had an awful headache due to the booze I had drunk and besides, it was so early. I had two cups of coffee before I set off, but they didn't make me feel any better. Obviously a few beers would always be the better remedy for a heavy hangover. We gathered about a hundred, a good mob for a second division away game. Some were still wearing tight jeans, black-and-white T-shirts, bomber jackets and the standard military boots. Gradually this fashion was fading away to be replaced by another trend in clothes and shoes. A good number of us were already wearing designer stuff, mostly shirts and trainers (copying the British casual scene). I remember I put on some Rifle tight blue jeans, a light blue Ralph Lauren shirt, Adidas trainers and an England cap then. I also had my black-and-white scarf. Before gathering at the station I had called some mates from the neighbourhood and we had arranged to meet up at the famous stairs (we described the place in the "7 Miles" Chapter). We would usually walk to the railway station as it only took us no more than 10-15 minutes going down those concrete steps. The others arrived in taxies as they used to live further away. We split into several groups and some sat in the nearby boozer. There was not much time to kill but still we had a few beers each. Hands held high, holding beers or other alcohol, we started singing out loud our club songs, put up a few flags on the streets and waited for the train to come.

As always, Tosh, I and several other lads started discussing a possible organised attack the very moment we would get off the train in Pleven. We had info that their fans would be waiting for us there. There were no mobiles or Internet then and so we weren't sure what to expect. Information would be word of mouth and on a number of occasions it would be just rumours and then all our plans would go down the drain. They announced the train departure time and the huge wave of fans spilled over the platform. Naturally, we were escorted by a few coppers patrolling the station.

We boarded the train and occupied the last few carriages. Sitting among old people, women and children, we draped our numerous flags on the windows and threw several bombs and smoke canisters out on the platform. People on and off the train got scared, wondering what exactly was happening. The cops could hardly find the words to calm us down and were at a complete loss what to do. Finally they decided to force us into the back compartments, moving their passengers into the front ones. So there, at the end of the train, we, loaded on booze and weed, had our party started. Songs were echoing all across the train and the atmosphere bordered chaos. The smell of weed and spilled alcohol was everywhere. Some were peeing out of the windows and others were sitting on the floor in the corridors. Bottles and metal ashtrays torn out from the compartments would occasionally fly out of the train windows. The Old Bill had not witnessed such scenes probably from 4th November 1987 when the mayhem caused by the mob from Gorna Oryahovitsa got into the chronicles of football hooliganism in Bulgaria.

We had police escort all the way to Pleven. The trip continued for about an hour and a half as the distance between the two towns is some 60 miles. Anyway, we managed to turn the train interior into a heap of debris even in such a short period of time. Most of us didn't have tickets and got accordingly fined. It was a novelty we found really hard to get used to. Of course there were lads who avoided the fines hiding in the toilets or beneath the seats or lying on the luggage racks covered in flags and clothes. In brief, we would always find a way to travel for free. Others were so stoned that they could barely stand on their feet and got warned by the cops that they would be either ejected from the train or not allowed entry to the stadium.

The moment the train reached Pleven, we started roaring like wild and we lit up several smoke bombs. To our surprise, there were no other policemen apart from our escort of 4-5 coppers. Imagine them and the hundreds fans in the background. We started getting off in groups. Full of energy and ready for more, we started kicking everything in sight and people rushed off in all directions. We smashed the windows of the ticket offices inside the station. A group of some 10–15 Spartak fans was waiting for us but they were just flabbergasted by our great numbers. We were also astonished by their small turnout. Probably they had been expecting us elsewhere. Despite their small number, we had a go at them and after a brief exchange of punches and kicks they quickly scattered. A few tables in the nearby cafes got overturned and we started throwing glasses, bottles, chairs, etc. at the runaways. When the police reinforcements arrived we had devastated everything around. Violence had taken over. I saw some of our lads diving in the street-side bushes laughing their arses off and they kept on doing that a thousand times. They must have started some weird kind of competition. As a result, we got heavily escorted all the way to the ground. There were police sirens wailing all around.

Two hours were left before kick-off time and the Old Bill made us take position in the stadium vicinity. There were a few boozers around where we went to have more beers. One could hardly call them pubs or bars as they were just small ex-garages converted into joints and they had those old-fashioned plastic chairs and tables outdoors. Typical meeting points for local piss heads. Some of us decided to take a rest in the park near the stadium. In just a few minutes a larger Spartak mob appeared and started throwing stones and debris at us. Chaos erupted so we grabbed our bottles (some empty but some still full) and stones to respond to the challenge. Chairs and tables also started flying around. The Old Bill intervened, baton charged and dispersed us. Finding it hard to deal with us, they forced us into the ground though there was plenty of time until kick-off. They pushed us into the away end. We put up our flags on the fencing, not higher than one yard in those days, and we wouldn't stop singing, our chants echoing all across the ground. We lit up a few flares and smoke bombs and threw them onto the pitch, making our end look like a battle zone. We were visiting supporters but one could get the feeling we were the home ones.

The ground was full, but it was only our noise one could actually hear. The distance between us and the Spartak fans was long. The game had just begun and we were already 2-0 down. Half time arrived and what we cared about was the much anticipated fight off the pitch rather than the score itself. What we eagerly awaited finally happened just before the second half began. Some of our lads were roaming around quite freely in search of potable water.

In those times there were those drinking fountains located around stadiums (not only) where people could quench their thirst, especially on hot days. Imagine the scorching sun blazing down the terraces where you stand having drunk lots of alcohol ahead of the game. It was real hell there with all that heat and sweat going down our bodies. Before they knew it, the blokes in question looking for water to freshen up found themselves in the home end and after exchanging some verbal abuse and gestures, went toe-to-toe with the locals. We could not respond that fast and besides, they didn't call for help anyway. They were just happily engaged in a fight with the home supporters, right there, in the very home end. I noticed several cops just standing there, chatting. I seized the opportunity and urged some 20 lads to come with me and have a go at the locals in the main stand. They must have thought I was crazy, but still they came along jumping over the low fencing. We made a dart for the opposite end crossing the pitch and shouting out loud. The cops saw us and started chasing us, but they could hardly catch us as they were too overweight. We were young and fast and most cops in those days looked like real pigs. We were almost half way through when utter mayhem ensued. A police squadron approached us, the players and team officials also intervened. Some of us were taken down under a rain of police batons and shields and some ran away in all directions. There were only three of us left against the enraged hosts and cops. We were showing them some obscene gestures and I yelled out loud, *"Come on, let's have it, you fucking bastards!"* Some of their lot started throwing objects and ripped-off seats at us. Three or four of them managed to break through security and had a go at us. I head-butted one of them while the rest were fighting my mates. We were throwing punches and kicks wildly, but they were hitting us, too. It went on for not more than 2–3 minutes when I got this severe blow in the head with a seat and blood spurted all over. The coppers also joined (I didn't know what they had been doing till then, but they must have been busy taking our other lads out of the ground) hitting us with their batons and kicking us hard. I was face down to the floor and one of them stepped on my neck and literally crushed my face while handcuffing me. Then they dragged me like a slaughtered animal to their police car. Behind me, they frogmarched the other two guys, one of them had his hands tied with a rope as the cops had run out of handcuffs. Fucking weird, isn't it?!

They loaded us onto the police van and took us to the local precinct. The drive didn't take long and we just laughed all the way wondering what was going to happen after all those brutal scenes. My only hope was to evade some severe punishment like a long stay in the nick. I was already 18, so as an adult things could get rather tough for me. Once you come of age you face all the dangers of being punished by the law. When we arrived, they pushed us into a cell that looked more like a cage with its wooden bunk beds. I got some medical aid for my head. We were told they would set us free in a couple of hours. Sitting down on the bunk beds, we were discussing how well things had gone and what we were to expect from the local police. We asked the coppers how the game proceeded in the second half as they were attentively listening to the radio bringing the news that our beloved Lokomotiv got battered 3-0. Despite that loss, we were absolutely pleased with ourselves and with what had happened. Well, it was not quite like the brawl we witnessed as kids in November 1987, when the black and white army (with our dads in their ranks) literally trampled down all that stood in their way, but I think we proved ourselves deep in enemy's territory, which meant a lot to us.

We got released later, when the game was long over and our mates had left for our hometown. Nothing happened as we walked along the deserted cobbled streets on our way to the train station in the late evening. It was pitch-dark and there was grave silence. What had happened earlier in the day just sank into the dark shadows of the night. After the morning hangover, now it was the headache from all the blows I had received. The place where the seat had struck hurt like hell. I also felt pains in my legs and body, probably the result of all those batons that had hit me. Once the rush of adrenaline was over I started feeling truly knackered and drained.

We hoped there would be one last train to Gorna Oryahovitsa as otherwise we would have to spend the night in Pleven, which was a dangerous venture in itself since we didn't want to stay alone even one more minute in the enemy's den. To our relief, there was a train and we managed to catch it. We slept all the way back, exhausted from the hard, but exciting day. When the train arrived in Gorna Oryahovitsa we were awaken by the loud cheers of our mates who were waiting for us at the platform. We got off the train and fell into their hugsas they were giving us this kind of hero's welcome. They asked us what had happened and if we had had any problems on our way back. Then we headed for our Domino Bar, where we stayed until dawn drinking and singing, looking forward to our next away game in the town of Pleven several weeks later.

Пияни фенове на Локо (ГО) атакуват трибуната в Плевен

Фенове на Локомотив (ГО) за малко не предизвикаха масово сбиване, след като нахлуха на трибуните на полувремето на мача на отбора със Спартак (Пл) в Плевен. Петима пийнали горнооряховски запалянковци пробиха до официалната трибуна и започнаха да редят обидни жестове и реплики към плевенчаните, които седяха там.

Плевенските полицаи обаче се намесиха и предотвратиха сбиване, което щеше да последва, ако скочеха и местните фенове. 15 минути преди края на срещата посърналата агитка на гостите кротко прибра знамената си и отпраши към гарата, за да не изтърве влака за Горна Оряховица.

НИКОЛАЙ ИВАНОВ

Drunken Lokomotiv (GO) fans attack the main stand in Pleven

Lokomotiv (GO) fans almost caused a mass brawl as they

invaded the main stand at half time of their game against Spartak in the town of Pleven. Five intoxicated supporters from Gorna Oryahovitsa made it to the main stand and started hurling verbal abuse and gestures at the locals sitting there. However, the police intervened and prevented the impending fight that would have surely started if the local fans had responded. 15 minutes before the final whistle the careworn visiting supporters meekly folded their flags and set off for the station in order not to miss their train to Gorna Oryahovitsa.

Correspondent Nikolai Ivanov

ПОЛИЦИЯТА ОТСТРАНЯВА ПИЯНИ ЗРИТЕЛИ

Група от около 20-ина привърженици на „Локомотив" (ГО) присъстваха на плевенския стадион „Славi Алексиев" при гостуването на любимия им отбор срещу местния „Спартак". На почивката между двете полувремена трима от тях в явно нетрезво състояние успяха да развалят доброто впечатление за групата, която се държа изключително коректно през първото полувреме. Държейки се неприлично, те успяха да стигнат до централната трибуна, отправяйки неприлични жестове и изрази към плевенските фенове. Само бързата намеса на плевенските полицаи успя да предотврати неприятен случай, а самозабравилите се хулигани бяха незабавно изведени извън стадиона.

Police eject drunken supporters

A group of around 20 Lokomotiv (GO) fans attended the away game of their beloved team at Slavi Aleksiev ground in the town of Pleven against the local Spartak FC. At half time, three of them, obviously drunk and disorderly, managed to spoil the good impression of their group, who behaved in quite a decent manner during the first half. Behaving in an outrageous way, they managed to get to the main stand showing obscene gestures and hurling abuse at the supporters from Pleven. It was only the quick reaction of the local police that prevented a nasty accident and the arrogant hooligans were immediately ejected from the stadium.

Storgozia (Pleven)

Only a few weeks later Lokomotiv (GO) played another game in the town of Pleven, this time against the other local club called Storgozia.

It was a relatively new club, founded after 1987 and it used to play either in the second division or in the Amateur League. Their nickname was the "greens". Their ground was called "White Eagles" and it could host a crowd of 12.000, but is now in ruins. Moreover, as far as I know this club does not exist anymore, or if it does, it must be playing in the lower amateur leagues that I know nothing about. A lot of such newly established clubs went bankrupt or were wound up due to financial problems.

During the 1995/96 season they were playing in the second division. There was not much interest in that game as compared to the match against Spartak, but still we decided to make the trip. There were some 25 of us, the usual suspects from our last encounter with Spartak fans. This time we decided to avoid the cops' presence so we had to be quick and cautious and keep as still as possible. The memory of our last battle was still fresh and I, personally, hoped to avoid any confrontation with the Old Bill as I was facing the real threat of being harshly punished by the law in the form of doing community service and being banned from football games for a certain period. Back in those years one could hardly be sent to prison for football related hooliganism. It would always be either a fine or community service. Now the picture is rather different as there are CCTV, videos, imprisonment and long-term bans.

In order not to attract the attention of the police we arrived at the station in small groups not wearing any scarves or flags. We had a few beers in the nearby pub and discussed any possible plans for attack in Pleven. Storgozia supporters often allied with Spartak fans so we expected to see some familiar faces. My group consisted of several lads. The others were led by Tosh. He had most of the hardcore lads with him. We also had this girl, whom we highly respected as she was the old school type of a real, genuine football fan. Each lad who turned up on this day had his contribution to our firm as an already experienced football hooligan.

At 7:30 am the train departed for Pleven. We had split up in smaller groups and probably for the first time in our lives we had bought tickets. We opted for paying the fare instead of getting into any trouble with police and ticket collectors. So we boarded the train and sat in different compartments in order not to attract the attention of others. One may say this was the beginning of the casual culture in Bulgaria as we started to travel in a more casual manner, without wearing any club colours or any other insignia.

There were a couple of cops patrolling the carriages, but they didn't have a clue we were going to a football game. Dispersed among the other passengers, without any excessive emotions, we surely didn't arouse anyone's suspicions. Truth to tell, we were playing away from home against a much weaker team, but we hoped something interesting would happen in Pleven again.

Surrounded by all those ordinary people, I found boredom and the monotonous rattle of the train along the tracks additionally irritating. I had the feeling the journey would last for eternity. First thing we did after arriving at the station was to look around and make sure no rivals were waiting for us. Alas, the platform was almost deserted but for a couple of passengers and two cops. We got off undisturbed and slowly made it to the exit, still in separate groups. The two coppers smelled a rat and followed those of us who were at the back. Tosh with a few other lads were in front.

Coming out on the street, they were the first to see some blokes hanging around on the opposite pavement. Tosh cried out, *"Here they are, let's do them bastards!"* There were about 10 of them beckoning us. They started throwing stones at us and we, never minding the two-cop escort, rushed towards our attackers. Once they saw us, they scattered in all directions hitting the narrow side streets nearby. We ran after them but couldn't get them and they vanished like a fart in the wind. Sirens started wailing, the cops were now on the alert and we had to sneak away fast. We arranged a meet in the centre of the town before heading for the ground as there was still plenty of time ahead of kick-off. We stopped in a restaurant downtown to have a snack and a few more beers. An hour before kick-off time we started for the White Eagles Stadium, walking in small groups at some distance from each other. We expected something would happen on the way to the ground as there was time for another fight, but actually it didn't.

On approaching the venue, several cops intercepted us and escorted us to the away end. It was unusually warm and sunny for the end of October. Some had to strip down to the waist because of the hot sun. Attendance was poor as if to prove the lack of interest in that game. Storgozia players were outplaying us, our team was easily losing the ball in midfield and so our opponents scored three. There were some strange decisions by the referee, but a 3-0 result showed expressively we had been outclassed. By the way, we were not surprised by the outcome of the game in view of the poor condition Lokomotiv was then. The memories from the relegation from the top division were still fresh and our players were finding it difficult to get used to life in the second division. Besides, there was a change of generations. Financial debts were accumulating fast, we didn't have a sponsor and our problems were getting increasingly worse. Some of the better players left and opened gaps to fill in.

To cut the long story short, we had fallen in a "black hole" and there seemed to be no way out of there. Disappointed by the score and by our failure to have a go at their supporters, we left the ground earlier and headed for the station to catch our train. On our way there we had scattered while chatting and discussing the game. No ambushes by local fans, no cops around, so we felt somewhat empty, having failed to do our duty.

The girl I told you about before was tall and had long black curly hair and a child's face. She was the first to arrive at the station along with a few lads. We, at the back, were far behind them. Approaching the station we heard a familiar voice calling, *"C'mon! Hurry up! B. is getting beaten at the train entrance and there are some 15 of them."* We got the shock of our lives so we ran like hell, not presuming anything like that would ever happen. We ran as fast as we could. This time we had to give those bastards a really good hiding. We reached our target and we hit them like a hammer. Punches were thrown and you could hear the sounds of teeth cracking. We punched and kicked them all over. The girl was screaming as they had grabbed her by the hair and were pulling it. Tosh threw a few mighty punches and took down the one who was holding her. He collapsed and got kicked even harder and longer by my mate. Two of their lot had taken down one of our lads and were kicking him real good. I managed to save him by kicking one of them right in the face and the other one straight in the chest. The others were also engaged in a brutal fight and the punches echoed across the concourse, where the brawl had spread. It was complete bedlam. Weird, come to think that both our mobs were few in numbers. People around were screaming, begging us to stop. Someone had called the cops as we could hear sirens in the distance.

We fought on like that for several minutes and finally we got the upper hand. When they saw the Old Bill coming they dispersed and ran away in all directions. We wanted to start a pursuit but the police intervened and stopped us. They remained in guard until our train arrived. B. was holding her head as she couldn't stand the pain from her hair being pulled for so long. The good thing was nobody got nicked. We were pleased and proud that we had managed to beat them hard on their own ground. Two successive away games against clubs from Pleven and we had been victorious on both occasions. Two derbies that we will remember for good and will keep on telling the younger generations of football fans what wonderful times the 1990s were.

Dunav (Ruse)

Dunav FC is one of our main competitors this season for promotion in the top flight. They are now top of the league and are one of the teams most likely to win a promotion for the first division next season.

The club is from the town of Ruse and was established relatively late, in 1949. Their kits are all sky blue and their nickname is the "dragons". Ruse is the biggest Bulgarian port on the Danube, situated in Northeast Bulgaria on our border with Romania. The most successful period for that club was when they played in the top division from the early 1960s to the early 1990s, finishing fourth in 1975 and playing in the UEFA Cup versus AS Roma, winning 1-0 the home game in Ruse. They have been crowned League Two champions five times and are one of the strongest sides in Bulgarian second division.

It was in those "golden" years for their club that we played them a few times. From the mid-1990s to the early new millennium they used to play either in the second division or in the amateur leagues and they went bankrupt twice. After 2003, supported by some local businesses, they started from the lowest level of Bulgarian football. In 2014 Dunav Ruse won the Amateur League and returned to the second division, where they are one of our greatest rivals for winning the title and getting promoted to the top flight.

Here is what a friend of ours, an eyewitness and participant in the events that happened in the Danube town in the late 1980s, has to tell:

"Apart from Etar (Veliko Tarnovo), Yantra (Gabrovo), Spartak (Pleven) and Litex (Lovech), probably this is the other Northern derby in our region, taking into account that the distance between the towns of Ruse and Gorna Oryahovitsa is only some 60 miles. A train journey is not so convenient for this particular destination and in recent years coaches have been hired. However, some of us chose the train on that occasion and arrived in Ruse the previous day. Unsurprisingly, in the early hours following their arrival, 10 of our lads clashed with 50 locals in one of the railway station subways and were naturally defeated and forced to seek refuge in an old, abandoned and rundown velodrome. As in those times there were no mobile forms of communication, they managed to reach us via payphone, inform us of what had happened and warn us of what we might expect. So, we prepared a serious invasion and I was kindly asked to make a dozen of my pyro specialties.

We let them know we had arrived in their town in our traditional way by lighting some pyro and then headed for the ground, where we occupied the Bordeaux beerhouse. We knew well that it was their territory and they used to gather in that boozer ahead of each game… Naturally, we were looking for confrontation with the locals in order to take revenge on them for the fight we had lost the previous night. We must have brought about 200 lads and the locals were nowhere to be seen. Evidently, they could not match our numbers and they had to put up with it. The pub was completely taken by us and we decided to go on a binge before kick-off. We happily started shouting and singing our then traditional "It's on the house" chant. In addition to being not so fond of buying tickets for the train, we just loved drinking and having fun in pubs for free.

The match was supercharged and we got all that hostility from the entire ground. Come the end of the game, it kicked off everywhere in the streets. Running battles with the locals, we reached the velodrome in question, where we had it toe-to-toe with their mob. Neither side could get the upper hand as our numbers were almost equal. 300 fought that battle, 150 for either party. Generally, such thing would rarely happen on our scene, or at least I could hardly remember any occasions when the numbers were even. Another surprising thing was that on the battle field there were no debris that one would usually use when the going gets tough. Though the place was in a wretched state (almost demolished) there was hardly a stone around. So what we had was a good old toe-to-toe, no weapons or tools used. I also decided to play fair and didn't resort to any of my gadgets. During all those years our teams almost never crossed each other's paths due to playing in different divisions and so there was no chance for either party to look forward to taking revenge. Anyway, believe it or not, call it fate or whatever, but at this very moment as I am writing these lines, Lokomotiv is playing away in Ruse."

After the events described we played Dunav Ruse once only. I believe it was in the late 1990s when both our clubs were in the Amateur League. Not many Dunav fans turned up then. They were in a severe financial crisis, had huge debts and as a result, had settled for mediocrity. The same went for us in those times, by the way. We had great games followed by some absolutely wretched performances. Their supporters had left the scene, as we used to say, so we weren't expecting any trouble.

We took the train again, some 50 of us. We arrived at noon and decided to have a drink at the already mentioned Bordeaux beer house. There was no trace of local fans in their favourite boozer. Having drunk loads of beer and sung our songs, we were off to the ground.

Walking down the Danube town street we went on chanting and some tired to stop the traffic on one of the boulevards. Bedlam ensued due to the constant sounding of horns, the cries of passersby and our shouts and chants. A hundred yards ahead we saw some Dunav fans, not more than a dozen. They kept at a distance, though. We exchanged some abuse trying to outshout each other and then a shower of debris thrown in both directions followed. Dustbins were being overturned, bottles and other objects hurled. We simply blocked the traffic and people around were begging us to stop it. Some fella got out of a car (a Trabant) and started shouting angrily at us. Then 6 or 7 of our lads grabbed the car and just overturned it! Imagine the expression on the driver's face, who just panicked and ran for help. Then the Trabant doors got dented after the rain of kicks that followed. Kicks and punches were also thrown at several passersby. We then regrouped and had a go at the home fans standing across the street. We dispersed them after we showered them with stones and other debris. They took to their heels into the narrow side streets, but we went on to chase them all the way. Then we heard the sound of sirens and in a few minutes several police vehicles arrived. The cops surrounded us, we had some verbal argument with them regarding the overturned car, and then they escorted us to the ground. There was no way for them to nick anyone for that accident since they would have had to nick our whole fifty-strong mob. Nothing significant happened until the end of the game, attendance was low and after the final whistle the Old Bill escorted us back to the train station.

As we were writing this (02.04.16), Lokomotiv (GO) was playing away in Ruse in the second division last round in a direct clash for winning the league. Some 100 hardcore Gorna Oryahovitsa supporters made the trip but there were no brutal scenes like that anymore due to the strict police security measures.

Nikopol and Lom

From 1997 to the spring of 2014 Lokomotiv (GO) played in the Amateur League, going up to the second division for only one season.

It was a period marked by a long and severe financial crisis, endless fights for power within the club, neglected youth academy, rundown training facilities and no interest at all in what was happening. The club hit rock bottom, there seemed to be no hope and we were on the brink of winding up. Loads of people left the football scene and attendance fell down to almost zero. Naturally, it was all due to the fact that the crisis went on for nearly ten years and nothing would ever change in that period. We would rely on local players who would play their hearts out on the pitch, but the lack of funds had taken its toll. Despite all those problems, the main core of 30-40 lads (a mixture of old and young generations) kept on supporting the team everywhere they played. Of course, there were some hooligan riots at games, but not as often as there used to be in the 1980s and 1990s. But even so, the Chief of the Regional FootballCouncil then used to say, *"Our only worry comes from Lokomotiv (GO) fans as they make trouble everywhere they go."* Trouble broke out in the town of Nikopol and Lom, where our away games were marred by brutal outrages. Since I didn't attend those games in the flesh, I leave it to two of our lads to tell the story of what they witnessed on those away days:

Nikopol and Lom are two towns located on the Danube River in Northern Bulgaria and their clubs Sitomir (Nikopol) and Marie Louise (Lom) played in the Amateur League together with our beloved Lokomotiv (GO). Both clubs were famous for nothing else but their hostile supporters, who would sometimes influence game results as they used to intimidate or even beat referees. In those towns football was the last thing on their minds during games, our players would often be maltreated and badly injured, which additionally used to make the atmosphere red hot. In spite of the number of letters of complaint, the Regional Football Council did not care to take any measures regarding safety at those grounds. It was more like rugby or wrestling witnessed there rather than football. Those games were usually not guarded by police and even if there were some cops they would usually take the side of the local fans. To cut the long story short, it was downright scary to visit places like those if we were to take small numbers. It was a kind of nightmare that kept on haunting us. They have never had any organized mobs or firms. There was just that crowd of people (I'd call them peasants), sometimes armed with planks of wood that they would wield in the air and they would keep on hurling verbal abuse at our players. It looked like a scene from the Middle Ages rather than our modern world. The footballers of those two teams looked more like gangsters or rugby players of similar body weight. Both our away games in 2011 were marred by outrageous scenes typical of action films that had nothing to do with football. We travelled by coach on both occasions, being not more than 20–25 people, which was considered a rather small turnout.

The game in Nikopol was in late autumn and the pitch looked like a muddy field. The conditions were simply horrible. Under the unremitting rain, the Sitomir players used all kinds of forbidden means to win the game. They kicked and pushed our players, their tackles were getting increasingly brutal and the referee kept on favouring their side under their fans' constant boos and insinuations. Emotions got really hot as one of the Lokomotiv players was continually being maltreated due to his fast raids and dribbles that made the home side players really edgy. During one of his raids, a home player viciously tackled him from behind but was not shown any kind of card. Our players' response was furious this time as they surrounded the referee, but he remained silent and then it got really nasty as some cops ran onto the pitch and started pushing our footballers away. It was an absolutely unprecedented outrageous conduct by the police. One of the coppers even threw a punch at our fouled player sending him down on the ground a whole yard away. We tried to invade the pitch and intervene, but were met with a shower of baton blows. Some local blokes carrying lumps of wood stepped in hurling insults and threats at our players and officials. The game was on the brink of suspension. To top it all, come the end of the match, the Lokomotiv (GO) coach had to go to local police precinct, where, to their greatest surprise, two of our players were taken down and taken in custody for 24 hours charged with affray!

The away game in the town of Lom was no different in terms of what happened on the pitch. It was another massacre as players pushed, kicked and tackled each other as if going for the kill. We were twenty-something againtravelling by a minivan. Ahead of the game we sat somewhere near their ground to have a few beers. We sang and chanted. Minutes before kick-off time, passing through this neighbourhood right next to the stadium, we saw a few dark-skinned boys who started throwing insults and threats at us. We immediately had a go at them and dispersed them in a shower of stones and debris. We went on walking but in just a few minutes some thirty men appeared and stood in our way. They were all carrying bludgeons, pitchforks and rocks and it was plain to see they were there to fight us. What could we, say 25 of us, do against such savages who had come to help the ones we had attacked earlier? They started throwing stones and rocks at us, but the Old Bill's quick response calmed things down. The angry mob continued shouting and wielding their weapons. Police reinforcements arrived, dispersed the crowd and even nicked those more unruly of their lot. Fortunately, we didn't have any casualties. I can only guess what a bloodbath that day would have turned into but for the cops' intervention. Someone would have surely died there! The game itself was not interesting at all, apart from the reckless tackles we witnessed. On top of it, we got beaten 3-1, two of their goals being scored from offside positions. Thanks God we do not play away games in towns like Nikopol and Lom anymore because if we went on doing it I just don't know what could really happen...

Here is what another Lokomotiv supporter has to tell about the experience he had on that away day in the town of Lom:

"One of our most remote away trips in those times was to the town of Lom, some 130 miles away from Gorna Oryahovitsa. It meant a long trip along the potholed roads of the Northwest. There were 4 carloads of

us and I and a mate of mine had primed ourselves with loads of booze, though we had drunk it all by the time we arrived in the Danube town. There we looked for a pub in the centre of the town as there was plenty of time before kick-off. With no coppers around, we started singing and chanting to the top of our voices and the locals would just stare at us in dismay. Some of us would take a pee right there on the grass in front of the boozer, which additionally irritated the bystanders and made them appalled at our behaviour.

An hour ahead of the beginning of the Marie Louise vs Lokomotiv (GO) game we headed for the ground, which was situated near a gypsy ghetto. We had scattered along the street and I was walking in the back along with my mate (the one we had started the journey with). Three boys came from the nearby hill and they were chased away by us with a rain of fists and boots. We two also had our contribution, you know. Some 15 minutes later we arrived at the ground where about 50 men were waiting for us in order to take revenge. We had a toe-to-toe with them and my opponent was a huge bloke who had clenched his fists and had so many rings on his fingers. We exchanged a few punches and I had my lips cracked, blood pouring down all over my clothes. For 2 or 3 minutes we stood our ground, but then more locals arrived and their number probably reached 100. We got encircled and they started throwing stones at us. Some were armed with bits of wood and other tools. We regrouped and tried to fight back by also throwing stones and debris at them, but we were heavily outnumbered. We were desperate, but eventually got lucky to see two police cars arriving at the scene. The locals went on trying to get at us and were still throwing at us whatever they could find and then a cop took his gun out and wielded it before the unbelieving eyes of everyone around. Things calmed down and they managed to finally separate us. More police backups arrived and they took us into custody while those injured were taken to the local hospital. We couldn't watch the game, but still it was a legendary away day...

футбол България
футбол свят
спорт
волейбол
форум
живот

коментари
е-7 Дни Спорт
Добави Коментар

информация
Реклама
Адрес
Webmaster

футбол България   Вторник, 19 Април 2011

Футболисти на Локо (ГО) арестувани на терена

Безпрецедентен екшън беляза поредния кръг в Северозападната „В" група. Двама футболисти на Локомотив (ГО) пренощуваха в ареста на РПУ - Никопол, след което им беше повдигнато обвинение по указа за борба с дребното хулиганство. Стефан Бакърджиев и Красен Славчев се оказаха с мярка за неотклонение „задържане под стража" за срок от 24 часа. Това се случи след мача на техния Локомотив с местния Ситомир (Никопол).

Пожарът пламна между 65-ата и 75-ата мин, когато няколко пъти Стефан Бакърджиев бе малтретиран от футболисти на съперника. При едно положение до самата тъчлиния Бакърджиев бе подкосен отзад. Той разпери ръце и подвикна на съдията: „А сега картон няма ли?" Той и съотборниците му изригнаха, когато реферът Никола Петров отсъди само странично хвърляне, и го заобиколиха да му търсят сметка.

- Да, може да сме го бутали, но не сме го удряли, не сме го и псували. Останахме безкрайно изненадани, когато нахлуха униформените и без да се церемонят, започнаха да ни блъскат - разказа Пламен Иванов от Локомотив.

След мача ръководителят на охранителната група разпоредил Бакърджиев и Красен Славчев да се явят в местния участък за снемане на обяснения. - Бяхме потресени, когато разбрахме, че Стефан и Красен остават в ареста. Какво му е престъплението на Стефчо? Че потърси обяснение от съдията за бруталните влизания на противника ли? - недоумяват неговите колеги.

Димитър Николов

7 Days of Sports Newspaper

Lokomotiv (GO) players arrested on the pitch

The latest round of the Northwest Amateur League witnessed an unprecedented action. Two Lokomotiv (GO) players spent the night in the nick in the town of Nikopol after being charged with affray. Stefan Bakurdzhiev and Krasen Slavchev ended up taken into custody for 24 hours. It happened right after the game between their club Lokomotiv and the local Sitomir FC.

Trouble started between 65th and the 75th minute, when Stefan Bakurdzhiev got maltreated by rival players on several occasions. On one of those occasions, right by the side-line, Bakurdzhiev was tackled from behind. He spread his arms and cried out to the referee, "Won't you show him a card now?"He and his teammates went ballistic when the referee Nikola Petrov awarded a throw-in only and they encircled him looking for an explanation.

"Sure we may have pushed him, but we neither swore at him, nor hit him. We were extremely shocked when the police invaded the pitch and without thinking twice started to shove us", said Lokomotiv player Plamen Ivanov.

After the game was over, the chief security police officer ordered Stefan Bakurdzhiev and Krasen Slavchevto appear t the local police department to give testimony.

"We were stunned when we were told that Stefan and Krasen would remain in custody. What crime did Stefan commit? Asking the referee for an explanation of our opponents' brutal tackles?", his colleagues are bewildered.

Correspondent Dimitar Nikolov

A football mob beats up gypsies in Lom

Lokomotiv (GO) fans storm a house and are driven back in a hail of stones

The Roma strike back with rocks, pitchforks, screwdrivers and claw hammers

Lokomotiv (GO) supporters beat up two fans in the town of Lom and then stormed a house shouting, "Charge!". The accident happened before the Marie Louise vs Lokomotiv

(GO) gamefrom the fatal 13th Round of the Northwest Amateur League. On route to the ground the belligerent Gorna Oryahovitsa fans started another fight. Some 30 men come to the rescue of their friends from inside the ground showering the aggressors with stones. It was only the quick reaction of the police that prevented more horrible consequences. However, it is still a mystery why the policemen didn't escort the away fans, who started shouting Nazi slogans the very moment they arrived at the train station.

Correspondent Petyo Petrov

Beroe (Stara Zagora)

Beroe from the town of Stara Zagora is one of the biggest Bulgarian football clubs. The town is located in South Bulgaria, in the Eastern part of the Upper Thracian Plain, between some hills and the Sakar Mountain.

The club was founded way back in 1916; they are nicknamed *Zaralii* and became Champions of Bulgaria in 1986. They play their home games at Beroe Stadium with a capacity of 12 000 that boasts the largest ground roof in Bulgaria, brilliant lights and is fully renovated to meet UEFA requirements. It was one of the grounds that hosted the Under 17 European Championship in 2015.

The club's glorious years were in the 1970s and 1980s when they, led by their legendary striker Petko Petkov, battered the Austrian giants FK Austria Wien 7-0. They also played for the UEFA Cup Winners Cup outclassing the Spanish side Athletic Bilbao 3-0. Beroe were eventually knocked out by the German FC Magdeburg who later on won the final game against AC Milan and lifted the cup. In the 1980s, and till the late 1990s, Beroe were a constant member of the top division, where Lokomotiv played them in all our 9 top flight seasons. Then, after the democratic changes in Bulgaria, Zaralii had some financial difficulties and were on the brink of going bankrupt, but some local businessmen saved the club and since 2009 their team has been playing again in the first league, winning the Bulgarian Cup twice, in 2010 and 2013.

We were to play an away game to Beroe Stara Zagora. I think it was the destination we would most frequently visit. My personal record was 9 away league games there, not missing a single away day (counting from their Champions year of 1986 and our promotion to the top flight in 1987) plus a cup fixture. Quite naturally, we started our party right there on the train, where some 200 "black-and-whites" repeated their weekly ritual going on the piss on wine, rakia and beer.

The usual squabbles with cops and ticket collectors were quickly over, or were in any case muted by the two huge drums that we used to carry everywhere we went in those days. Of course, the problem was that, as always, we were travelling with a 100% discount, which had become a kind of craze and was broadly discussed with the law enforcing authorities. We would almost every time get away with it finding an excuse in the fact that we were "railwaymen" and it would be pretty absurd to pay any railway fare!

However, some had had too much to drink and got taken off for a breath of fresh air waiting for the next train. Along that particular line, it would usually happen at some mountainous train station, where the offenders were given the chance to get sober pretty fast breathing in the fresh air from nature and so the next train would always bring some old, but so to say refreshed reinforcements. On such occasions I have always looked forward to the train departures and arrivals. These are simply great moments and I remember quite a lot of them. The song we used to sing every time we entered their town, which began like that, "*At the train station in Stara Zagora, shouting out loud...*", coming for the noon train made the locals wonder whether some animals had not been accidentally let out of some zoo!

The train had not come to a standstill when we all started getting off through windows and doors and some ended up rolling down the platform. One could see some half-naked and barefoot lads, but the climax was definitely a geezer who got off the train like a real magician. He climbed down a window when the train was still in motion holding a bottle of wine in each hand, rolled out onto the platform and got up triumphantly keeping the two valuable bottles intact! In just a few seconds, the surprise on people's faces turned into fear and horror and their curiosity vanished fast. The station got deserted, the number of coppers grew and we occupied the famous large park next to the station singing on the next part of our song *"... we kicked Beroe's ass again carrying bombs in our hands..."* and then we put up our flags on all the trees around.

By tradition, we decided to stay there and wait for the ones who had been taken off previously and were expected to arrive on the next train and besides, it was too early to go to the ground. Suddenly, word went out that huge numbers of "green" fans were heading our way. The park was immediately ravaged and turned into a fortress. We overturned benches and made piles of collected stones and whatever else we could use as weapons. We were looking forward to facing the enemy that never came anyway. Two hours after our arrival there was still no trace of any home fans. Our missing part of supporters arrived on the next train and got quite a shock when they saw our preparations for defending against the local fans. What followed were bits of wild laughter and self-irony at our stupid idea to put our trust into some fucking rumour.

So this away day, understandably, became famous later on among our fans by the name "The Barricades".

On another occasion involving similar invasion (about 180 people) of ours, we followed a similar scenario in the park and decided to wait for our mates who had been taken off the train during the journey, killing time by playing rugby with an old frayed and torn cloth football we had found, which, only God knows how, had taken the shape of a rugby ball.

We were just having the time of our lives, playing so passionately that even the "All Blacks" could have envied our skills and zeal. We were having fun running all over the park and got so involved at some point that the ball started flying across the adjacent streets.

Before long we had a crowd watching us, which made us even more inspired. Judging by the clamour around, the locals started to like it. Unfortunately, the Old Bill appeared and, as they always do, they spoilt the party and I dare say there were no problems whatsoever before their arrival. We were just letting off steam playing rugby in a park in Stara Zagora. After we almost started a fight with the cops, our mob got extremely aggressive. We started for the ground going on a rampage and destroying everything that stood in our way.

Naturally, our first victims were the shops and their shop windows. The shop assistants only just managed to lock the doors and run away. It turned to absolute bedlam, the height of it being an overturning of a green Moskvich (a big and heavy Russian car), which could surely be envied by even the strongest powerlifters. I said to myself, *"Never underestimate the power of alcohol"* and I saw a man standing on a nearby balcony holding his head in disbelief and shouting insults at us. All along the way to the stadium the locals would hurl all kinds of household items such as flower pots at us and even pour buckets of water on our heads! However, nothing could stop the ravaging mob on its way to watch their beloved team.

On another away day we directly started a fight with the coppers. I remember we arrived at the ground rather early (as we were no longer allowed to stay in the park) and by and large, we were wondering what mischief we could do. We chose to jump over the fencing and enter the ground ticketless. Out of the blue, a dozen cops appeared and started taking us off from the stadium fence by pulling our legs and hitting us hard with their truncheons. Some had already climbed over the top and were caught in a dead-end street situation. The local guards also appeared from the inside of the ground. They started rocking the fence violently as if they expected our lads to fall off the fence like ripened fruit would do off their trees.

Never before in my life as a football fan had I seen anyone rock a fence with such rage and spite (taking into account that after all, those were security guards that were supposed to prevent such incidents). Understandably, we tried to help our mates and several lads got nicked. However, we persevered and, truth to tell, were smashed by the police truncheons! It was also the first time I had seen a truncheon break into a human head and it was a funny thing as we were all waiting for the geezer to stagger and collapse, but to our great surprise and also much to the surprise of the cop with the broken truncheon, not only didn't he fall down, but started shouting angrily in the copper's face, *"Why are you hitting me, you pig?!"* For a brief moment everyone paused and went silent and the policeman kept on staring in dismay at his broken truncheon. Seconds later, rage found its way into our heads again and we had a go at the cops and guards in a wilder and even more violent manner. It continued all through the game and come the end of it we went so fucking mental that after we got escorted to the railway station, we decided to take it out on a nearby club where we had a good ruck with the locals before catching the midnight train.

As a whole, during our 8 or 9 trips to Stara Zagora we didn't meet any proper opposition. There were a couple of minor accidents involving not so many people, but, generally speaking, I would surely give no credit and pay no respect to *Zaralii*, especially as we all know about their alliance with the "violets"!

Sliven

Sliven FC is a club from the town bearing the same name, situated in Southeast Bulgaria and also known as "the town of the 100 voivodes", closely related to the resistance movement in our country during the times of the Ottoman Empire.

The club was founded in 1949 and their nickname is the "Voivodes". Their most successful period was after 1974, when they won the second division title and got promoted to the top flight where they played for not fewer than 19 season, relatively well at that, and even finished as high as third in 1983/84 season after Levski and CSKA. It was then when Lokomotiv (GO) played them in the top flight. Their team was a hard nut to crack for most other clubs and we also had problems playing in the town of Sliven. Their greatest achievement was in 1990 when they won the Cup beating CSKA in the final 2-0. In the late 1990s they found themselves into a severe financial crisis and were relegated down to the Amateur League. Eventually the club went bankrupt. Their rebirth was in 2000, when the famous Bulgarian player form the USA'94 golden Bulgarian generation Yordan Lechkov was elected President of the club and after a couple of seasons they won the second division title again going up and playing in the top flight for three seasons in a row. The played their home games at Hadzhi Dimitar Stadium (capacity of 15 000) that was later also renovated and hosted the Under 17 European Championship in 2015. Since 2012 Sliven FC have been playing in the amateur league after another severe financial crises.

There are always two sides to the history of any town or club. We already told you briefly the story of Sliven form a purely historical point of view. We, as visiting fans, have always been interested in the other side. That is where we were going and who would be waiting for us there! In addition to the above mentioned nickname, Sliven was also known as the "town below the Blue Rocks" **11**. What we and all the other travelling supporters could expect to encounter in Sliven was only "wind, rocks and people from the minorities." And we were about to experience exactly those kind of difficulties.

We were travelling by coaches, some 180-strong hard mob. We were met by several huge groups of gypsies who started throwing stones at us right away. We had a go at them in front of the ground, but the coppers quickly regrouped and took control. They dispersed the locals and pushed us inside the ground. Stones immediately started flying in all directions over the ground outer fencing, behind the away end, and when I say stones, I mean rather large cobbles and pieces of rock! All you could do was wonder which way to run to and hide in order to avoid being hit on the head. The game started and we already had a few injured. Anyway, we still did our best to support our beloved club with all our might.

I remember we had a couple of huge drums and when the players went out for the warm-up they just couldn't believe what numbers and quality we had brought. The drums echoed all around under the Blue Rocks and one could think we were the home side. At half time we got showered with loads of debris again and when the game was over we were forced into the coaches not being able to make a single step aside. The cops just ordered the drivers to set off and drive without stopping anywhere. We felt like animals stacked into a narrow shed and, in turn, started challenging the locals with insult and obscene gestures.

On the outskirts of Sliven there are some hills and just when we thought we had made it safely out of the town, a volley of stones and rocks followed. Hidden somewhere in the Blue Rocks, they were throwing stones and rocks at us like mad. I thought that if the coach had had no roof, they would have filled it with stones right to the top and only God would have been able to count the injured. In the end, we arrived back in Gorna Oryahovitsa on a coach that looked like a convertible, no window panes on, wind-swept and carrying bits of Blue Rocks.

---

11 BLUE ROCKS – A NATURAL PARK AND PHENOMENON SITUATED NEAR THE TOWN OF SLIVEN

Shumen

In late September 1994 Lokomotiv (GO) played Shumen FC a first division game away from home. They used to be one of our major rivals in the 1990s since their "golden era" coincided with ours. They are one of the oldest football clubs in Bulgaria, though one could hardly call them successful. They have had a couple of seasons in the top flight, they have reached the cup semi-finals twice and their greatest achievement is finishing fourth in the first division during the 1993/94 season.

That away day was one of our most memorable ones not only because of our huge turnout away from home, but also due to the scenes of violence that followed. It was unusually hot and sunny for the end of September, something we would call Indian summer. We had a whole football special train organised especially for us! A great number of black-and-white supporters were expected to travel on that antique passenger train that looked more like those trains in the old Western films. About 400 fans had gathered at the train station since the early morning, which was an impressive number for travelling supporters in those times.

All around the station one could see only Lokomotiv fans scattered across an area of 100 square yards in the nearby cafes and boozers. Some were quenching their thirst with cold beer and others were oiling their throats with homemade rakia and wine. The clatter of beer glasses, the constant singing and chanting in unison with the beating of the drum, the sound of bottles shattering and the loud and heated arguments contributed to that unique atmosphere ahead of games that we all adored and that was our reason to go and watch football. Some blokes' faces had already turned red, others were barely standing on their feet and still others were lying meekly on the pavements naked from the waist up, drinking their beers and basking in the warm autumn sun.

At noon things were already getting out of control. There were empty bottles and litter everywhere and the size of the crowd had increased significantly. I think that this was our second biggest away day turnout, after Pleven in 1987. I just couldn't see how this raving crowd could be appeased and squeezed into the train and only time could tell whether such a train would reach its destination in one piece. The train station in Gorna Oryahovitsa resembled a scene from Beirut in the early afternoon! The platforms were all flooded with the black-and-white sea of supporters and I had enormous doubts whether that train would be able to accommodate all those willing to board it.

Getting on the train looked more like a naval boarding. There were no separate compartments on board and we all flocked like animals while watching more and more people steaming in. Some were riskily crossing the tracks with one hope in their minds only, i.e. to get to the departing train, and so they'd rather be pulled up straight through the open windows instead of waiting in line to get on through the doors. An absolute bedlam! Inside the train the temperature was probably 40°C. Most were waist-up naked. I stuck my head out of the window and I thought I was in India, where passengers traditionally travel on overloaded trains. The sounds that followed were more like the sounds made by a sinking ship rather than a departing train.

Slowly and sluggishly, the locomotive tried to get going. A horrible screech was heard as it set off only to stop a few yards further, which made the "passengers" roar with discontent and anger. As if on cue, everybody bellowed unanimously and started thumping with their hands and feet. The rumble was deafening and the station roof reflected it, sending it back to us as a mighty echo. The roar gradually turned into a song and the rumbling sound grew even more unbearable. The windows gaskets were worn out and the panes were rattling as if were about to fall down any minute. The first debris started flying: tables, backrests, ashtrays, lamps, etc. The train made a second, this time successful attempt, which was celebrated with 2 or 3 blasts from homemade bombs of red lead and bronze. Everyone at the station ran for cover and I was sure they were praying that we finally left the station. All broken off items started swishing through the windows.

Pulling out of the station, the train interior looked somewhat brighter and more spacious. All the windows were open (some were already smashed) and the wind mightily blew in as if to freshen and cool us down. I took a look around and saw that half of the furnishing was already gone and that was the reason why the carriage looked more spacious, but who cared anyway. The booze kept raining down, the songs were getting louder and louder, adrenaline rushing to our heads, and the events from the departure were repeated over and over again at each small station. What could the station in Shumen expect!?

Getting off there was rather unloading (as described in the article about the game). Several hundred blokes got simply unloaded from the severely devastated train and then they all, in a purely tribal style, roared like one and started ravaging the very town of Shumen. Having made our first steps in the town, the first fences, stalls and booths got shattered and smashed. I remember one of our lads, in a most offhand manner, in order to cross the street, raised his hand and stopped a bus moving towards him. When the bus halted, with a mighty kick he ripped off the Mercedes emblem in front, which was immediately raised high in the air as a captured trophy and once again everybody roared with approval and satisfaction.

I do confess that on that day we didn't behave like humans, but rather as pillagers. On our way, people started leaving the cafes and pubs looking for shelter. By the look on their faces one could tell they thought we were some kind of lepers. It was as if some infection had come upon their town and they all dispersed in horror running to and fro. However our target was clear – the stadium. We quickened up our pace and all efforts by the police to subdue and escort us were in vain. It was an unstoppable invasion! We were walking in small groups along some busy streets and the cars were just slowly stopping to make way and wait for us to pass.

On approaching the ground, we found ourselves on a main multi-lane road that could only be crossed by going down a subway. However, it was not our idea to cross it this way! The lads in front had already crossed the first lane and were getting over the road restraints when we saw a coach approaching in the distance. Someone cried out loud, "*Those are our players!*" So everybody rushed like madmen towards the lane the coach was driving in. What act of sheer madness, isn't it!? The driver slowed down as he couldn't believe his eyes. I will never forget the expression on his face. He stopped the coach on the main road and we encircled it jumping around as if it was an Indian campfire. The players were also shocked and didn't know how to respond as we kept on jumping around in frenzy. We were so exalted that if we had all tried to, we could have surely lifted the coach and carry it to the ground!

In the vicinity of the ground some ticket offices got damaged. A very good friend of mine drove his huge head through the small window asking for tickets and the seller immediately fled in horror and was gone. He wasn't that lucky, though, as his head got stuck inside and almost lifted the ticket booth in question as he was trying to take his head out.

The atmosphere at the ground was more than hostile. It seemed the entire town had become aware of our rampage and the locals came searching for revenge. The cops found it hard to suppress tensions and the very buffer zone between the two sets of fans was, to put it mildly, ridiculous. Just a low railing panel that could easily be overcome by any small child. To the locals' credit, they were the first to dare storm the railings but they were met by our old school boys there, veterans that had long mastered the art of terrace fighting.

Few people can be called real fighters, but on that day we had brought the crème of the crop and we felt invincible. An exchange of punches followed and two or three of their lot were down. The typical sounds of hitting jaws and heads could be heard all around. One of those hooligans was the brother of a close friend of mine and was recognised by the Old Bill as the man who had orchestrated the riots back on the train and caused a lot of damage both on the train and during our march through the town streets. He was also the man who had victoriously kicked the Mercedes emblem off the bus earlier in the day, which meant he was the perfect scapegoat for the cops and so they nicked him. Instead of taking him out of the ground, however, the brainless coppers did something unheard-of, which was more characteristic of Bulgarian stadia in the previous decade. To obviously serve as an example to all the others, they decided to handcuff him to the fencing in the home end lower part and it looked more like a scene from a film about the Middle Ages and the mob lynching. The home crowd started hurling at him all kinds of objects, they spat at him, insulted him and, generally, one could imagine them taking him to the gallows after being sentenced to death.

Naturally, there was no way for us to just stand there and watch such humiliation, so we responded rather aggressively. If the cops wanted it, we made sure they'd get it. The entire second half was marred by our endless surges forward in the direction of our mate tied to the fencing and our fights with the Old Bill, and meanwhile the locals kept on throwing at us all kinds of missiles. After the game (we lost 2-1) our mate was taken to the police department and we refused to leave the ground without him. They forced us out and hitting us with their batons goaded us all the way to the station in a never ending aggro.

After what it seemed like hours, we arrived at the station guarded as if we were some global threat, and there we had our Western style train waiting for us. We were all pretty irate as a result of the beating we received from the police, who loaded us onto the train and ordered the train drivers to start off. Everything on board was ripped off and thrown as missiles at the cops, but that wasn't the end of the day.

Five minutes after the train had pulled out of the station we got bombarded with stones from all sides! The train was moving very slowly and the locals, having made an ambush, were sending us off with a hail of stones. Without a moment's hesitation, I pulled the emergency brake and the train made such an abrupt stop that we thought it would be derailed. We were mad with rage and decided to finally take it out on the locals. Probably more than a hundred of us jumped off the train into the emptiness and ran after our enemy. By emptiness I mean acres of land with various crops like maize, wheat and sunflower. The perfect place for two mobs to have a fight undisturbed by the police. There were only a couple of helpless cops with us on the train and so they called for backups. We still had time to get at our opponents and give them what they really deserved. We saw them hop into several cars and drive off past the arriving police patrol cars. We darted off back to the train. When the cops caught up with us, to our surprise, they just delivered our mate that had been nicked at the ground, pushed us back on board and sent us home with the words, *"Never come back to Shumen again!"* We, of course, hands held high in the air, all gave them our middle fingers and set off on our return journey happy that we were in full strength again and that we had done our job well on yet another away day.

Shumen – Lokomotiv (GO) 2-1

The midday train unloaded a carriage of diehard Lokomotiv (GO) fans, who added colour to the football game. Even before the game started, they had a fight with Shumen supporters. The timely intervention of the police and the secured safety area between the two sets of fans prevented any further trouble, but the atmosphere remained tense.

The supporters from Gorna Oryahovitsa sang their voices out of shape all game long, but couldn't help their team. The two sets of fans clashed ahead of the game, exchanging a couple of kicks, but the police quickly took control of it.

Svetkavitsa (Targovishte)

The truth is that Lokomotiv (GO) has played Svetkavitsa **12** (Targovishte) only in the lower divisions and never in the top flight.

Targovishte is a town in Northeastern Bulgaria, approximately 60 miles east of Gorna Oryahovtsa. The club was founded way back in 1922, but generally they are a small and modest club, without any major achievements. The "Thunderbolts" (that was the club's nickname) played their home games at Dimitar Burkov Stadium with a capacity of 12000 in all blue kits. Their claim to fame was the record-breaking number of seasons they have played in the second division, i.e. 43. Their first season in the top division was 2011/12, their sponsor being a local businessman, but they got immediately relegated after winning one game only. Plunging into financial debts and crisis, Svetkavitsa soon went down to the amateur leagues, where they play at present.

In 1989, the cup draw sent Lokomotiv to play in Targovishte, which eventually turned into some grave hooligan rampage the stories of which are still being told to this day.

Here is the account by one of our old school supporters, a Lokomotiv top face at that time, of what he witnessed and experienced on that away day:

"I started going to football in the early 1980's together with a good mate of mine, who I am attending games with up to this day. I have been involved with Lokomotiv organised mob since 1986, even before our club got promoted to the top flight. It was actually on the eve of our promotion from the second to the first division! Those were tough times for the terraces and the very game was following the "attack is the best form of defence" rule and to some extent the law of the jungle was in force, i.e. "Eat or be eaten."

I have been fond of pyro stuff ever since I was a little boy and, as they say, I loved playing with fire in both literal and figurative meanings. Everybody knew that I was involved in the making of some serious explosive shit, used quite often at stadia in those times and almost every single mob had its expert in that field. I would often even exchange expertise with our enemies from neighbouring Tarnovo, for example.I remember that when I was younger I used to go downtown during the New Year celebrations when, traditionally, everybody would use any kinds of firearms and blasts and shoot like in the Wild West all sorts of hunting and air rifles and guns and, in particular, exactly that type of homemade bombs. Some of my older friends, without being fully aware of the real danger, would celebrate by throwing randomly such handmade blasts everywhere. One evening I went out to meet them and when they saw me coming in the distance they started throwing bombs at me just like they would throw snowballs in winter (just for fun) and I started running about wondering which way to go to in order to evade the bombs that were falling down like meteors. Probably it was then I became immune to that stuff and I have never been afraid to make it, carry it and use it. I know what people might think when reading these lines, but that was the whole truth and the actual way of life in those pretty rough and tough times.

I would often practice those skills of mine and the lads from the mob would take advantage of my services as football grounds were the most common places for using that shit. I don't say I was proud of myself, but I was just skilled in doing that and I really did it with the greatest pleasure. They would regularly come asking, "Vic, there's a game coming, so would you mind making some explosives for our next away game?", and, of course there was no way I could possibly say no.

It was a cold November day in 1989. The Bulgarian communist government had just been overthrown and the times were turbulent, to say the least. Some 70 people made the train journey away to Svetkavitsa (Targovishte) for a cup tie. The evening before the game I did not have the time to make the pyro so I just decided to take the materials I needed with me and make the stuff on the train. Getting off at Targovishte station, I blew up one or two bombs to test them and to notify the locals that Lokomotiv (GO) had already come to their town.

At the ground, we were stood behind one of the goals. No fencing, segregation or escorts of any kind. Just a good old time away game when you could smuggle almost anything into the ground. When you could drink to excess, fight the locals at large and blow up a bomb or ignite a smoke canister.

At some point, out of the blue, the locals started crowding all around us. The atmosphere got more hostile and the police found it hard to keep tensions under control. By and large, there were not many cops inside the ground anyway.

At half time things seemed to get out of control and I took out a bomb just to scare the shit out of them and make them retreat. Without any doubts or fear I blew it up right there, amidst our ranks, as I did not mean to aim it at anyone in the crowd or hurt anyone. I just wanted to make them go away... In the chaos that followed one of the locals managed to steal my rucksack (full of explosives), probably thinking he was nicking our flags (another common practice in those times).

Absolute mayhem ensued and the cops, being at a complete loss, were pushed onto the racetrack together with us by the locals. Some of us even had to invade the pitch and cross it diagonally just to get arrested at its opposite end seconds before the second half began. The rest of us, some 30–40 boys, were confronted by about 200 local fans who kept on pressing and pushing forward driving us towards the pitch. We were caught in a huge trap and there was no way to have a toe-to-toe. It was rather a hell of a jam and the cops just made matters worse as they blocked both sides and didn't let us get away, making the situation even more confusing.

We got that dreadful feeling of some terrible impending fatal crush. Just then, the one who had stolen my rucksack thinking he was capturing a war trophy, decided to express his triumph by tossing it high in the air... no need to tell you what followed - a deafening blast that shook everyone and echoed thunderously. I turned around and saw something I would hardly ever forget: there were people who quickly dispersed but there were also those who were simply crawling out to safety. Some 10 of our lads still remained and most of them were surrounded by the cops on the pitch. And I hadn't even made it to the racetrack and was still standing on the terraces, all by myself! After the explosion, some of the locals pulled themselves together and had a go at us even more aggressively. They knocked me down, but my biggest worry was that I still had a few bombs on me! They started kicking me. I just coiled up thinking, "if they blow up now, that will be the end of me!"

Making a last-ditch effort, I managed to take one out and blew it right in front of my face, simply turning my head away in order not to get blinded by the explosion. I felt everyone around took to their heels and I took advantage of it and stood up. I then threw another bomb and raised my hands high wondering when the hell they were going to finally arrest me?!My last effort turned out a success as two cops handcuffed me and frogmarched me past the main stand. I thought they were going to lynch me… All sorts of missiles started flying at me and I really felt the star of the day. They pushed me into a police UAZ minibus (a Russian vehicle). The game was naturally suspended, and a few of our players and officials came to the minibus trying to understand what was going on and negotiate my release. No chance! The coppers were absolutely infuriated and they drove us to the local precinct, where their rage totally got hold of them and they beat the shit out of us. I got some serious charges and I had to go through several court instances in order just to mitigate them. Eventually I found out that there were a lot of injuries, some being grievous bodily harms.

I got through loads of interrogations and investigations and my case was classified as gravely as a second degree attempted murder and even terrorism. One of the injured fellas had suffered serious damage (potential disability) and so I immediately got a lifetime ban from attending football matches…"

Haskovo

"Two carloads of fanatic teenagers poisoned the atmosphere at the stadium in the town of Haskovo. No matter how strange it might sound, they were one of the reasons behind the defeat of their allegedly beloved Etar FC". That's how we started our conversation with Ivan Stoychev, our correspondent in the town of Haskovo.

The accident at Haskovo vs Etar game is rather serious to not share our apprehension that the triumphant vulgarity has been inadmissibly tolerated and that in case of such approaches we could witness some stupid football related wars.

We will start the summary of facts: taken into custody are: Nikolai Boyanov (aged 17), Tsanko Kolev (aged 18), and Ventsislav Varbanov (aged 22), who is the ringleader of the Veliko Tarnovo mob. A trial has been initiated against them on grounds of Art. 325, Par. 2 of the Penal Code for "hooligan acts of extreme obscenity and arrogance occasioning actual bodily harm". One of the fans attending the game had his arm broken and another one received burns as a result of which they have been rendered medical aid.

So how did things end up in hospital and… in court?

It all started at the train station in native Veliko Tarnovo. The minor and adult offenders, intoxicated, blew up a couple of bombs as a warm-up, and overturned dustbins. Police officers talked to the violet fans and let them board the train only after being explicitly assured that they would behave properly while on the train. That was actually what really happened as they slept off their hangovers. Then, on Saturday morning, in the town of Haskovo, they started drinking the famous local brand of beer and showed the cloven hoof at the morning game between Haskovo and Chernomorets veterans by blowing up a few bombs, breaking down benches, smashing bottles and hurling verbal insults at the players. After that, at the "big" game, more bombs were thrown, one of them injuring a football fan. The violet hooligans started a fight on the terraces using hidden tools such as chains and knuckledusters. The game was suspended for 10 minutes and eventually the police restored order.

This is the brief summary of the "case", about which we would address the police with the famous words, "Elementary, my dear Watson!"Elementary it is, as it all could have easily ended back at the station in Veliko Tarnovo. However, the "bombers" continued on their way to Haskovo. What also continued was, to put it mildly, the inappropriate educational conduct of the police officers as they held peaceful talks with people who had already proven their aggressive and violent intentions, trying to make them promise they would "behave" while in Haskovo, instead of at least searching them for any "gunpowder stocks"…

In this story you will once again have the pleasure of meeting the Boyar mob ringleader (nicknamed the Pedagogue), who, as we see from the article above, was a major participant in all the events from those times. Here are the thoughts he has to share with us about this occasion:

"I can say that being the ringleader of the Tarnovo supporters in those times was not something I had intentionally sought after or tried to achieve as a major goal in life. I just had it in me and I believe it was my destiny. As the years went by I gave proofs of my keenness on fights and organisational skills.

The Haskovo incident was, let me put it this way, a grotesque event in the history of our fandom, which had serious consequences, but, anyway, that was how things went in those times and there was nothing we could do to change them.

In 1990 our team was in great shape (coach, management and players). We had been making great advance in the title race and were definitely going for the gold, which eventually we did win.

We had some serious organisation for that away day. We travelled on the night train and things started to go wrong at the very beginning as we pulled the emergency brake at some point in order to protest against the cops taking off several of our lads.

In those years we had the habit of using some homemade explosives (bombs) and no matter how stupid it may sound nowadays, we had primed ourselves well for that match as we were well aware that we were going to a district of rather serious ethnic tensions and had good reasons to expect provocations. Though it is a different story described in the article, we did face some provocations and we were really forced into using the bombs in question, which we generally meant to blow up on the ground racing track. Ahead of the game, pretty smashed, we threw a few bombs just to test them and probably that was the reason for the locals' aggressive reaction as they had a go at us at half time. We are not talking about any innocent victims at all... I had the feeling that the entire ground would steam in at us and we just had to defend. We were simply forced to use all tools and means to save our asses.

We managed to collect such tools breaking off bits and debris that we could use for that purpose. There were no seats at grounds back then; it was just benches made up of three long timber woods so I grabbed one and started wielding it in the air. It was sheer madness and in spite of our brave resistance, the locals started to prevail and, heavily outnumbered, we started losing ground.

Then I saw one of our lads take a homemade bomb (they were kind of advanced and the explosive mixture was put in an empty beer can) out of his backpack and throw it amidst the crowd, which sent two of them locals straight into the air... there were a number of injured.

We got nicked right away and they tried to give us sentences in fast-track trials, but our lawyers managed to rebut some of the charges. In addition, for better or for worse, I had lost my IDs during the fight so as a matter of fact neither I, nor they could verify who I really was. As I was being nicked a copper asked for my IDs and then I realised I had lost them.

His second question was where I came from and I lied to him that I was a pedagogy student unintentionally involved in the incident. Hence my nickname the Pedagogue.

We were taken into custody for 48 hours and later on sentenced."

A year after the Boyars' case in Haskovo and two years after our similar experience in Targovishte, we also played an away game in the town of Haskovo. We had booked two coaches and, as always, we met downtown, had a few drinks and set off for Southern Bulgaria.

I guess you already got the idea that the Stara Planina mountain range, which divides our country in two geographic regions, is also a kind of unseen border separating the people from those regions in terms of mentality, customs and traditions. As in most places, Southerners are more hot-blooded and Northerners – more reserved and severe. However, towns like Haskovo and Kurdzhali were more special as they also had this Turkish influence due to their proximity to the border with Turkey. This, in turn, facilitated the formation of large ethnic groups in those areas that had rather different temper and behaviour.

There are, of course, exceptions to this rule, and beyond the mountain range up north one could also find similar regions (like Shumen and Targovishte), but somehow, away days in those southern towns would always have this particular sense and taste of hatred and hostility. We could feel it in the air right after we got off our coach there. So when you add the Pedagogue's story above describing their bitter experience the previous year, we were not surprised at all that we were met by full riot gear police the moment we set foot on their southern ground. The cops simply stood us against a tall wall and lined us up like terrorists.

Meanwhile, the locals started flocking around and piled together along the nearby fence ready to lynch us. I tried to talk to a copper asking him what the reason for their hospitable reception was and he reminded me of the incident with football supporters from our region the previous year. We had a bad reputation among them locals no matter that we were actually Etar's greatest rivals and though we are separated by just a few miles we have had this hatred for each other since times immemorial! I tried to explain all that to the copper, but he just wouldn't listen, telling me to explain it to the blokes on the other side of the fence. I looked over my shoulder and to tell you the truth, there stood the ugliest creatures I had ever seen in my life... horrible, distorted faces and pikey-style clothes (most of them wearing cheap tracksuits they must have bought from the nearby flea market), and when you add to that all the gestures and insults hurled at us, as well as some weapons they were carrying, you'd get a really nasty picture. Some tough 90 minutes lay ahead.

We got frisked from head to toe and some half an hour later they let us at least turn around only to shove some pump guns into our faces. We couldn't move an inch and the hostile mob behind the fence were getting more and more vicious and revengeful. In the meantime, we pulled ourselves together, the drunken sobered up quickly and everybody became fully aware where we were and what was expecting us. Then we also pushed to the fence in question and it all got fucking mental. For the first time at football, a gun had been pointed at me and, believe me, the feeling is not pleasant at all! However, adrenaline rushed in our heads and some started climbing the fence in an attempt to get at the locals behind it. The fence was made of metal bars placed at quite a distance between one another, leaving gaps probably wide enough to throw a punch through it. If someone had the fast, accurate and sharp punch of Bruce Lee, one could have bashed some ugly motherfucker's face at the opposite end.

We decided not to risk having a toe-to-toe as we saw the blades in their hands and so we started throwing all kinds of missiles at them. I remember a very funny incident when I friend of mine, who was standing next to me, came closer to their lot and spat in the face of one of those ugly bastards who also happened to have thick moustaches. You should have seen that hideous crooked face, spittle hanging down his moustaches. The locals went fucking mental and started throwing bottles at us. It was as if two warring camps of inmates (of different races and backgrounds) were trying to get at each other but were divided by bars. They were ready to tear us apart if they had to.

It all went for let's say ten minutes and after that they escorted us into the ground. We were so heavily guarded that at half time we went to the toilets in small groups, like children, always accompanied by policemen carrying rifles! The very game was completely left in the background and forgotten as the atmosphere was depressingly warlike rather than football related one. It was actually in the town of Haskovo and at the place we are going to next tell you about that I have witnessed such enormous hatred and menace that were not only football related!

---

12 The Bulgarian word "svetkavitsa" means "lightning" in English.

Arda (Kurdzhali)

Arda (Kurdzhali) was one of the teams we played away in our first campaign in the second division after being relegated from the top one in 1994/95 season.

The club is named after the Arda River on which the town of Kurdzhali is situated in southern Bulgaria. The club played in the second division for many years, but nowadays it is to be found in the Bulgarian amateur leagues. In terms of football the game was not very important as it was the beginning of the season, but what happened after the match will long be remembered.

I think it was autumn as it was a wet, miserable day. As not many people were expected to make the trip and due to the lack of convenient railway transport to the town of Kurdzhali, we decided to book a coach. We were not more than 30–35 fellas. The trip was not that long (approximately 150 miles), but the road passes through a big mountain and a number of towns and villages, which would normally take some 5-6 hours by coach (mind you, coaches then were not as fast and luxurious as they are now) and that meant a rather tiring trip. Most of the lads who were to travel to that away game were from my former neighbourhood.

The trip was like the majority of other trips we had made by then. There was plenty of alcohol, songs and loads of black-and-white flags draped along the side and back windows of the coach. Some slept all the time, while others were discussing the forthcoming game and mostly what we could expect from the local Arda fans. They were not famous for being passionate football supporters, but it was another town with a high percentage of minority groups.

After the fall of the totalitarian regime in 1989, there were a lot of riots caused by minorities in towns like Kurdzhali, but 6 or 7 years had passed from those turbulent times. To be honest, I was a bit afraid as I knew what such people were capable of, although it was now democracy and peace. No matter how strange it may sound to some, those times were still tough and people should know the truth. I don't give a damn about the current attitudes of the EU to minorities as we are football fans and we don't deal with politics. So let me go back to that rainy day we travelled to Kurdzhali.

Druzhba Stadium was in the very centre of the town, situated in a huge recreation park. The coach driver parked his vehicle in one of the side streets and we agreed to meet there right after the game. Loud shouts and chants broke the silence of the town and the locals started wondering what was going on. We wouldn't stop singing and chanting despite the sounds coming from the noon prayers going on in the surrounding mosques and echoing in the distance. It was a rather tense atmosphere not only because of the rain, but also because we could hear more Turkish rather than Bulgarian words. The match itself was not a spectacular one and it ended in a 1-1 draw, though there were some controversial situations.

In general, we played relatively well, though it was hard to play brilliant football on a wet and muddy pitch. The rain wouldn't stop, which made the conditions even worse. We were separated from the home crowd, which was not big at all, and a few cops were taking care of the order. Our unending support and all the flags along the fencing were an interesting sight for the locals that I thought they had never seen before.

Anyway, we could hear their constant hostile boos and abuse directed at our players. We had to put up with it somehow and though we would hit back, we just wanted to get out of that God-forgotten place as soon as possible. After the final whistle we headed downtown, but in a side street we came across a few local fans gesticulating and abusing us. We had a go at them and a rain of fists followed. They were fewer than us (8 or 10 blokes), but we showed no mercy and beat them hard. Some were already screaming for help, others were writhing with pain on the ground covered in mud, but we just wouldn't stop beating them. A couple of them managed to escape. The others were left lying on the pavement and we hurried back to the place where our coach was waiting. In just a few minutes, out of the blue, some 20 men appeared armed with bits of wood and knives and they were wielding them in the air shouting out loud. They started running towards us and we didn't hesitate at all, but took to our heels as fast as we could. They started chasing us still shouting and, believe me, I have never run as fast as I did on that day. I can only imagine what would have happened if we had started a fight with them!

Somehow we managed to get to our coach and the first ones to get on told the driver to start the engine and set off immediately after the last one of us boarded the bus. The locals started throwing all kinds of debris at our vehicle, but fortunately no window got smashed and none of us got injured. Police patrols arrived and dispersed the angry natives. We were escorted by the Old Bill out of town and for the first time in my life I had felt glad to see the police. What an afternoon it was though kickoff only went on for a few minutes!

Lomomotiv (Mezdra)

Life in the lower divisions in all those long years seemed to have made us support our club even more ardently. 2004 was proof of that and probably our climax in those times in terms of riots and hooliganism. Pitch invasions, brawls and fights on the pitch. No matter whether we had opponents or we just wanted to beat up the referee as a result of some mistake of his and we would invariably and quite naturally end up fighting the police...

A similar occasion we had on an away day in Northwest Bulgaria, in the town of Mezdra. Traditionally, they would always meet you there in their proper, though weirdest manner, as fans of other clubs from that region would unite against intruders, despite being one another's opponents in general!

That sunny day in late May was no different and we made the trip by coach (our major means of travel after the beginning of the new century) and not by the National Railways, our usual "general sponsor". Well, as far as our free journeys were concerned, we didn't travel for free because we had some special discounts, but simply because we wouldn't buy tickets with the intent to save money for nothing else but booze! Those were the exact reasons behind the majority of us having the railways as their favourite means of transport. However, times had changed and our away days had become much more civilised and sophisticated... but let this not mislead you. It would all end the moment we drew closer to our enemy's territory and headed straight to the centre of their town, usually blowing up homemade bombs. I know how dangerous that practice was, but as I told you before, we had those enthusiasts who made them and it was only some ten years ago that such things would still happen across Bulgarian stadia!

It was scorching heat when our coach finally arrived in the centre of Mezdra. Out of it came some waist-up naked savages bellowing like wild animals. A horrible boom was heard when we got off and I felt the bomb fragments hissing past my ears. Usually that was the result of the mixture of ferolite, red lead, bronze and flints joined together! Car alarms went off and in just a minute we had not only onlookers (perched on the tower block balconies around), but also the first ones willing to fight. They turned out to be not natives, but our "good old chaps" from the neighbouring town of Vratsa (who we are going to tell you about a little bit further below). It will be an exaggeration to say that those clubs were our primordial and fierce enemies, but life in the lower football leagues really meant making some new enemies.

We then started singing *"You only came here to watch us..."* and the coppers hurriedly restored order and put an end to the petty arguments between our two sides. We settled in the nearest boozer and our songs started to entertain the fellas on the balconies around while the sounds echoed across the blocks and returned to us even louder, like a boomerang.

Our "pals" from Vratsa joined the show as bystanders remaining on the pavement opposite and probably wondering whether they had come to fights us or just meet us. I recognised a lad or two from the Sofia Levski vs CSKA scene as I knew they were members of one of CSKA firms. What I saw in the eyes of the rest was admiration for what they were witnessing and they looked like as if they were going to ask for our autographs any minute. It was not far from the truth actually as in just a few hours we were going to be the stars of the day both on and off the pitch.

Probably an hour before kickoff time, our escort, kindly provided by the police, was so impressive as if the game was to be played between top of the table teams in the first division rather than clubs from the third echelon of Bulgarian football. There was even a special Sofia Police unit (something not typical of that squad) and several vans stood there full of riot police who, quite naturally, were wearing masks and full riot gear.

We got escorted all the way to the ground and our Vratsa companions followed us as if they had never seen such a sight before. Attendance was very high (in our standards) since it was the end of the campaign and both clubs were struggling for promotion. The local ground was an absolute shit hole and one could hardly imagine it as a sports facility of any kind. The same went for their team, too... It was just one of those numerous short-lived football clubs in Bulgaria. Anyway, both teams eventually got promoted to the second division. They even went as high as our top flight, though didn't leave a very impressive mark there.

It was the perfect place for us. We felt like wild animals let out of their cages into the wilderness. By wilderness I mean the large area of un-mowed grass behind one of the goals that looked more like a picture taken in a savannah rather than at a football ground. It was somewhere amidst that tall grass that a red fire engine was proudly parked, probably with the intention to put out any possible fire that we could start with our pyro or to cool down our passions on that hot day by dispersing us with its powerful water cannon. There was no fencing or safety netting whatsoever and I could tell from the very first sight that it was going to be the ultimate stage for us to show our abilities.

Believe me, I've seen greater shit holes among Bulgarian stadia, some of which are located right in the middle of corn, wheat or other cereal fields, but that ground in particular is definitely among the top five ugliest venues I have ever attended. We knew well the referee as he had robbed us in several previous games, but when he awarded a ridiculous penalty for the home side in the opening minutes of the game after a foul was committed clearly outside the penalty box, all hell broke loose and set upon him. His very whistle signalling the foul was a spontaneous challenge for us to invade the pitch and try to take the law into our own hands.

I was one of the first to invade the pitch and I saw that almost all our mob followed me galloping like a herd of enraged bulls trampling down everything that stood in their way. Facilitated by the absence of any obstacles and the belated reaction by the police, our first lads almost caught up with the villain in black and then I saw several cops literally lie down on the referee pressing him down with their shields and covering him like a turtle would use its shell to protect his life. *"Come 'ere, you son of a bitch…"*, I yelled almost out of breath and I swore at him vulgarly. I had not looked back until then but when I saw the impenetrable wall of shields on the ground around him, I slightly turned aside trying to evade them and then I had 3 or 4 cops in pursuit, their batons making those unmistaken hissing sounds before hitting my back! I made a few manoeuvres and managed to turn around making the way clear for my return sprint. It was as if a whole corridor opened in front of me and I started running as fast as I could towards the away end. I could already see that the majority of the pitch invaders had been nicked or knocked down while others were being pushed back onto the terraces. However, I kept on running and managed to get back unhurt, even intact.

The rest of our mob gave me a hero's reception with standing ovations and hugging and simply made me dip into a sea of mates.

The cops were not able to identify me and they even gave up any attempts to do so as they already had troubles with the ones nicked, who had started to protest and go wild. Some 10 minutes later, order was restored and the one who was to blame for all the riots resumed play and then our goalkeeper saved the penalty kick, sending us into delirium and over the moon. We just went fucking mental and once again some of our lads invaded the pitch, but were quickly sent back.

Even to this day, there are people who make me tell this story and still wonder and cannot understand (as I am rather overweight) how I managed to get away from the cops on that day without even a single scratch, not to speak of being beaten up and nicked. Lads, to be honest with you, I cannot explain that, either. When I analyse the events that happened on that day, I believe it is some kind of force that makes you do everything spontaneously and instinctively on such tricky occasions. Occasions like that, after which one of the greatest stars of Bulgarian football (ex-Manchester City & Bolton player) Martin Petrov, who was born in the town of Mezdra and was a VIP guest at the game, would say, *"Those were the ugliest scenes of football violence I had ever seen in my entire life."* Taking into account that he used to play for CSKA for quite a long time!

A week later, after our last home game from the campaign, Lokomotiv got promoted into the second division after an almost 10-year exile. Come the final whistle, we invaded the pitch again, this time celebrating with our players and our joy was even doubled as it happened on the official holiday of our native town. Though it was going to be a brief moment of happiness, no one could take it away from us!

Botev (Vratsa)

Our away game in the town of Vratsa against the local Botev FC was one of the most anticipated ones because we had been swimming deep into the sea of mediocrity between the second and the third division for so long.

They had just been relegated from the top division. They were rather infamous for being an unwelcoming host and had played in the top flight for as many as 26 years in a row between 1964 and 1990. There we were going to meet some like-minded supporters and a few notorious hooligans and that was the reason why we had always tried to have a decent turnout in that remote place.

We were about 30–35 lads and the game was to be played on the official holiday of their town. There were lots of people on the streets of Vratsa, having in mind the event they were celebrating. We settled in a boozer near their ground (Hristo Botev Stadium) and started drinking cold beer, singing songs about our beloved Lokomotiv and chanting at the locals sitting at the tables around. Not before long, the ringleader of Botev mob appeared followed by several of his mates. He was also a renowned leader among CSKA hooligans as he supported that team from Sofia along with his local club. They saw that our group was not a small one, woke up to the situation they were in (they must have expected not more than 10–15 fans to arrive from Gorna Oryahovitsa) and started a kind talk with us.

During the game, their ringleader sent a youngster to us with a message proposing a 10 vs 10 fight outside the ground. Unfortunately, Vratsa boys have always had fewer numbers in spite of living in a bigger town. On hearing their proposal, one of us asked their youngster what the rest of us, say 20-25 people, were going to do, stand back and watch or take turns in participating in the pre-arranged fight they were offering us. So their messenger was sent back with loads of mockery and we showed their fans standing in the opposite end a number of indecent gestures. There were no further confrontations as they chose to stand aside and watch the football. Although they had a good number of tough boys, they had never turned up for an away game in the town of Gorna Oryahovitsa.

Montana

One of our remotest away games in the first division was in the town of Montana situated in Northwest Bulgaria on the Ogosta River (their ground had the same name as the river), amidst some foothills north of the Stara Planina mountain range.

Montana FC played for the first time in the top division during the 1994/95 season. It was our second away game in early September in the third round of the new campaign. They didn't have any significant achievements, besides becoming second division champions twice. Montana is also the birthplace of the famous Bulgarian footballer Stiliyan Petrov, who made great impression in the UK playing for Celtic and Aston Villa.

We organised a coach trip to that remote and God-forsaken place and there were some 250 of us. It was one of our best turnouts for that campaign. Our next similar invasion was to the town of Shumen at the end of the same month, of which we told you about earlier in this book. It was a hell of a tiring trip that took about 6 hours, us finishing our drinks half way through it. Besides the usual songs and chants, there were those long-lasting arguments involving Tosh and another lad. Their quarrel didn't end before we arrived in Montana so you can imagine the verbal fight they really had!

The ground was located in one of the suburbs surrounded by the river and some agricultural buildings (the former cooperative farm). We arrived shortly before kick-off time. The atmosphere was somewhat depressing, dreary and drab. It looked like the end of the world, a rundown place encircled by some old dilapidated structures and buildings. There were some blokes going to the Ogosta Stadium, but they looked more like peasants than football supporters. They were dressed in shabby clothes and by the look of some of them you could guess they were coming straight from the fields after work. I thought I was dreaming, never before had I seen anything like that.

The moment we set foot on their ground we started bawling and yelling rather than singing. A group of locals appeared in front of us and started hurling obscene gestures and stones at us. They were rather angry with us, which kind of surprised us as we had never met their lot before. We expected some peasants armed with pitchforks, axes and hoes to appear any moment! We hit back by throwing some debris and empty bottles at them. We went on firing at each other from a distance until we decided to have a go at them and disperse them. Some of us started a toe-to-toe, which didn't last long as the Old Bill appeared.

We continued to hurl abuse at each other, but there was nothing else we could do in the presence of so many cops. One of our lads got arrested for the small scuffle we had had with our local opponents. He was detained until the end of the game that our Lokomotiv (GO) lost 2-0. Nothing worth telling about happened during the match apart from the awful refereeing mistakes, all of which were to our disadvantage. A defeat, outrageous referee decisions, a long and exhausting journey in both directions, a failed attempt to get into a fight at some cursed place; that was what we were going to remember about Montana.

Minyor (Pernik)

The southwestern part of Bulgaria was the region that, believe me, nobody wanted to travel to on an away day. In the next lines we'll make an attempt to explain why. There are three large towns in the region that we can surely call "the triangle of death". Truly hostile places and a real challenge to all visiting football fans.

Minyoris a football club founded in the town of Pernik in 1919. The town is situated in Southwest Bulgaria, in the Pernik valley surrounded by Vitosha mountain. It is near Sofia and is famous for being the biggest coal mining town in Bulgaria. The club's nickname is "The Hammers" and they were a real horror during their five seasons in the top flight in the late 1990s. Pernik has become a sinister and almost impossible destination for the majority of its opponents. The derby games they play with teams from Sofia have always been real actions involving smashed bus and train windows.

In 2001 they were kicked out of the top division after they played Levski as a torrent of stones simply poured over the pitch on the players, referee and linesmen. After a 7-year exile, the "yellow-and-blacks" (the club colours) returned to the top flight, where they played until 2012/13, when they got relegated down to the second division.

As a youngster (13–14-year old kid) I visited that town since I have some relatives living there and I decided to combine the away game of my beloved Lokomotiv with a visit to my cousins. One of them was a Minyor fan. I caught a train and took the long journey to Pernik, changing trains in Sofia. In those years, typical of that region was the use of narrow-gauge railways. The distance between our capital Sofia and Pernik is a couple of dozens of miles only, but the means of transport mentioned above (slow as a snail) would turn each railway trip into a real nightmare lasting for almost as long as my journey from Gorna Oryahovitsa to Sofia did.

After a long and troublesome journey, I stepped off the train and immediately sensed that distinct smell of smoke and burning. The sky was dull and overcast and it seemed that something was drifting in between the earth and sun. It was all coming from the mines and coal processing plants, where the local Minyor **13** got its name from.

My cousins gave me a hearty welcome and naturally were very hospitable, but in general, the locals were not famous for being friendly, but rather notorious for their hostile nature, and to be more precise for their Shopimentality (wrongly adopted as a common noun for the citizens of the Bulgarian capital Sofia). To really feel the difference between life in North and South Bulgaria I will tell you that in order for me to have a decent conversation with my relatives, at times I simply needed a translator! I know that everywhere you go you'll find some marked accents and slang, but in my case it was a whole different language.

On the next day I went to the game with my cousin, who accompanied me as an elder, and we were sat among the home supporters. There, they could easily smell a rat and tell you're not one of them without even having to ask you the time and hear your accent. Lokomotiv opened the score and I impulsively jumped for joy. I suddenly felt the withering looks of everyone around and my cousin quickly made me sit down. The blokes around started giving me a look and asking who I was and what I was doing amidst their lot, provided I was just a kid and my cousin was really one of them lads!

A few years later I was foolish enough to go to another game there and this time we even dared to take a firm, wear scarves and fly flags. Actually, we couldn't watch the entire game anyway as 6 minutes into the first half Lokomotiv scored an opener and we went mental...

In just a few minutes, however, we were surrounded by a mob of enraged Orcs (that's how fans of other clubs mockingly call them) and got simply pushed onto the racing track and taken out of the ground by the Old Bill with the words, *"Why the hell did you come here? Don't you know that everyone gets done here?!"*

---

13 THE BULGARIAN WORD "MINYOR" MEANS "MINER".

Pirin (Blagoevgrad)

The same hospitality and nice words we witnessed in the other big town in this part of the country. If in the southeast you could feel the influence of neighbouring Turkey, here it was the influence of Greece and Macedonia.

Pirin FC is a long-standing participant in the first and second divisions of Bulgarian football and one could call it a football talent cradle as a number of famous players have come out of their academy, among which names like Ivaylo Andonov and Petar Mihtarski, representative of the USA'94 golden Bulgarian generation. Undoubtedly, the most famous football player whose career started with the "eagles" (the club's nickname) is Dimitar Berbatov, who made his mark playing in England.

The club was founded in 1922 and has won recognition as one of the strongest sides in Southwest Bulgaria, being a constant top flight team, though not winning any significant silverware. They have earned fame as a tough opponent and a top flight mid-table finisher. In 2005, the club from the mountainous town (located between the mountains of Rila and Pirin) was sent down to the third division due to its huge debts, but after 2014 they returned to the top division having won two successive promotions.

Unlike Pernik, the cops in Blagoevgrad asked us, right there at the gates, why we had gone there and we really needed a translator to understand what they were asking us. I think I'd have had a better communication with a Macedonian rather than with any of them locals. To our amazement, the coppers at the gates would even sample the booze the locals were bringing into the ground and would simply raise a toast with them, letting them freely and in a most friendly manner smuggle in whatever they would like to!

There were about 30 of us and we felt like lambs before the slaughter. The atmosphere was more than hostile and we all got fully aware that our major and probably only goal would be to get out of there alive. Come the final whistle, we were kept inside for almost an hour, but coming out of the ground it seemed as if the game had only ended five minutes ago. They were all there waiting to lynch us! Luckily, one of the coaches that our team was travelling on had not left yet and, finding it half-empty, the cops told our club officials that if they didn't take us with them, the police couldn't guarantee our safe advance to the train station and, respectively, our safe return trip home. So we ended up on board our players' coach and one of them asked us in surprise, *"Guys, did you really make it all the way down here?",* and then he concluded, *"You're surely the most faithful bunch of supporters there could ever be!"* Our coach was seen off with a shower of stones smashing one of the side windows, but that was the least we could get away with on that day…

Vihren (Sandanski)

Going to away games further south, you actually can't tell for sure whether you're still in your own country or you are abroad and there was a glaring difference between us and the locals in terms of fandom, clothing, etc.

Vihren FC is a small and modest club from the town of Sandanski, which is a pretty tourist town visited by crowds of tourists from neighbouring Greece and, especially in summer, one could more often hear foreign speech than Bulgarian language. The club now plays in the amateur league. The "Gladiators" as they are called had always been wavering in the sea of mediocrity between the third and second division until they reached their memorable 2004/05 season, when, for the first time in their history, they won promotion to the top league as champions of the second division. A

fter several years playing in the top flight, the club got relegated down to the amateur leagues, where they still play up to this day. It was during the season they were crowned champions that they played against Lokomotiv (GO).

Despite the enormous distance and probably the remotest destination we had ever had to travel to, this time we were well organised and several coach loads of us descended on the centre of the resort. The locals just didn't stand a chance against such a mob and many of them would steer clear of us, scared stiff.

We had some top faces returning to our ranks on that day, lads who had not had any football related fun for quite a long time and they were the first who struck up some old songs and romped about the pubs and cafes of the shocked town. It seemed the tourist season had just begun, the weather was fine and all the tourists were watching in dismay the waist-up naked invaders from Northern Bulgaria. The picture was rather grotesque as most of our older lads had huge bellies and would not stop chanting *"The beer monsters are here"*. After literally ravaging several boozers downtown we headed for the ground. It was a sheer riot. Some of our lads would make passes at the beautiful girls and once again I got the feeling we were some pirates cast on a paradise island and indulged in rampage and pillage.

Inside the ground we were stood behind one of the goals, but on a few occasions we invaded the home supporters section to be driven back by the police batons. The game was turning into a nightmare for the home side and when we scored a huge load of bodies poured down the fencing, which gave in and we all found ourselves on the pitch. The very stand was elevated and probably a yard of concrete mould made our landing quite painful, especially for those who were up front and, after the fencing collapsed, ended up being at the bottom of the pile of bodies.

Our joy was next door to madness and for a few minutes complete chaos ensued all over the pitch. Some were rolling over on the ground, turning handsprings, others were showing obscene gestures to the home supporters, still others were hugging our players, and there were, of course, those of us who started chasing the home players down the pitch, just for the sake of change and... fun!

Cherno More (Varna)

A week before the final round in the first division, our Lokomotiv, which had already secured its place in the middle of the table, played away from home to Cherno More **14** in the town of Varna.

It was spring, in late April 1994. The "Mariners" (as Cherno More were called) had already been relegated from the top division, but that didn't stop them from beating us 1-0 at their ground called "Ticha", though both teams had nothing to play for but their honour and pride. Their club is one of the oldest in Bulgaria and it is the first official football club. They were famous for being a strong and inhospitable side and a great number of Sofia clubs' away games would turn into a real nightmare in Varna.

Cherno More was not a largely successful club (winning the title way back in 1938) despite being one of the top league regulars. The 1990s were undoubtedly the hardest part of their history. During the whole decade the team from Varna played in the top flight only once, in 1993/94, and the rest of the time they spent playing in our second division. Probably that was the reason why we didn't cross paths with them as when we played in division two they were in division one and vice versa.

In 2000 the "Mariners" returned to the top flight, where they play up to this day. Last year (2015) they won their first Cup ever, knocking us out of the tournament at the quarterfinals, 6-0 on aggregate. The truth, however, is that though playing in the first division for more than 15 seasons in a row, their ground is one of the smallest (an 8250 seater), only their south stand has a roof (partially installed) and on the whole it is a rather unattractive venue. As far as I know, Ticha Stadium does not even meet the most basic UEFA requirements.

But let us go back to that spring day, 30th April 1994. As we said, the game was not a crucial one for either club. We were to finish eighth in the first division table and they had already been relegated. There was not much interest in that fixture and probably that was why only about 50 of us chose to travel to Varna and Lokomotiv management booked a special coach for us.

It was a late afternoon fixture and that was why we set off at noon. Besides, the distance between Gorna Oryahovitsa and Varna is approximately 140 miles, which meant that the trip was going to take more than three and a half hours. We had gathered in a boozer right next to the bus station and we were drinking beer and dining, looking forward to our next adventure. A police patrol vehicle was there to keep an eye on us until we depart, but we wouldn't listen to their warnings not to make too much noise around, if that is the correct expression for singing and chanting our repertoire. In general, they were just trying to find a reason to nick someone and spoil our fun.

We bought some more cold beer they were selling in the shop next to the boozer and got on the coach. As it was leaving the station, we all started banging on the side windows and thumping on the floor, screaming to the top of our voices *"Loko, Loko…"* The vehicle was not very comfortable and I remember we made the driver occasionally open the door in front in order to let some fresh air in. Half way through, the cold beer was finished, which further made us feel as if wearing spacesuits. From time to time one could hear some screeching or see dense smoke come out of the coach exhaust, which just made us pray to reach our destination on time…

Upon arriving in Varna we got off straight at Ticha Stadium western gate, which was the ground away end. There were a few cops, but not that many as they were probably not expecting us to turn up right there. We got off in a mighty roar and blew off a few bombs, which scared the shit out of the bystanders who could not even imagine that anyone was going to disturb their afternoon peace with such explosions. We noticed a boozer with plastic tables and chairs opposite the ground gate, but we had to cross the boulevard to get there. We saw some coppers coming so we darted off bringing the entire traffic to a halt for several seconds. A few cars braked sharply and their drivers got out cursing and swearing at us, but nobody gave a fuck.

We crossed the boulevard as cheeky as we could be and took over the boozer without a single worry, leaving behind the onlookers to stare in shock and disbelief. The Old Bill arrived and started with their usual warnings for us to behave and so on. We had a few beers and started for the stadium western gate escorted by 4 or 5 cops.

Along a nearby street leading to the northern end of the ground we saw some Cherno More fans coming. They were not more than 15 blokes heading towards us, probably having heard the blasts and the songs we were singing. Our front row lads had a go at them kicking and punching. You could hear the routine sound of punches hitting jaws and heads and the muffled thuds of kicking feet. The locals were watching from the sides of the street and kept on shouting at us, *"peasants, peasants…"* A few of their mob were already down, but the others kept on fighting toe-to-toe. One guy had made a chokehold around my neck and was squeezing so hard that I could hardly breathe. I made several attempts to hit him in the ribs with my elbow, all in vain. Then I bit him hard, sinking my teeth into his forearm until he let go of me. He screamed in pain and I, out of pity, kicked him in the head. Meanwhile, a copper bashed me across my ribs with his truncheon. I went down holding the place the dumb cop had just battered.

The scuffle went on for a couple of minutes until police backups arrived and baton charged, drifting the two sets of fans apart. We had a few casualties, some with split lips and others with cuts and bruises. They set us apart and a couple of our lads got nicked and detained until the game was over. The locals also had some casualties, but they just scattered in random directions. Heavily guarded, we were taken into the ground and nothing worth mentioning happened until the final whistle. Same old shit after the game. The police escort had us boarded on the coach that was waiting for us in front of the ground and off we were on our way back home. As we were leaving Varna we kept on hitting and kicking the coach interior walls, shouting to the top of our voices, *"C'mon Loko, C'mon Loko"*, and showing the middle finger to all passersby who dared to look at our vehicle...

Nearly 20 years later, Lokomotiv (GO) played Cherno More again in a cup quarterfinal fixture, the first leg being played at Ticha ground in Varna, where we lost 1-0 as the home side scored in the dying seconds of stoppage time. The interesting thing was that we were playing in the second division while they were in the first half of the table in our top flight. In general, it was a tough game with a few goal scoring chances. Our team had come with the intention not to lose the match. Lokomotiv played with passion and heart and had their good chances to score in the second half, but on the whole the game was dominated by both defenses. Our aim was to go for the win at the second leg, but the home game turned into a disaster for us as we lost 5-0.

About 400 supporters from Gorna Oryahovitsa made the trip to Varna for the first leg, and in particular, there were representatives of our younger firms, i.e. GO Boys and JRF Youths, who occupied the entire away supporter pen. Among them there were several old school fans who had taken part in the events described way back in 1994. Our lads were joined by lads from Spartak (Varna) hooligan firms, who are Cherno More's archenemies and are on friendly terms with our young ultras. There was an exchange of obscene gestures and verbal abuse between the two sets of rival fans, but the game was not marred by any riots or street scuffles between mobs. No chance of that happening as the security measures were now too tight, not like it used to be in the good old days. The only thing worth remembering was the incredible atmosphere and the tremendous support by the black-and-white army in the form of songs, chants and choreo involving smoke canisters and flares. We all prayed for a miracle and an advance to the semifinal, but unfortunately the "Mariners" managed to score in the 93rd minute...

After our cup fiasco against Cherno More, fate decided to cross our paths again, this time for a summer friendly before the start of the 2015/16 campaign. Naturally, not many fans were interested in such a game, but I decided to attend it, especially as I was already living in Varna at that time. This friendly will be remembered for its suspension due to the home supporters' pitch invasion in their effort to have a go at Lokomotiv players.

It was a hot July day and I sat near the southern stand, usually occupied by the home diehard supporters. I was impressed by the fact that there was no police at all, probably due to the game being just a friendly. The "Mariners" scored an opener quite early, but the atmosphere was getting increasingly tense as all the referee's controversial decisions were in their favour and the home side was strongly determined to win the game at all costs. Those disputably awarded free kicks made our players even more agitated and uptight and one of them eventually lost his temper and kicked the home side goalie. Up to that moment, Cherno fans had been constantly hurling abuse and threatening our footballers. I could do nothing else but stand there and listen to all that crap as I was all alone.

When the Lokomotiv player was leaving the pitch after being sent off, he made an obscene gesture to the local fans. Then some 30 people invaded the pitch. There was nobody to stop them and although the referee, linesmen and managers tried to do something, the local louts started punching and kicking our players. More players intervened with the aim of stopping the melee and it resulted in complete chaos. I couldn't see who was punching who, but a Lokomotiv player was knocked down and they were kicking him all over.

The brawl went on for probably five minutes until the Old Bill arrived. Passions subsided, but our player Antoniy Balakov, nephew of the former Bulgarian football star Krasimir Balakov, had his nose and cheek-bone broken. Naturally, the summer friendly was suspended as early as the 36th minute. The police arrested two Cherno More fans who were among the most active in the fight...

Бой прекрати контролата Черно море - Локомотив

11 юли 2015, 18:18 | Ивайло Борисов   f Харесва ми

Фенове нахлуха на терена и потърсиха саморазправа с играч на гостите

Бой на терена прекрати контролата Черно море и Локомотив Горна Оряховица в 36-ата минута. При резултат 1:0 за домакините, футболист на Локо получи директен червен картон за фаул срещу Марк Клок. На излизане от терена играчът Иво Харизанов провокира публиката с неприличен жест и над 15 ултраси на домакините прескочиха оградите и нахлуха на терена.

В следващия момент те опитаха саморазправа с играчите на гостите и въпреки че футболистите, треньорския щаб на Черно море и реферите опитаха да тушират мелето, двама футболисти на Локо бяха ударени и ритнати. В крайна сметка двама от играчите на гостите са пострадали, като Антоний Балъков, който е с подута скула и разбит нос. След секунди страстите утихнаха, но треньорът на Локо Сашо Ангелов прибра своите подопечни в съблекалните и проверката бе прекъсната.

Голът за "моряците" реализира Симеон Райков от фаул в 21-ата минута. Малко след това Бакари получи тежка контузия и бе изнесен на носилка от терена.

Fighting suspends the friendly between Cherno More and Lokomotiv (GO)

Fans invaded the pitch in an attempt to have a fight with a player from the visiting team

---

Fighting on the pitch resulted in Cherno More vs Lokomotiv (Gorna Oryahovitsa) friendlybeing suspended in the 36th minute. With 1-0 for the home side on the scoreboard, a Lokomotiv player was directly shown a red card for committing a foul against Marc Klok. When leaving the pitch, the player in question, Ivo Harizanov, challenged the home crowd by showing an obscene gesture and then more than 15 home ultras jumped over the fencing and invaded the pitch. In a few seconds they tried to engage into a fight with the visiting playersand although Cherno More players and coaches, the referee and linesmen tried to stop the brawl, two Lokomotiv players were punched and kicked. Ultimately, two of the away players got injured, Antoniy Balakov having a broken nose and a swollen cheek-bone. Shortly afterwards the tension subsided, but Lokomotiv manager Sasho Angelov ordered his boys into the dressing room and the friendly was suspended.

The goal for the "Mariners" was scored by Simeon Raikov, converting a free kick in the 21st minute. A little bit later, Bacari was severely injured and had to be taken out of the pitch on a stretcher.

Correspondent Ivaylo Borisov

"С очите си видях как група побеснели лумпени събориха на земята Мицаков, а после започнаха да го ритат, кой където свари."

Това разказа за "България Днес" треньорът на "Локомотив" (Горна Оряховица) Сашо Ангелов, след като уж приятелска среща между неговия тим и "Черно море" беше прекъсната от страховито меле.
Контролата на стадион "Тича" бе прекратена при резултат 1:0 в 36-ата минута, след като фенове на "моряците" нахлуха на терена и започнаха да бият играчи на гостите.
"За мен проблемът дойде от това, че на официалното си предсезонно представяне "Черно море" искаше задължително да победи, а съдията отсъждаше всяко спорно положение в тяхна полза - каза Ангелов. - Но ние винаги играем сериозно и не сме склонни да подценяваме нито една среща, дори и приятелска. Обстановката се нагорещи от обратните отсъждания на рефера. Бакари, за когото се твърди, че е контузен, падна, без дори да има допир с нашия вратар. След поредния фаул в наша полза, който не беше отсъден, Харизанов наистина ритна лошо футболист на "Черно море". Получи директен червен картон и когато напускаше терена, направи обиден жест към публиката. Нещо, което в никакъв случай не биваше да прави.
Тогава около 30 души нахлуха на терена. Нямаше кой да ги спре, защото срещата не се охраняваше от полиция. Започнаха да бият и удрят нашите футболисти, всичко продължи около пет минути. Белезите от боя ясно си личат. Знам, че Антоний Балъков има намерение да съди нападателите, и подкрепям решението му.
На Харизанов вече обясних, че е недопустимо така да провокира публиката. Жалко, че не си говорим за футбол, а за побой. Наясно съм, че такива случки няма да върнат хората по стадионите."
По неофициална информация полицията е задържала двама запалянковци на "Черно море", участвали в мелето.

"I saw it with my own eyes! A mob of outraged louts knocked down Mitsakov on the ground and started kicking him all over."

This is what Lokomotiv (Gorna Oryahovitsa) manager Sasho Angelov told the *Bulgaria Today*Newspaper after the so called "friendly" played by his team and Cherno More was suspended due to a fierce brawl.

The pre-season test played at Ticha Stadium was suspended after 26 minutes, with a score of 1-0, when "Mariners" fans invaded the pitch and started beating the visiting team players. "I explain all that trouble with Cherno More's ambition to win the game at all costs during its official pre-season presentation of the team. In addition, the referee would award each disputable situation in their favour", Angelov said, "but we always play seriously and are not inclined to underestimate any game, be it a friendly.

The atmosphere got red hot due to the referee's totally unfair decisions. Bacari, who is said to have been injured, went down without even being touched by our goalkeeper. After another instance of foul play that went unnoticed by the referee, it is true that Harizanov kicked a Cherno More player really bad. He got a single direct red card and as he was leaving the pitch, showed the home crowd an obscene gesture. It was something he shouldn't have done by any means.

Then about 30 men invaded the pitch. There was nobody to stop them since no police were in charge of the security of this game. They started beating and hitting our players and it went on for approximately five minutes. One can clearly see the scars resulting from that beating. I know that Antoniy Balakov is thinking of suing his attackers and I do support his decision. I have already told Harizanov that he can't provoke the audience like that. It's a pity we are discussing a fight instead of football now. I am fully aware that incidents like that are highly unlikely to make people come back to the grounds to watch football games."

According to some unofficial sources, two Cherno More supporters who took part in the melee have been arrested.

14 Cherno More in Bulgarian means the Black Sea

Neftochimic (Burgas)

During our last season in the first division, i.e. 1994/95, we played away to Heftochimic (Burgas) for the first time as they had won the second division the previous season.

The "Sheikhs", as they are nicknamed, were a newly established in 1962 club, founded by workers in the Neftochim chemical plant. They started from the amateur leagues and in the 1980s they used to play in the second division. In the early 1990s a millionaire called Hristo Portochanov took over and in just four years managed to take it to the top flight, where they successfully played for ten years in a row. In addition, they also made their mark in the Cup tournaments. They played in green and white and were the local bitter rivals of the other club from the town of Burgas, i.e. Chernomorets, whose fans are our allies.

The president's millions not only brought success on the domestic scene, but also facilitated the complete renovation of their ground called Lazur, which turned into a real football jewel in those times. Both the northern and the southern stands had roofs. The ground also had powerful lighting and the immaculate pitch was used by a number of other Bulgarian clubs playing European games as it met the UEFA high standards. Even the Bulgarian national team used it for its official games while Vasil Levski Stadium in Sofia was under repair. It used to be one of the best grounds in our country and in 2015 it hosted a number of Under 17 European Championship games.

Let us go back to that game we played in the town of Burgas in late September 1994. Though autumn had come, the weather was still warm and the last tourists were relaxing on the beaches in Burgas and the nearby resorts such as Sunny Beach and Ravda. Eventually these destinations became favourite places for the English to spend their summer holidays. It was quite understandable, taking into account what was offered to foreigners: cheap booze, posh hotels, wonderful sandy beaches and great nightlife with plentiful of young and pretty girls. To put it briefly, everyone felt like being in the seventh heaven and fully enjoyed their holidays.

We made a decent turnout for that game. There were 30–35 of us travelling by rail and the same number going by cars. We set off early in the morning as we wanted to take advantage of the warm and sunny weather promised in the forecast. The distance between the two towns is not so great (about 140 miles), but a train journey usually takes a long time. As always, we spent it singing and drinking. We arrived at Burgas train station at noon.

Getting off the train, there was that smell of petroleum everywhere, making you feel as if you were in Libya! We had a rally point with the rest of the black-and-white supporters, who had already arrived at the seaside. With plenty of time ahead of the game (kick-off time was around 7:00 pm) we decided to relax on the nearby beaches. Loaded on cold beer, we set off for the beach, our loud chants and shouts echoing all around. The holidaymakers on the beach were quite surprised to see the approach of some one hundred long-haired geezers dressed in black-and-white T-shirts and drinking bottoms up as if it was water in their bottles.

We dispersed, put up our flags on parasols and on the sand (much dirtier than the sand in Varna). Gradually those tourists started sneaking out, folding up their beach towels and looking at us in anger as we had spoilt their afternoon rest and precious nap under the scorching rays of the autumn sun. They were puzzled by the look and behaviour of the long-haired hooligans, who were hurriedly taking off their jeans and in their underwear (no one wore bathing trunks) were rushing to the surging sea waves. There were also those who went swimming without a stitch on. Imagine what kind of indignation and disgust those onlookers had in their eyes! Some of us could barely stand on their feet, others would throw up and then once again raise their bottles of beer and drink and there were those who we standing up and pissing right there, where the sea met the sand!

Once we had finished all those excessive amounts of alcohol, we headed for Lazur ground, much as I regret to admit, leaving behind a complete mess. Of course, we were now escorted by a police car after all that noise and hell we raised on the beach. We were walking and chanting *"C'mon Loko, C'mon Loko"*, the passersby were staring at us in dismay but we just didn't give a damn, especially after we had cooled down in the pleasant waters of the Black Sea. The road to the ground was across a residential quarter also called Lazur, which is located next to the stadium and is surrounded by gardens and parks. One of our lads, obviously rather pissed, decided to have some fun on the swings at a children's playground despite our calls to go on. The people on the balconies of the nearby residential buildings were watching him disbelievingly, laughing their heads off. In a few minutes he fell over (he had his arm plastered), threw up on one side and pleased with himself joined us again.

As we were approaching the gates, most of us started complaining that they demanded us to pay for our tickets. Some lads tried to climb up and get over the high fencing, but didn't make it. More police arrived and we had to reach into our pockets and pay the fare. Our mate with the arm in plaster was almost at the top of the fencing in his attempt to get in, but at some point he just dropped down to the ground and remained there motionless for a couple of minutes. We stood him up and supported him as we were entering one of the stands.

In those times they didn't have a separate away sector so we were simply stood in the first sector we found ourselves in. A few minutes later some 30-40 local fans turned up right above us and started throwing missiles at us. They also began threatening us and showing indecent gestures and then those of our lads that stood closer had a go at them, exchanging some kicks and punches. We rushed towards the enemy but the Old Bill responded fast and a dozen of cops surrounded us separating the two sets of rival fans with their shields.

After that they drove away the locals, sending them to their seats. We remained heavily guarded until the end of the game that we miserably lost 2-1. Their winner was scored by their leaded goalscorer Stancho Tsonev, who then approached our end and started challenging us with his hands. We hit back by throwing at him bits of plastic seats that we had ripped off during the game. The cops intervened again with a baton charge and eventually restored order. We had no mercy for the player in question during the return leg in Gorna Oryahovitsa when he got booed at by the entire home crowd throughout the game that Lokomotiv won 3-1! Following that defeat in Burgas and the not so successful confrontation with the Neftochimic fans, they became one of our bitter rivals though we didn't play each other for quite a long time after that...

At the end of 2005, Neftochimic was relegated to the second division following repeated protests by both its fans and the supporters of their town rivals, the "Sharks" **15**, after an idea was coined to merge both clubs. After numerous scandals, financial difficulties (their millionaire owner was gone) and debts, they even went down to the amateur leagues. After Lokomotiv (GO) returned to the second division in 2014, and respectively they did the same in 2015, now the youngsters from JRF Youths & GO Boys are on the watch for Neftochimic fans ahead of the fixtures to be played after the release of this book...

---

15 THE NICKNAME OF CHERNOMORETS FC, THE OTHER CLUB IN BURGAS

EIGHT

ALLIES

Chernomorets (Burgas)

CHERNOMORETS (BURGAS) IS THE OTHER FOOTBALL CLUB ON THE southern Black Sea coast.

The club was founded in 1919, but as the years went by it went through a lot of changes due financial difficulties and litigations. The "Sharks", as they are called, host their games in the town of Burgas at Chernomorets Stadium with a capacity of 22 000. In 2008 a project for building a new covered stadium was announced. However, construction works never commenced and their current ground is now dilapidated as the team plays in the amateur leagues. The best period for the Burgas club was between 2007 and 2014, when they played in the top flight. As a whole, they take pride in their youth academy where local talents thrive.

What is typical of Chernomorets supporters is that they also copycat the English football fan style, focusing on choir singing, chants and flags. They are one of the oldest organised sets of supporters in the country and have left their solid marks in Bulgarian fandom. They have had regular serious clashes with fans of the Plovdiv clubs, as well as with Beroe supporters. Their main hardcore firm is called BS

Crew, and in recent years they have had some young blood joining their ranks under the name of Blue Sharks Young Crew.

In the beginning, our relations with them (just like in the case with the "Blues" from the seaside town of Varna) were far from friendly and the "everyone is an enemy" principle completely prevailed in those years.

Here is what one of them thinks of the evolution in our relations:

"When my mate Tosh from Gorna Oryahovitsa phoned me to ask me of my opinion of their firm and our alliance in general, I thought he was joking! Hundreds of pages can be written about that. Anyway, I will try to briefly express the Blue Sharks' attitude telling some stories involving different mates belonging to Chernomorets supporters' big family. Now, before our acquaintance turned into a long-standing and euphoric friendship, it was a whole different story.

Way back in 1994, in late April, we were to play an important away game to Lokomotiv (GO) in our fight to avoid relegation from the top league. There were two coach-loads of us, some 100 fans, travelling to Gorna Oryahovitsa in a dense fog. The small, hilly town with a prevailing working-class population was completely uninteresting for us and we had no hatred for them whatsoever.

Our mob was a mixture of old school hooligans with long criminal records and beardless youngsters on their first away day. Fans from small towns in the interior of our country have always envied us for living on the Black Sea coast and all the things that go with that such as better jobs, beautiful girls, etc. Our younger and rather naïve lads did not listen to the advice they were given by our"old dogs" (as they say), namely that they'd better be cautious in Gorna Oryahovitsa. They just wanted to go on the rampage the way they found best. However, the locals must have been looking forward to the game with much more enthusiasm and were much better prepared than us in terms of tactics. They knew where our coaches would park, they knew our numbers and took the most advantage of that.

Come the end of the game, the black-and-whites mobbed up, started stalking us in smaller groups and finally had a go at us. They tried to capture a Union Jack flag from one of our lads, but failed as he broke through their siege comprising of 6 or 7 local fans (mainly metal-heads and some older blokes) by throwing a couple of well-aimed punches. Among the locals, there was this young but very muscular lad with long curly hair who was pretty active and up for it and you could tell he was one of their ringleaders.

In the end, after exchanging loads of punches and kicks, we had several casualties while they only had one! It was back then that those guys impressed us as they had been only a mystery for us before that unfortunate encounter. That was surely one of the few places where we got defeated and saw such hostile and aggressive fans!

At the end of the season Lokomotiv (GO) came to play in Burgas. The night before we drank at our favourite pub called "The Sailor" and we didn't assume that the black-and-whites would arrive on the night train (they used to travel mainly by rail). We decided to go to the train station and meet them. I personally had never seen such hardcore group of 40–50 lads, all of them up for it. We raided the train and a mass brawl started. It was too dark to see anything and all you could hear were the sounds of punches thrown and the loud shouts and screams of people fighting. Then the Old Bill arrived and the chaos grew even bigger. Both sides had casualties and some of our lads even got jail sentences. The railway station in Burgas has never seen another midnight battle like this!

Years later, the student quarter in Sofia accommodated both our Chernomorets fans and supporters from Gorna Oryahovitsa. Our paths crossed. Supporters of all kinds of small clubs would attend our European games to meet new people and to get a feel of the thrill to be part of a bigger mob. Alcohol, heavy music, light drugs, acts of hooliganism and our mutual obsession with British casual culture permanently bonded us with the boys from the railway workers' town. Before we realised it, the 1994 fight was forgotten and we would meet each other at parties or football games. The fact that we found hardcore lads and football hooligans in such a small working class town makes us, Chernomorets fans, filled with admiration up to this day! United, well-organised and loyal, that's what they really were. Naturally, we would attend their derby games on days full of football violence such as their away game in Veliko Tarnovo (a mass brawl in front of Etar ground) or in Mezdra (pitch invasion and tearing off police uniform insignia)!

As the years went by, our friendship grew even stronger. They would come to Burgas on their summer holidays and we, whenever we found it convenient, would visit them in Gorna Oryahovitsa, on which occasions we would almost always end up in Veliko Tarnovo looking for trouble. Actually, that hatred between them and the Boyars is a rather notorious one and I don't know if any other hatred between Bulgarian clubs could even come closer to theirs! The truth is that they have it in their blood and hatred was their daily routine even when they didn't play derby games. I've seen it and I've felt it a thousand times.

There are hundreds of occasions spent together at chalets and campsites, or right there in our former capital Tarnovo, on which ringleaders of the Boyar mob would simply fly off the balconies of their boozer called "The Street". We have also got into trouble together in Sofia underground life or at gigs such as the one of the Agnostic Front band, where we made a joint attack on some Beroe fans. It was a brilliant fight as it had everything you'd ever want, i.e. kicks and punches, bottles thrown, injured and nicked guys! We always laugh out loud when we remember that incident in Sofia.

I definitely place JRF at the hooligan top level. They have never backed off and they have always stood their ground side by side with us even in fights that have not been football related. They were an absolutely crazy bunch of lads as if they were on some weird kind of drugs of their own taken underneath the Kamuka area and they really are a wonderful number of lunatics and hooligans for such a small town they come from! I hope they keep up the good work!"

Spartak (Varna)

During our nine top division seasons, Lokomotiv (GO) several times played against the other club from our seaside capital Varna. Its name is Spartak FC.

We played pretty well against them in games such as our home 3-2 victory in 1988 and away 3-3 draw in 1993. In those times they would alternate the first and the second division of Bulgarian football. The "Falcons", as they are nicknamed, have been one of the regular participants in the top league since they were founded in 1918 and they have also been champions of Bulgaria.

The period between the 1970s and the late 1980s is considered as one of their most glorious ones, and in the second half of 1990s they established themselves as one of the strongest country clubs in Bulgaria. Now Spartak have been playing in the amateur league since in 2015 the club went bankrupt due to a series of financial liabilities and debts and so they had to start from scratch.

In recent years, both our clubs' younger generations of fans developed a friendship. Our JRF Youths & G.O.Boys firms and theirs Brigade Hools & Semper Fideles quite often pay each other friendly visits. In fact, this mutual respect has its roots in the late 1990s when one of our lads moved to live in Varna and later on became one of their ringleaders. At that time actually everyone was everyone's enemy and though now we consider them as our allies, back then we were pure enemies with them.

It was like that way back in the autumn of 1993, when Lokomotiv (GO) had to play away in Varna and we just stole a point from them after a spectacular 3-3 draw in a first division fixture.

We brought some 60 lads on that away day trip, a tight firm travelling to Varna on an early morning train, which was our favourite way of travelling to remote destinations in those times. Our journey was made much more pleasant thanks to the usual huge amounts of booze and a good number of songs that we sang standing in one of the back carriages. The black and white flags were flying out of the train windows and we were all in good mood after our first two games after the beginning of the campaign, i.e. a win and a draw.

We arrived in the seaside town at noon and decided to head straight for the beach and from there catch a bus to take us to their ground, which was also called Spartak (capacity of 13 000), a stadium relatively smaller than the one they hosted the English giants Manchester United at way back in 1983. The game between Spartak and Lokomotiv was to kick off in the early afternoon and so we had time to relax on the beach and cool our bodies with a beer or two.

I remember we used to have the tradition of putting up a huge hand-sewn Union Jack and in general the cult for the English game was in fashion back then so many other firms would also put up British flags to pay their respect to the motherland of football. We found out that the beach was within a guarded zone due to a nearby waterslide. When we approached the fencing some guards tried to stop us at the gate demanding tickets and so we surged forward, knocked down half of the fence and simply poured into the sandy strip. We then draped the huge flag on the ground and lay down around it, devouring more and more of the ice cold beer. Though we are not figured as "children of the sea" (as our town is not near the sea shore), a large number of us (I mean Jolly Roger Firm members and the followers of pirate romanticism in general) have always considered the shore as a special power of attraction and so we just loved to drape our flags on beach parasols and proudly watch them flying in the breeze.

I remember someone had brought a battery powered cassette recorder blasting out Running Wild's Under JollyRoger album, which added atmosphere for us as somehow that music was in unison with the beach and the sea.Come the early afternoon, most of us had lost control and decided to take over the nearby waterslide! In just a few seconds, some brutal shouts and screams came from that direction and all holidaymakers just started leaving the beach. The guards had phoned the police telling them about our violent invasion and so the Old Bill came to escort us out and onto the ground. We chose to split into small groups (in twos or threes), sneak out of the beach unnoticed, and catch a bus going to the stadium. We had carried out an investigation and knew that Spartak fans ahead of their home games usually gathered in the small boozers situated around and opposite their ground main entrance.

In those times Spartak brought good numbers but they were not as organised as they are now. Nowadays their firm is pretty tough, they have some young hooligans and their future looks bright. After several minutes on a public transport bus people started looking at us in their strange ways. The way we looked then, I mean long hair, tight jeans and military style boots, and the loud singing, which sounded more like screaming and yelling, made all those passengers get off the bus and walk on.

Shortly before getting off at the bus stop near Spartak Stadium we noticed their boys drinking undisturbed. We started chanting *"Loko! Loko!"* and hitting the bus windows with our fists, eager to get off as quickly as possible. They saw us and started hurling insults and threats at us. Tensions rose in that hell of a noise we were making and after the gestures they showed us we went fucking mental. Before they even realised what was happening we stormed their pubs.

There were no more than 30 of them and they surely got a fright upon seeing some 60 black and white mad louts running towards them. We steamed into them throwing punches and kicks. Plastic tables and chairs started flying about, the sound of smashing bottles filled the air and all kinds of debris were hurled from both sides of the boozer. We went toe-to-toe with them, though some were still throwing bottles and fragments of broken gear and stuff.

A massive fight started and the sounds of punches thrown and our loud shrieks had attracted the attention of the passersby and the regular supporters on the opposite side of the street, who were first watching only, but then started joining the brawl. It was getting way out of control. Though Spartak fans almost equaled our numbers, at some point they flew into a panic and some of them fled. The fight lasted no more than ten minutes when the police intervened with their usual truncheons and shields. Lads from both sides were bleeding, the entire pub was ravaged, there was smashed glass all around and everything had been turned to ruin. The cops separated the two rival sets of fans and kept us on the spot under a heavy gendarmerie escort. We went on singing and teasing them with some mocking chants. Some of us got nicked, others sought medical care, but by and large, that was one of our best away days to be remembered for long after that…

In the years to come, we would visit some of the boys who took part in the events described quite a few times and, naturally, we had full respect for each other, which we further developed into the good friendship we have with them these days. Spartak (Varna) became strong allies of ours, especially when we would play away to the other Varna club, i.e. their sworn enemies Cherno More, which you already read about in another story in this chapter.

Levski (Sofia)

I remember us hosting Levski and there were 22000 people at the 15 000-capacity ground. There were people on the light towers and up the tall poplars all around the outer fencing!

A whole week before, we would shred old newspapers and gather cash register tapes. We had sacks full of such stuff ready for the big event and once the game kicked off, the pitch looked like as if it was not us throwing it from the terraces, but someone pouring out those sacks from the very sky above. The pitch was all covered with the stuff and the play was delayed for some 30 minutes until they cleaned up.

When we played in the top echelon of Bulgarian football, we would quite often successfully challenge (in terms of football) the two Sofia giants, but it was a totally different story on the terraces due to the huge numbers both "reds" and "blues" used to bring.

I have always shared the opinion (and openly declared it) that the so called "eternal derby" of our capital Sofia poisons the rest of the Bulgarian football fan culture in general. I believe things could be on a much equal basis and there could be much more interesting and tougher games if the two clubs in question did not "steal" fans from other towns. I don't say that we haven't got any friends and acquaintances supporting CSKA or claim that we have more friends and acquaintances supporting Levski, but we did have an affinity with the "Blues".

Now I'd like to make it clear. I don't mean in any way that Gorna Oryahovitsa is either "blue" or "red" as some modern-day moronic fans would claim. It was just that the bipolar model of Bulgarian fandom would always force you into making your choice and most young fans nowadays prefer to support the more famous and celebrated club instead of their local teams. This is the main reason why so many small teams sink into oblivion. It's not only the financial difficulties, but because they have no devoted fans to stand behind them and support them in hard times. A great pity indeed!

Here is what a good old friend of ours thinks about that, about us, Lokomotiv, and about the development of our friendship with the supporters of one of the two Sofia giant clubs:

"My name's Ivan and I support Levski (Sofia). I am writing these lines at the request of my good mate Tosh. He has set himself the difficult task to describe part of the Ultra-Hoolie movement in Bulgaria and in particular the football related events involving the Jolly Roger Firm. I am not into words that much, but I will try to brief you on my relations with them.

*My first memories of meeting Gorna Oryahovitsa boys date back to the beginning of the third millennium. The majority of them had a liking for Levskiand so it all began in the legendary Sector B **16**. For those who are not familiar with the Bulgarian scene, football is almost a two-way race all over our country, so there are Levski, CSKA and… all the rest. JollyRoger Firm was probably the cream of the crop among the smaller towns in the countryside.I was mostly impressed by their enormous love, devotion, fervour and self-sacrifice to football and their unconditional support for their beloved club. A core of absolutely faithful* *and loyal mates, ready to do anything to stand for what they believed in and support the people who stood close to them. Gorna Oryahovitsa lads (as they are also known in our circles) have repeatedly proven with their attendance and acts their unreserved support for us, Levski fans, and they have always been given a hearty welcome in Sector B. I remember the great number of invitations they'd send us to visit their home and especially their thrilling away games. All the parties and the fights ahead of and after games, well, I can hardly find the words to describe and convey the emotions we have been through together. There was this particularly awesome occasion for us during the 2005/06 season when my beloved Levski reached the European cup quarterfinals and played Schalke 04 and the boys from Gorna Oryahovitsa categorically supported us! In order to demonstrate how remarkable that achievement was in itself, I'll say that Levski started playing in that tournament as early as in the second qualifying ground. Our games were played on Thursdays and after each one we'd go to a live music night club together with them and we'd go on partying till the break of dawn.*

My relations with Jolly Roger Firm evolved and so I made new friends from their town, lads that did not support Levski. Our parties and meets became more frequent, 3 or 4 of them being particularly important and memorable in my mind in spite of the huge amounts of booze devoured. The respect and willingness they showed while supporting a couple of my ventures made me feel I am a rich and happy man in terms of loyal friends. I invited them to two of my birthday parties and I'll tell you about them in a few lines.

The first time we were at the Kapchuka chalet, where I used to celebrate my birthdays. Let me tell you a few words about the chalet. It is located in a natural canyon near the town of Pleven used in ancient times as a Roman road. The chalet is secluded amonst magnificent nature and fully met my guests' expectations to feel cozy and in peace. I had invited about 50 people and I was glad they all turned up. Friends of mine came from Varna (Ultra Varna is a Levski Firm I am a member of), Sofia, Pleven and Gorna Oryahovitsa.

We played football on the meadow in front of the chalet, and there was a lot of heavy music, food and drinks and of course, plenty of fun. The prefect party! The second time I had invited guests to the Srebrostrui chalet situated in the Kailuka Park in the town of Pleven. That park is the biggest man-made park in Bulgaria. The chalet hall looks like a hunters' lodge, which made us feel warm and comfortable enough to have a great party. There was a beer drinking contest so lots of lads had a blackout and on the next morning we had to help each other recollect the events from the party.

And finally let me tell you a few words about one of the authors of this book, Tosh, who in my opinion is the ringleader of Jolly Roger Firm. We took to each other immediately. I don't know whether it is due to our similar age, or because we were born under one and the same sign, or simply because we have similar beliefs, mentality and interests. Anyway, I don't think that matters much since I am just happy to know him. He is a reliable man, caring of his wonderful family and friends. Creative, versed, responsible and ready to stick to his guns whatever the cost. We would regularly try to out speak each other (he just likes to talk) and after we'd get tired of talking (I found it so hard to out speak him!), we would challenge each other in arm wrestling. Life separated us in terms of space and we haven't seen each other for several years, but I do believe that we will soon right this wrong. I wish him good luck in his new venture!

I am thankful for the opportunity and the invitation to take part in this project and I would like to wish my friends from Jolly Roger Firm best of luck and let them keep on being strong, loyal and resolute!"

---

16 Sᴇᴄᴛᴏʀ **B** ɪs ᴛʜᴇ ɴᴏᴛᴏʀɪᴏᴜs Lᴇᴠsᴋɪ ᴜʟᴛʀᴀs sᴛᴀɴᴅ

Notts County (Nottingham)

"In April 2012, me and my wife Kath decided to leave our home in Nottingham, England, and fulfil our dream of living abroad. Our choice

of destination was Bulgaria, which came as a surprise to our friends and relatives. We immediately settled down in our new environment and we really found ourselves living a leisurely, peaceful and easy life, which beautiful Bulgaria can definitely offer with its unique nature.

And yet, there was something that I missed a lot and that was football, having followed Notts County all my life, and that left a huge blank in me. I have always loved the game and despite all the disappointments resulting from my support for Notts County back at home, nothing could replace or even compare to attending a football game with my mates. The early meets, a few beers and the support for my native team, I missed all of that awfully.

Anyway, after a quick search on the Internet I found my local team called Lokomotiv (GO). They played in the third division and guess what… they were black-and-white, too! Just fine! I had attended a few home games before I and my father, who'd come to visit me, went to an away game in the town of Svishtov. To be honest, I didn't know what to expect and I wasn't sure whether anyone else from Gorna Oryahovitsa was making the trip. Upon arrival, we were immediately approached by a group of lads dressed in black and white who were extremely curious to find out who the two foreigners following their modest club were.

The game finished 1-0 for Lokomotiv against one of the top teams in the division, Academic Svishtov and I was really fascinated. Watching the fans and players celebrating together after the game was really out of this world, something absolutely different from our English game, where I knew from experience that most players avoid any contacts with the supporters, if possible.

It didn't take long to get a message from one of the authors of this book, Tosh, who in turn had chosen London as his destination and was already living in England with his family. He was also wondering what an Englishman like me was doing in Bulgaria and I told him I would sometimes attend his local club's games. He immediately helped me get in touch with some of the local lads and after a few weeks I would already feel at home.

Ahead of games here, fans also meet in pubs as early as possible in order to have as much beer as possible (and not only, cause they have a unique homemade drink they call rakia and, truth to tell, I started to really like it) and discuss the game! Several things made a strong impression on me and one of them was those lads who'd support their club and town with such passion and pride that could even make the most die-hard English supporters jealous. One of them local lads told me long ago that, "Supporting Lokomotiv (GO) is not only about watching football, it is about being a part of a large family."

Lokomotiv (GO) is one of the few clubs in Bulgaria that get a travelling support everywhere they go. There is always at least one coach-load of fans in their usual good mood no matter the score. Probably this is largely due to the huge amounts of alcohol (rakia) they'd always drink ahead of games. Never before and nowhere before had I seen people drink like and as much as they drink here. Mind you, I come from a country that's famous for its drinking habits and trends. However, that would always make your day happier and funnier like a recent away day in the town of Vratsa.

It was a fine warm day and I and a mate of mine had just sat in the sun, beer in hand, when one of the lads joined us slightly pissed and then he started stumbling upon the tables and finally fell over. Upon seeing that the owners simply threw everybody out of the bar!

It happened a short time before kick-off time and my friend and I tried to pick him up. After several unsuccessful attempts he finally got up and we left him there happily swaying down the street at the speed of a snail. Anyway, we got near the gates and then some of the youngsters lit up some smoke bombs and flares and all hell broke loose in seconds as the Old Bill quickly surrounded the culprits. Meanwhile, the drunken kid somehow managed to do a 100-metre sprint directly bumping into the coppers telling them straight what he thought of their mothers. They got him nicked and he was almost unconscious when they put him in the squad car!

Come the end of the game, everybody's attention turned to releasing the offender and after a couple of phone calls the cops agreed to let him go and return to the coach that was waiting for him at a lay-by out of town. He was given a hero's welcome as he was telling us how the cops started beating him hard and the only way he could stop them was by farting out loud!

I'd like to say a big thank to all Lokomotiv (GO) fans who accepted me as one of their lot, and especially to Koko, Nikolai (though a Forest fan), Radoslav and Tosh for initiating our first meet. Come on LOKO!"

Lokomotiv (Plovdiv)

A lot can be said and written about the railwaymen's football club from the City of the Seven Hills as they call Plovdiv, who we have a lot in common with not only in terms of symbols and colours (black and white), but also in view of the great friendship we started and the respect we have had for each other through all those years.

Plovdiv is the second biggest city in Bulgaria, located in the central part of the Upper Thracian Plain lying on the banks of the Maritsa River between two majestic mountains, the Rhodope and Stara Planina. Lokomotiv (Plovdiv) was founded in 1926 and the club's nickname is the "Smurfs". They play in the top division at their Lokomotiv ground with a capacity of 12 000 (the same as ours). They became champions of Bulgaria in 2003/04. It was their first title ever and they also won the Cup of Bulgaria in that season. The club from Plovdiv made another unprecedented move in the history of Bulgarian football as a supporters' association got hold of 96% of the club shares and so they became the first Bulgarian club to be managed by fans.

They have played several times in the European club tournaments, their most successful season being 1964/65, when they knocked out two teams, Vojvodina and Petrolul, before getting done at the 1/8-finals by Juventus. In 2005/06 they played a UEFA Cup tie against the English side Bolton Wanderers, and there were a number of street fights between hooligans from Blighty (Cuckoo Boys) and Lokomotiv thugs who call themselves Lauta **17** Hools. Those scenes are described in details in Doug Mitchel's book "Walking down the Manny Road" (Inside Bolton's Football-Hooligan Gangs).

The black-and-white supporters from Plovdiv are leaders in Bulgaria in terms of good organisation and they have been the first to introduce in our country all new European football subculture trends. It was not accidentally that the first formal fan club in Bulgaria was founded by Lokomotiv (Plovdiv) fans in 1988. Their bitter rivals are the other football club from the City of the Seven Hills, i.e. Botev (Plovdiv), who later on became our great rivals by default.

Our acquaintance with Lokomotiv (Plovdiv) dates back to the early 1990s. First it was a game our two clubs played in Gorna Oryahovitsa, when, at half time, several of us just went to their lot and following long negotiations with the Old Bill they finally let us enter their away end, also persuaded by the Plovdiv supporters' calls *"Let them come, don't worry!"*, which were a clear sign that they, just like us, had good intentions only. I keep some great memories of that meet since they showed their respect for us in the very beginning. They are simply true gentlemen and absolutely down-to-earth guys, while as far as fandom is concerned, you know what they say, *"What is seen is not pointed at!"* A second meet followed at the central Plovdiv ground when we played another club from that city, Spartak, and then our alliance was legitimised, once again in their city, during our game against yet another Plovdiv club, Maritsa FC. It was then I met one of their lads called Donch (RIP), who, unfortunately, is not among the living anymore. It is him we will pay tribute to further below in this book.

But here is what another fan of the Plovdiv Smurfs has to tell about us and our second meeting. A founder and current leader of one of their firms called NUP (Napoletani Ultras Plovdiv):

"Since I belong to the so called "old-school" generation, I will tell you about an occasion in Plovdiv, when Lokomotiv (GO) played Spartak (Plovdiv). I remember we had been drinking by the rowing canal, which was a fairly cool place in hot weather, as the game was to be played at the Plovdiv city ground situated right next to it. There were about 25 of

them. I remember it was extremely hot and they could barely carry their rucksacks full of flags, smoke canisters and bombs. They must have had 2 or 3 each! They had primed themselves pretty well for a football game. The heat made us drink huge amounts of beer and soon it was "everybody naked from the waist up", a quite spontaneous and rational decision. I already knew a couple of Lokomotiv (GO) lads, having met them a few months before during our game in their town of Gorna Oryahovitsa. It was then they had come to our away end to show their respect to us and their devotion to the "black-and-white" idea.

We oiled our throats well and stood along with them on the upper tier behind one of the goals. In only 20 minutes after we entered the ground, about 30 flags (most of them British) were draped all along the curved railing in front, some of them hanging down as low as the lower tier. They were afraid someone could pull and nick them from below, but actually they had no reason to worry as soon it became clear that the city ground was virtually empty. They anticipated the game as if a huge crowd was going to enter the sector any minute ahead of kick-off time, but alas, it was only us and them, our black-and-white brothers in arms.

I think there's no need to tell you that there was no organised home support of any kind whatsoever! The game began and their voices erupted. Only their echo answered them, quite loud at that, due to the wonderful venue acoustics. One could only hear the constantly repeated shouts "Don't stop!" and "Everybody! Louder!" When you're in a small firm as theirs you simply can't even think of remaining silent or having a rest! No one is there to replace or substitute you and after the game your voice will certainly be gone and you'll need a whole week to get it back for its next trial! However, I was greatly impressed that they sing loud, clear and most of all correctly! Their chants were accompanied only by the deafening bangs of the bombs thrown and the distinct clapping of their hands.

The scorching sun found it hard to break through the thick clouds of ammonium nitrate smoke spreading all around. Even the few home supporters lost interest in the game and were staring in disbelief at what was going on behind the goal, most probably thinking "Are those blokes *sane!?" They sang like that non-stop for 90 minutes. One could surely tell they considered it as their duty and vocation, like we all do, of course. It is that particular thing, i.e. the thing that is worth travelling hundreds of miles and looking forward to each week, and the thing you cannot afford to miss or discredit yourself with. You rely on yourself and on a small circle of close mates only. This is exactly what I saw in them and, truth to tell, I was more than impressed.*

I find all those comparisons between the so called small and big teams as highly tentative and that useless game proved my idea as it was the perfect example of brilliant support and choreo despite the total lack of atmosphere and charge due to the small numbers and the absent opponents.

Full respect to our brothers from Lokomotiv (GO)!

B.H.

They were also interested and it has nothing to do with what some people say that we were kinda fawning and stuff. We are not like those who always try hard to prove themselves somewhere. We earn friendships in a true and honest way. It is a matter of reputation and respect. Quite recently, one of their lot said, *"The black-and-whites" from Plovdiv are friends with Gorna Oryahovitsa and Napoli only."*

A few times afterwards we have been invited to Plovdiv derby games and I am more than fascinated. They have always given us a hearty welcome there and I also believe we kinda brought them luck in their games against Botev. By and large, I think that the Plovdiv derby by far outweighs the Sofia derby between Levski and CSKA.

In the lines below I will try to briefly summarise my experience with such derby games and the development of our long-standing friendship.

There was this period when me and my mates would regularly visit

Plovdiv not only because of football, but also because of the old town charm, its nightlife and last but not least, because of our true friends. According to a generally held view, people from big cities are always considered as, let's say stuck-up, in comparison with people from smaller towns like us. However, our case was totally different.

I remember a game Lokomotiv (GO) and Lokomotiv (Plovdiv) played on a freezing winter day. There were some 15 of us at the railway station in the early morning and everyone around would ask us, *"Are you going to a football game or are you going skiing?!"* However, as always, we didn't give a fuck about any weather forecasts and the half a metre of snow on the ground. We decided to make the trip to Plovdiv anyway. When we were at the highest train station in Bulgaria called Krustets, where the railway crosses over the Stara Planina Mountain, the train unexpectedly stopped and they said there had been a railway electrification system breakdown that was impossible to repair under the given circumstances as at some points there was already a metre of snow cover!

We jumped off the train and sank into some waist deep snow! We had to wait for an alternative means of transport to be organised, but it was not clear what it would be. The whole country was declared in a state of emergency and everybody was advised to go into the tiny waiting room and stay there until the problem was solved. However, it didn't suit us as there were only few hours left before kick-off and we just had to find a way to move on. Finally we made it!

We made a deal with an all-terrain truck driver to take us with him to some major road from where we could continue our journey hitchhiking. So, out in the freezing cold, we got on the vehicle (just like soldiers) and very slowly, but surely we reached a busy road, from where we were given a ride to our much cherished destination, i.e. the Lauta Stadium in the town of Plovdiv. There's no need to tell you how chilled to the bones we were and to top it all, we were half an hour late for the game and our team was already down. Naturally, the pitch was in an awful condition and the Smurfs (obviously much better adapted to the weather) would simply score one after another. I'll never forget their players' dives after each goal they'd score, leaving a trail of mud behind as they were happily gliding down the pitch.

After the final whistle they wildly celebrated their much deserved win. Understandably, we were simply devastated and we left the ground with our heads down, wondering how the hell we were going to get home and then we heard someone calling and whistling to us. It was several of their lads, who, having seen the kind of situation we were in, offered us to stay with them for a couple of days until the weather got better. In the evening we went out clubbing together and had a wonderful time. That's the kind of friendship we are talking about, friendship that is not only football related or limited.

Hospitality has always been our priority when they visit our town so I would tell all the haters out there: *This is the perfect football related friendship between supporters of two different clubs. What is different from many others is the fact that we share one and the same philosophy, a black-and-white one!*

Though earlier in this chapter I mentioned the superiority of their archenemies Botev in all those years before we formed our black and white alliance, after that our friends definitely grew and developed in terms of fandom and soon they were the ones who wouldn't care about the others in Bulgaria. I remember that when they came to Gorna Oryahovitsa before the 1990s they were, to be honest, nothing special, either as numbers or as quality. However, I remember well how they marched through the Borisova Garden in Sofia, right in the heart of CSKA, and how they wouldn't bow their heads to none of the big clubs in Sofia. I'll leave aside the hatred existing between the two Bulgarian biggest cities Sofia and Plovdiv for another book maybe, cause now I am going to take you back to one of the bloodiest Plovdiv derbies ever, where even we, being only guests, fell victims to the fierce rivalry.

It was another invitation by our friends. Some ten of us took the train to Plovdiv. We were in an excellent mood and had great expectations. Adrenaline kept on getting higher with each minute on the clock. We got off at Plovdiv railway station and headed for the place we had arranged to meet our friends, an Irish pub called Dublin. Afterwards we found out that the particular venue had been chosen with the purpose of confronting the "yellows" (that's how they call their blood enemy) as it was situated on the borderline in terms of territories and was closer to Botev ground than to Lauta.

We arrived at noon to find out that we were late as the two sides had already been running battles. There were huge riots as cars and dustbins were being overturned, an exchange of every kind of missiles imaginable like bombs, bricks, stones and flares was going on, and of course, a toe-to-toe involving pipes, belts, etc. was raging all around. In general, the place looked like a war zone and some of us had the bad luck of being at the wrong place at the wrong time when the cops started nicking people. The worst thing was that some lads got arrested without even taking part in the battles. For example, a few of our boys got nicked in Hristo Botev Blvd (I was not present there) just because they were walking along with the crowd at the time of the riots. What was interesting in that case was that the future Chief Secretary of Police General Petrov in person (at that time Chief of Plovdiv Police Directorate) got an urgent call to appear at the crime scene (which he did in his house clothes) and so he specified our lads as major participants and even as the ones who orchestrated the violence.

Afterwards they were taken into custody, convicted of hooliganism and ended up doing community service for a few weeks, sweeping the grass in parks and gardens and paving the old town streets with setts. You can watch footage of both events on YouTube. So we also had our considerable contribution to those derby games and the Plovdiv "black-and-whites" really loved inviting us and were happy to see us attending their games. Moreover, I personally have never witnessed Lokomotiv get defeated on all those 7 or 8 derby games I have attended. Probably they were in a good shape in those days, but such are the facts.

At another derby between the "yellows" and the "black-and-whites", played at Lauta ground, I witnessed an old school scuffle between both sides, though Botev were probably in their decline then. Anyway, they brought some really tough lads on that day and, if you ask me, they even got the upper hand as they ambushed their opponents and came from behind a school wall. The Smurfs were definitely caught by surprise and couldn't move at first. Opposite I saw the same faces I had seen several years ago when Botev came to play in Gorna Oryahovitsa in the early 1990s (an occasion we described in our story about them earlier in this book). What followed was a real, classic, masculine, aggressive fight with no weapons or tools used. All you could hear was the heavy thumps of kicks and fists and the performers were both sides' top boys. It was probably the best they could bring, two tight and tough groups of 20-30 lads each. A real masterpiece when it comes to football related hooligan fights in general.

As I already said, in the years to come, Lokomotiv (Plovdiv) fan structures (firms and clubs) grew up fast and simply started terrorising their rivals from the other side of town. It was no longer a fight to prevail on a derby day; it was now a struggle to rule an entire city. I have attended several, let's say, "crusades" all over Plovdiv, veritable manhunts for "yellow" fans when groups of Lokomotiv hooligans would patrol the city streets for 24 hours for two or three days in a row ahead of and after derby days in search of the local enemy's top boys. Botev FC then moved its ground to a nearby village called Komatevo, everybody started calling them "non-urban people" and Lauta Hools turn their away games there into real invasions.

In the mid-1990s, during one of my regular meets with Lokomotiv (Plovdiv) fans while we were playing Maritsa FC (another Plovdiv club), I was introduced to a lad that eventually I became so close to that we became like brothers. We officially strengthened our friendship and alliance. He was an idealistic person, but most of all a real football fan. Besides being a proper Lokomotiv (Plovdiv) supporter, Donch also had an affinity with the Scottish Hibs and

French Bordeaux and he was also a very keen collector of all kinds of souvenirs and items related to his favourite clubs.

In the first part of this book I already told you about my obsession for posters on the walls and flags on the windows during the parties I used to throw at home, but he would go much further than that putting stickers on doors, cupboards and kitchen appliances, collecting hundreds of pins and badges, pennants, football jerseys, scarves, etc. and making direct hits (as he used to call them) in casual scene designer apparel. He would even call me at 03:00 am to show me what Stone Island jacket of my size he had come across or where he had stuck the new Lokomotiv (GO) stickers I had given him.He did such things right until his last breath on this Earth and hours before he passed away (having fought an insidious disease for almost two years), he phoned me and said, *"Bro, I don't know whether I'll make it this time, and if I don't, I'll leave all those things I have collected all those years as a legacy to you!"*

Upon hearing that, I, of course, started crying but the legacy he left was not only those objects. Donch was very erudite, he used to read a lot and he would tell his stories in an absolutely fascinating way. He knew a lot about terrace football culture. I dare say he was the Bulgarian Pat Dolan.

In 2015 fate decided to take away both my great friends but I am sure that the sad loss will unite and bond even more people in football related friendships both in my own country and abroad.Throughout all those years he showed me the sense and meaning of true friendship on the terraces and beyond. He would often be a guest of honour in our town and together we would go to parties, clubs, concerts and seaside holidays. He knew how to really entertain his audience and was a true expert in a number of topics. He was the one who introduced me to many other "black-and-white" brothers who nowadays we have legitimised our alliance with. He was the kind of guy who'd always prefer to speak to you directly and plainly and to do it sensibly, without a trace of hypocrisy and two-facedness. He was also frank and straightforward with me and he would never spare me any constructive criticism, and at the same time he'd help me out in a number of ventures and endeavours and he would often advise and guide me. Although he was younger than me, I always listened to his words and I considered him as a man whose opinions and attitudes could teach me a lot.

Words and pages here would not be enough for me to express my grief over the loss of this man so that's why I'll let a close friend of his from Plovdiv do the talking, a man who Donch introduced to me in the dawn of our friendship with the following words: *"I have found a great new recruit for our stand and, mark my words, one day he will be a true leader."* Years later, it turned out that his scouting talent was quite good and I took at his word.

I remember when I first met that young boy sluggishly dragging his school bag on his way home from school. Bored to death and probably looking forward to finishing the Friday lessons and going to the Saturday game at Lauta Stadium, where, years later that grumpy little became founder of the GMU (Gott Mit Uns) firm and its major ringleader.

Here are his words about idealistic Donch and our friendship:

"I met Doncho many years ago. I remember his long hair that he'd always wear in a ponytail. He was older than me and I admired him a lot. He was my role model as a man and a football fan. He would always give me fatherly advice and teach me what it means to be devoted to your favourite club and to the "black-and-white" idea in general. As time went by we became closer and we started going out quite a lot to have a beer or two in our neighbourhood. He was the man who introduced me to fandom in general and to Lokomotiv top boys. I'll never forget how I felt when I first went to an away game with him and the rest of Lokomotiv supporters. At that time we loved to travel by rail and I'll always remember those good old days with nostalgia.

Ahead of one of our derbies with city rivals Botev he came and told me that he was going to meet some friends of his from Gorna Oryahovitsa.

We agreed to meet in our neighbourhood and then go to the train station to wait for the Gorna Oryahovitsa boys. The train arrived and a few lads wearing black-and-white scarves got off. They were absolutely positive though it was our first meeting. I got this feeling we had known one another for years. We oiled our throats with beer before the game and then headed for the ground. I can't remember well, but I think we beat Botev 1-0 or 2-1. After the game we labeled our guests as bringing good luck and if I have to be honest, we still haven't lost a single city derby game attended by Jolly Roger Firm lads.In the years that followed, we exchanged a number of visits. I won't forget how before a game we played against Etar in Veliko Tarnovo, I, Donch and several other lads went to Gorna Oryahovitsa the previous day. We were met at the station by Tosh, Turnip and some other mates of theirs. In the evening we had a party in their legendary boozer called Domino, where their entire firm had gathered. We sang songs all night and got pissed. On the next day, about 10–15 of us caught a coach and went down to Tarnovo a few hours ahead of kick-off time with the intention to look for troubles with the Boyars, who never turned up anyway. As the years went by, this friendship further developed for both me and Donch, and Tosh is really like a brother to us!"

Here is what the co-author of this book Gilly Black has to say about Donch:

I first met Donch (Doncho was his real name, or Donyo as everybody used to call him) during the game between Lokomotiv (GO) and Lokomotiv (Plovdiv) in October 1993, which the "railwaymen" from Gorna Oryahovitsa won 1-0 against the Smurfs from Plovdiv. Our meeting was due to the mutual respect between the two sets of supporters, which later turned into a real friendship.

I remember him as a quite lively lad with an incredible sense of humour and one of the leaders of their black-and-white army, which eventually became the notorious Lauta Hools hooligan firm. He was also very sociable and cheery; a quite funny guy and a real gentleman. He would always find a way to cheer you up and make you smile. He would talk with passion about fights on the terraces all over the country, but most of all he was ready to do anything in the name of friendship! I won't forget his typical goatee, charming smile, and the sunglasses and cap he'd always wear. He used to follow his beloved Lokomotiv all over Bulgaria, but he was also a follower of the English casual culture and a devoted supporter of the Scottish side Hibernian. He won the affection of so many people becoming a real top face in the City of the Seven Hills.

He would visit us quite often in Gorna Oryahovitsa, be it football games, parties or concerts. We'd also return the visits to Plovdiv attending derbies against their city rivals Botev. That's how we got to know the rest of their hardcore boys. I have never heard a single bad word about him. He was a true terrace legend!

Unfortunately, Donch passed away in the summer of 2015 following a long fight with an insidious disease, when he was only 37. The sad news brought sorrow to a large number of football fans, not only in Plovdiv, but in the entire country. I learned it from my mate Tosh. I was abroad at the time and couldn't attend his funeral. It was one of the saddest days in my life as we lost a true friend and a wonderful person! He is still talked about and his name lives on! He will never be forgotten! We will always miss him!

REST IN PEACE, old friend! May God bless you and one day we'll meet on the other side!

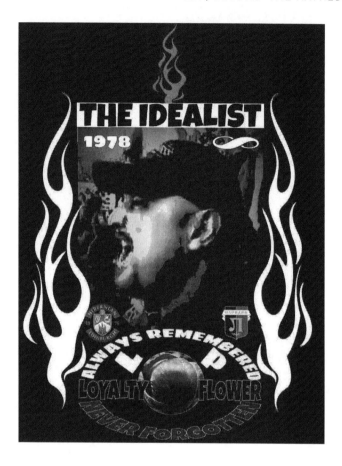

17 Lauta is the name of a residential quarter and a park in the city of Plovdiv

EPILOGUE

NO WAY OUT

SINCE THE MID-1990s, WHEN WE FORMALLY FOUNDED THE JOLLY Roger Firm, a lot of things have changed and we have seen so many lads come and go. The sad thing is that some friendships that we valued and relied on unconditionally have been ruined and as a result we have felt more or less betrayed. Others have remained as strong as ever and there have been also boys who just got bored and withdrew from the football scene.

For us (me and Tosh) the ideology we set and still develop has turned out to be a real (call it if you like) addiction and just like some kind of drug we have fallen deep into the hands of its dependency. We have incessantly fought against those who have lower instincts and those who have been trying hard to break down our unity, solidarity and loyalty. People have called us mindless thugs or loons trying to turn everything upside down on Saturday afternoons fighting their opponents.

To all those who don't understand and are not familiar with these issues, we would like to say that football firms comprise of quite clever, talented and bright individuals. We were football hooligans (may be still are, who knows?) for several reasons: the adrenaline rush, the fights against our enemies or just for the very thrill of spending a day out with your beloved club and your mates. All those reasons came hand in hand and made our weekends complete.

Everyone has a different view on hooliganism and football related violence as a whole, but we personally liked the idea to fight and protect your city or town, stand your ground and last, but not least, to fight for your favourite football club. That rush of adrenaline running through your entire body in an instant before starting a fight is the indescribable perfect feeling that we would dare to compare to the sense you get after climbing the highest mountain.We had to convey all of this to someone who would carry on the name of Jolly Roger, a name that is to remain forever as a synonym of respect in the football hooliganism chronicles. We just couldn't erase so easily what we have created with so much hard work, what we have been through and what we have permanently established on the football scene.

The future lies in the hands of the newly founded JRF Youths firm and it is relatively optimistic, taking into account that Lokomotiv (GO) once again plays in the top divisions. The future looks inspiring in the person of several praiseworthy boys who recently entered the hierarchy. We have tried to make these lads feel welcome and respectively introduce them to that ideology and I hope we've been successful. What they should know is that friendship is the strongest bond in any firm. When you know that there is always someone standing beside you, side by side, no matter how good you are at fighting, when you share both good and bad or when you can fully trust each other and when you feel your mate as if he was your real brother. Those are the principles that make football related friendship unique.

Hooliganism and football will always be there in our daily routines. It is true that the 1980s and 1990s will never be back again, modern times will never reach those heights, we will never be able to experience it again, but I seriously doubt and I do not believe that football related hooliganism will ever die.

Nowadays you can go to football matches without having any confrontation for months, while in those days, be it home or away, it just happened almost on a daily basis. Many clubs are now followed by lads wearing expensive brands like Stone Island or Fred Perry, trying to get noticed, but they would not get into a fight in order not to screw up their attire and there is nothing unconditional in that. We also wore such clothes, though it was difficult for us to find them in the beginning because of the totalitarian regime, but the fights and the desire to prove ourselves were of primary importance for us so that we can show everybody on the scene that we deserve some respect (something we believe we have achieved).

It is true that times have changed and fights on and off the pitch have also changed considerably. Security measures at stadia, video surveillance cameras, bans and fines play much more important roles now, but the ideology to follow what you love is still the same. They can ban us from attending games, but they cannot take away our memories. Nowadays information is much more easily accessible to the police, be it through social networks or any other sources and yet, there will always be youngsters, 14–16 years of age, who will believe in the ideology and try to look for ways to continue and further develop it. This is an irreversible process and when the core of a firm is deeply rooted and has one way or another been renowned for its reputation, there will always be seeds that will eventually grow into plants, which will hardly be uprooted.

A number of blokes have left the scene for the last twenty years, but none of those severe punishments, imprisonments and far-fetched bans will ever be able to destroy hooliganism. There is a light at the end of the tunnel, as they say.

Everybody sees things in a different way, from a different angle and we all know that there aren't two identical opinions on any issue. This is how we have seen things through our own eyes, this is how we have depicted them to you and no one can change that. We make no claim to have been precise, accurate and comprehensive. Neither do we consider ourselves as true writers. At times, things may seem slightly distorted in a fiction style, but everything is within the limits of the truth... or at least our truth we stand behind with our words.

This is not an autobiography. This is just a humble attempt by two boys from the country to describe what they have experienced at Bulgarian stadia.

All we could say in the end is that everyone has the right to form their own opinion and judge other people's experience and hard work on their merits without any personal prejudice. This is our opinion and we stand behind it with our reputation. We have also shared a number of personal things along with our experience with the JRF lads in those days when we were all together and stood like one.

Respect to everybody who has one way or another been related to our firm, while to all those that betrayed the ideology we would like to generally say: You were wrong!

Respect also to all enemies of ours who let all those events happen. We would also like to thank all our ill-wishers for making us even more motivated, for giving us the strength to finish what we started and fulfil our dreams by completing this project.

To all those who would undoubtedly say that what we have written is bullshit, we would like to say to stop criticising, move their fucking arses, spend 4 or 5 years, month in, month out, searching, reading and writing and write their own book... we wish them good luck wholeheartedly!

Also, if anyone reading this book has ever had the misfortune of being punched by us, you must have been at the wrong place at the wrong time or... you simply deserved it!

We sincerely thank all those who like us, properly appreciate our hard work and enjoy what we have written, for sparing the time to read our book! We hope you have also been a part of it one way or another and we do hope we have managed to bring back memories to you.

In conclusion, we would like to tell all JRF Youths that if they get the bug when they first enter a football ground or get off a train on their first away day and feel that wicked adrenaline in the form of a mixture of anticipation, anxiety, fear, excitement and aggression (all of it together), knowing that somewhere out there, in the strange town, the others are lurking, waiting for them, then somewhere deep inside you, the seed of a real hooligan has been sown.

In the end of it all, being a hooligan is not only about looking smart and wearing fashionable clothes. The question is to feel like one, to have it in your mind and soul, to have it inside, be it innate or acquired. And when you come to know the score from the terraces, I am sure you will agree with us. We will stay close to you, all you young and active lads, in order to guide you until you leave your remarkable trail on the scene.

We hope this book will live up to everyone's expectations and Jolly Roger Firm will secure its future through the young lads.

For us it was the last page and we have already turned it!

ABOUT THE AUTHORS

TOSH McIntosh (pseudonym) is Todor Stoychev (real name).

Born in 1977 in a small industrial town in Northern Bulgaria, called G.O. His father (deceased) was a structural iron and steel worker and his mother a medical nurse (now retired).

Married to Desislava with one child – a daughter – Nadya (age of 15).

Currently working as a Security Officer at Tally Ho Centre – London – North Finchley (Control Room – CCTV Operator).

Degreed in electrical technologies. Used to work as an electrician for nine years. Now he's doing 'Close Protection' courses for security businesses.

Author of two books in football-related – 'Hoolie-Ultra' – lit genre with many publications in Bulgarian newspapers.

A few auditory appearances on radio & TV in Bulgaria, no honours and awards yet.

GILLY Black (pseudonym) is Philip Bakyov (real name).

Born in 1978 in a small industrial town in Northern Bulgaria, called G.O. His father is a construction technician and his mother a piano teacher. Married to Mariya with two kids – a daughter – Eliya (age of 1) and a son – Antony (age of 11).

Currently working as a coating inspector on behalf of PPG

Protective & Marine Coatings. Master's degree naval architect & marine engineer. Certified marine & protective coating inspector with over 12 years of experience in the ship building & ship repair market.

Author of two books in football-related – 'Hoolie-Ultra' – lit genre with a few publications in Bulgarian newspapers & the society for protective coatings network.

No auditory appearances or honours and awards... yet.

31040719R00201

Printed in Poland
by Amazon Fulfillment
Poland Sp. z o.o., Wrocław